Cosmopolitan Rurality, Depopulation, and Entrepreneurial Ecosytems in 21st-Century Japan

Cosmopolitan Rurality, Depopulation, and Entrepreneurial Ecosytems in 21st-Century Japan

John W. Traphagan

CAMBRIA PRESS

Amherst, New York

Requests for permission should be directed to
permissions@cambriapress.com, or mailed to:
Cambria Press
100 Corporate Parkway, Suite 128
Amherst, New York 14226, USA

Library of Congress Cataloging-in-Publication Data on file.

ISBN: 978-1-62196-502-2

For Keith Brown, mentor and friend

Table of Contents

List of Figures

Acknowledgements

I would like to thank several colleagues and organizations who have been helpful in developing this project. Art Markman at the University of Texas at Austin has been supportive of my research and my participation in the Human Dimensions of Organizations program at Texas for many years. Thanks go to the IC^2 Institute at the University of Texas at Austin, which provided an office during my sabbatical leave in 2019, during which much of this book was written. Colleagues in the Department of Religious Studies at the University of Texas have also been important interlocutors in relation to many ideas that take shape in this book. Several individuals have assisted me with various aspects of the research and writing, including Jamie Gunderson, Tomoko Hetherington, Kumiko Kawachi, Tomoko Traphagan, and Sarah Summers and their advice and work are greatly appreciated. Tamotsu Kawamura at Miyagi University provided very useful help related to government policies on rural revitalization.

Finally, I want to give my sincere thanks to the many people in Iwate with whom I have shared hours of enjoyable conversation and friendship over the years. Ethnographic fieldwork is, on the one hand, a scientific endeavor in that the ethnographer is trying to systematically collect data and generate an understanding of the lifeways and ideas of people living in a particular place. However, it also involves developing close relationships, and often long-term and deep friendships, with people who choose to take the time to help with the research. After more than thirty years collecting data in Iwate, the line between research participant (or whatever other word is in fashion at the moment—subject, informant, interlocutor, etc.) and friend has become quite blurry and many who have, over the years, helped me with my research as teachers have also become close friends.

Elements of chapters 1 and 2 appeared in different form in the journals *Asian Anthropology* (16(2): 77–94) and *The Journal of Anthropological Research* (56(3): 365–385, copyright University of New Mexico). Research for this book was funded by grants from the Wenner-Gren Foundation for Anthropological Research, the Michigan Center for the Demography of Aging at the University of Michigan, as well as the Mitsubishi Heavy Industries Endowment and the IC^2 Institute both at the University of Texas at Austin. I am also appreciative of a Franklin Research Grant provided by the American Philosophical Society and a travel grant provided by the Northeast Asia Council of the Association for Asian Studies both of which supported research specifically related to Chapter 7.

Note on Translation and Naming Conventions

In general, I have included both Japanese and Romanized Japanese when I make use of Japanese terms or phrases in the text. Also, I follow the Japanese convention of using the family name first, followed by given name, when referring to individuals who have participated in my fieldwork. In many cases, I only make use of given names, because when writing about couples or members of the same family, it avoids confusion. All names of participants in my research presented here are pseudonyms; this is done to protect the identities of those who kindly gave their time and energies to help with my research.

Cosmopolitan Rurality, Depopulation, and Entrepreneurial Ecosytems in 21st-Century Japan

Chapter 1

The Narrow Expressway to Oku

草の戸も

住替る代ぞ

ひなの家

kusa no to mo
sumikawaru yo zo
hina no ie

Even a thatched hut
May change with a new owner
Into a house decorated with dolls[1]

—Matsuo Basho, *Oku no Hosomichi*

About 500 kilometers north of Tokyo one can take exit 36-1 off of the Tōhoku Expressway (東北自動車道 *Tōhoku Jidōsha-dō*), pay a toll of about 11,000 yen if you've driven from Tokyo, and emerge into mantis green expanses of rice fields dotted with ceramic-sided houses and parking-lot clad shopping malls. In spring and summer, the emerald hues permeate everything, only to yield to autumn shades of harvest gold and orangey reds that retreat into the inevitable gray-white shadows of winter with its crystalline trees and slush-strewn roads. As one twists through the cloverleaf exit and enters National Route 4, the assault of trucks and diesel fumes is intense. Route 4 is not a toll road. As a result, a seemingly endless line of dump trucks, other commercial vehicles, and cars often forms in both directions along stretches of the two-lane road. Many of the trucks lug loads so heavy that ruts have formed on each side of the road where tires tread.

To the north of exit 36-1 is the City of Kitakami, with, as of 2017, a population of about 93,000 and a population density of 212 persons per km^2 and to the south is the town of Kanegasaki, with a population a little under 16,000 and a population density of 87.8 persons per km^2. When I exit the expressway, I normally head south to Kanegasaki, where I have been visiting for both research and family reasons since 1988. Over the past thirty years, much has changed. In fact, when I first arrived in the area, Interchange 36-1 did not exist; its construction in the 1990s was a major accomplishment of then-Mayor Takahashi, who worked hard to situate the interchange in Kanegasaki, as opposed to Kitakami, in the hopes that it would bring development to the area. It did. Today a large Aeon department store, several chain restaurants like Marumatsu, and one of Japan's ubiquitous 100-yen shops have been built close to the interchange along Route 4. The area that was largely rice fields when I first visited Kanegasaki is now a major shopping district for people both from Kanegasaki and Kitakami. If one continues south on Route 4, the next town is Ōshū, which has a population of about 119,000 and a population density of 120 persons per square kilometer.

This book is an attempt to work through ideas that have been brewing in my head over much of the past thirty years as I have tried to find ways to adequately describe and discuss, from an analytical perspective, lifeways in Kitakami, Kanegasaki, and Ōshū and to some extent the region of Tōhoku where these cities are located. For me, this is much more than an analytical and academic exercise; I have spent at least four years of my life in the region, have family there, and have made many close friends among the residents as I have conducted ethnographic research. Despite that deep and long-term experience, as I have tried to understand the lifeways of the area through participant-observation over the years, I have found myself often confused about how to characterize my experiences. When I first visited Kanegasaki, the town where I have done the majority of my research over the years, the geographical and social context seemed very much rural and agricultural—any culture shock I felt probably had more to do with a Boston-raised suburban kid visiting an agricultural landscape that seemed far removed from the mainstream of global society than it did with the differences between Japanese and American cultures. In fact, I have always found Tokyo to be much like any other big city, although with its own distinct charms; Tōhoku seemed truly different from my experiences of life in the US. But is that perspective a product of my upbringing in suburban Boston? Or is it in some way a feature of the place and its lifeways that distinguishes it from the city? These are important questions, because they point to the problem of how we characterize and experience the rural and the urban, rustic and cosmopolitan in a globalizing social, economic, and political environment.

No doubt, most anthropologists struggle with these types of questions over time—the more one comes to know about a place, the less one seems to understand it. Humans are complex animals who never really stay put socially or geographically—the world we create is one of constant change, which makes that world impossible to capture in any objective or even lasting way. But there is value in trying to work through and contemplate the features of a particular place, time, and its people as one way of thinking more generally about the nature of humans as social and creative animals. Generalization is difficult, at best, and I make no effort here to draw broad conclusions from the very specific cases I will explore. However, while this book is about one place and period of time in Japan, it deals with a topic—human creativity expressed in the form of entrepreneurialism—that I think is a universal feature of human behavior. Humans are creative beings who usually look for ways to maximize their advantages in social ecosystems; even behaviors that are ultimately self destructive can also be quite creative. It is the overwhelming use of creativity as an adaptive tool that, in my view, most distinguishes us from other animals. We are not alone in being creative, but the extent of our dependence upon creativity as a way to cope with our surroundings seems to be singular in its scope as compared to other animals. In addition to my focus on entrepreneurs, the exploration of the relationship between the rural and the urban, rustic and cosmopolitan has implications for understanding human social and economic behavior well beyond the confines of northern Japan. Generalization is difficult, but research that provides a basis for comparison across human settings is analytically and methodologically useful, even if the primary aim of the work, as is the case here, is not comparative in nature.

In writing this book, I am largely concerned with one rather simple question: What does it mean to talk about rural spaces in reference to contemporary Japanese society and how can the study of entrepreneurial ecosystems help us in understanding those meanings? This question is embedded in a broader theoretical question that I want to explore here: From an analytical perspective, is the concept of the rural an adequate category for thinking about social and geographical spaces found in the countryside of modern Japan? I have little doubt that the concept of rurality is a meaningful social and geographical category in the minds of Japanese when they think about different regions of their country, and I will discuss this later in the book. However, that is a different sort of issue from the analytical one of whether or not rural and urban function as adequate categories for thinking about people's lifeways in a particular geographical and social space. As I work through this book, I will consider both of these perspectives—the analytical or etic and the native or emic—as they relate to the conceptualizations of rurality, and my primary goal is to make use of the ethnographic data I have collected over the past few decades to interrogate the notion of the rural as a descriptive and analytical category by exploring the experiences and identities of entrepreneurs and the manner in which an entrepreneurial ecosystem has evolved during that time period.

Entrepreneur vs. Small-Business Owner

I will use the term "entrepreneur" throughout the book; therefore, it will be helpful to offer a brief discussion of how I conceptualize the nature and meaning of entrepreneurship. Within the academic literature on entrepreneurs and entrepreneurial activity, the term *entrepreneur* tends to be variously defined and has come to be used in several different ways. The idea of the entrepreneur was initially defined by French economist and mathematician Léon Walras to describe individual or corporate entities who engage in agricultural, industrial, and commercial arenas of economic activity and the purchase of raw materials or productive services, transforming them in some way, and then selling those on the market at either a profit or loss.[2] Quite a bit has been written since Walras developed his ideas in the late nineteenth century, but as Howorth, Tempest, and Coupland point out, theoretical developments in the study of entrepreneurialism have been slow. As a result the definition of what constitutes entrepreneurship or identifies an entrepreneur continues to be debated and discussed in academic literature.[3] The idea of the entrepreneur has taken on a variety of categorizations such as social entrepreneurs, technoentrepreneurs, venture capitalists, the self-employed, and so on. Some have even argued that individuals such as college coaches can be understood in terms of entrepreneurialism.[4] In some cases, even institutions such as General Motors or universities have been identified as entrepreneurs.[5] The list of definitions is long and analytical precision at times rather sparse. Key concepts that typically are used in defining entrepreneurial activity include: 1) risk openness and risk management, 2) innovation, 3) ability to recognize opportunity, and 4) ability to access and use available resources.[6]

In terms of typical definitions today, a key element of entrepreneurial activity involves the starting of a business within an environment of risk, with risk usually being conceptualized in terms of the potential loss of economic capital. When it comes to individuals, the emphasis on risk-taking has been one of the primary factors used in differentiating entrepreneurs from managers and small-business owners more generally, particularly in psychological research. Entrepreneurs sometimes are viewed as forming a subset of managers and small-business owners who tend to have a high achievement orientation, propensity toward risk-taking, and a proclivity for innovation as compared to others in these general occupational categories.[7]

The small-business owners I will describe throughout this book reflect elements of an achievement orientation, willingness to take risks, and an attraction to innovative behavior, but it is important to recognize that these tendencies do not necessarily manifest themselves in terms of risk related to economic loss or gain. While to some extent the potential loss of economic capital characterizes the entrepreneurs I will discuss here, I think it is important to keep in mind that much more is going on when we consider entrepreneurial activity in rural Japan (or anywhere else). In each of the cases in this book, the decision to start a small business in a social, geographic, and economic space perceived as rural involved the potential for not only economic loss but also personal risk in terms of giving up a career, losing relationships established in other parts of Japan, and (in the case of one individual) long-term separation from one's family. Each of these represent situations in which individuals risked loss in the form of social and symbolic capital, while there was also potential for gain in these forms of capital. From an anthropological perspective, I think it worthwhile to take a broader view of entrepreneurial activity and think of capital in the form of symbolic and social capital as being components of risk-taking and innovative activities. Entrepreneurs in the postindustrial age are often people who risk their economic and social livelihoods (and even physical and emotional conditions) to pursue the acquisition of knowledge and skills that allow them to build alternatives to the institutional frames of life experienced prior to taking said risk, while at the same time building institutions that create new forms of confinement, even when they are still small businesses. I am following Bourdieu's formulation of social capital as the aggregate of actual or potential resources tied to access to and control over networks of social relationships.[8] This form of capital provides members of a particular network with power in the form of credit that can be exchanged for social, financial, and labor-related assistance. Throughout this book, I will be focusing on small-business owners, which are sometimes differentiated from entrepreneurs. However, given both the theoretical and definitional imprecision of the term entrepreneur and the social conditions and attitudes of small-business owners observed at my field site, as I move through the chapters that follow, I will largely use the ideas of the entrepreneur and the small-business owner interchangeably.

Ethnography and Rural Japan

One of the first ethnographies of Japan I read as a graduate student at the University of Pittsburgh was Edward Norbeck's *Takashima: A Japanese Fishing Community.*[9] Norbeck's study follows the pattern typical of other ethnographies of Japan (and other places) written in the 1950s and, in fact, well into the 1970s. It is situated in a small community in Okayama Prefecture and describes the details of household, community, religion, and work in the village. It is what I call a compact ethnography that keeps itself limited to the lifeways of a close-knit group of people living in an environment that allows them and the ethnographer to interact daily on foot or, perhaps, by riding a bicycle. The field of view Norbeck adopted as an ethnographer reflects his perspective on the place as an outside observer from a very different cultural setting. "The Western traveler," writes Norbeck, "marks the narrowness of the roads. He notes the manner in which buildings are compressed together so that as much productive land as possible may be used for raising crops." The Westerner, according to Norbeck, is also likely to be struck by images of rusticity, seldom missing from the Japanese rural scene at the time he conducted fieldwork, "of male bicyclists stopping unconcernedly along the road to urinate."[10] Many ethnographies of Japan, including Ronald Dore's contributions on urban and rural contexts,[11] Theodore C. Bestor's *Neighborhood Tokyo,*[12] and my own book *Taming Oblivion,*[13] to name a few, follow this basic approach of compact ethnographic writing focused on the details of community life among a small group of people whose lives are closely intertwined in a seemingly neatly defined web of social interactions and confined geographical space.

More recent ethnographies of Japan have moved away from this approach, reflecting the changing patterns of social interaction and community construction that contemporary Japanese experience via modern technologies of communication and transportation and often focusing on specific types of communities or social issues and patterns of identity expression, such as Karen Nakamura's work among the Japanese deaf community or a group home for schizophrenics in northern Japan.[14] A good example of work specifically focused on agricultural or rural areas is Donald C. Wood's study of the planned farming community, Ogata-mura, which extends the community-centered model of ethnographic writing by situating the people and place he studied into national agricultural and industrial flows as well as government policy frameworks that influence patterns of life and work.[15] Another good example is Scott Clark's *Japan: A View from the Bath,* which geographically decenters ethnographic writing by focusing on "the bath" in its various forms throughout Japan, without being tied to a particular village or town.[16] While there is still much intellectual and ethnographic knowledge to be gained by focusing on single villages—things change over time and the nature and lifeways of village Japan in 1955 has both differences and similarities with lifeways today—modern Japanese living in agricultural areas do not experience their world the way they did when Dore was collecting data in Shinohata in the mid-twentieth century.[17] And both urban and rural Japanese inhabit a mobile landscape that allows them to traverse multiple communities both in physical space and within the globalized social and virtual space of the Internet.

These changes necessitate rethinking how anthropologists approach both data collection and analysis and the modes of interaction and transportation that we use to engage in ethnography. Like the people I know in Kanegasaki and its surrounding towns, when I am there for research purposes I drive from place to place, moving not only through various villages (and, yes, there are still many compact and tightly knit villages in Japan) but also through towns and cities throughout the Tōhoku region. It is not unusual to start my day driving to neighboring Ōshū or further south to the temple complex in Hiraizumi, with stops at restaurants or to pick up groceries on the way home. When I return to the US, I continue to stay in touch with my friends in the region through email and Facebook, which was not possible when I started systematic fieldwork in 1994—at that time, the only contact I had with residents occurred when I was physically there or through the occasional letter. Ethnographic research for me today no longer involves heading to my field site, living there for a year or more, and returning to write up my results, although I do believe that remains the best way to obtain robust ethnographic data that allows for nuanced analysis and interpretation. For the most part as of 2019, ethnographic research is for me an ongoing endeavor that includes not only regular visits to the region I study but also technological innovations such as Google Maps to explore the area while sitting at my office computer in Austin. In a sense, I can be in Kanegasaki or any other part of Japan whenever I want by simply calling up Google Maps and shifting the perspective to surface level, which allows me to actually move through images of the town captured at a particular point in time. And if I see something interesting, I can drop a friend an email and ask about the object displayed on my screen or even dial her up on Skype or Facetime to have a conversation about it.

The issue here, however, is not only how I as an anthropologist can easily access my field site to collect data. The important point is that my informants and friends in Tōhoku are equally connected and equally able to explore other places, like Austin, and many have travelled overseas at least once in their lives and often multiple times; in fact, one person I know well has visited me in Austin, and in the summer of 2019 I met with another couple in New York City who happened to be visiting as tourists at the same time I was there for a conference. People move about in cars throughout the region and often travel to distant places. While their lives often continue to be focused on their local village, in some ways the depth of field that characterizes the scope of their daily experience, as well as their occasional experiences of travel, is much greater than it was even in the 1990s. In other words, the flow of change is complex, with eddies and currents that lead the ethnographer along with his interlocutors in many directions, and I have struggled as a scientist to arrive at a manner of characterizing this region that does not rely upon standard academic dialectical tropes that juxtapose frames of experience in terms of categories like rural and urban, agricultural and industrial, rustic and cosmopolitan. As I have spent more time in the region over the years, it has become clear to me that, whatever it is, Tōhoku—like any other place—cannot be easily fit into a particular phenomenal frame of experience, because the temporal and embodied structure of experience is limited by the fact that humans are "emplaced in a world that always outstrips the expanse of our being."[18] We live in a world that is itself in change and we lack the capacity to experience either the entirety of that world or the entirety of its constantly evolving nature.

KANEGASAKI AND TŌHOKU

Cold and cloudy in the winter, hot and humid in the summer, Kanegasaki and the neighboring cities where I have conducted research are in the southern part of Iwate Prefecture, one of six northernmost prefectures on Japan's main island of Honshu that together form the region known as Tōhoku. The area seems to radiate a pastoral vibe that captures feelings of the rural (*inaka* 田舎) and traditional (*dentōteki* 伝統的)[19] for both the Japanese and foreigners who visit as tourists and for locals who are raised and decide to live out their lives in the region. However, if one spends some time in many parts of the Tōhoku region, evidence of what I will refer to throughout this book as *cosmopolitan rurality* can be seen at almost every turn. Farmers fly drones over green rice paddies, dousing their crops with pesticides and fertilizers that help to increase yields, although there has been an interest in organic farming since the 1990s.[20] Bullet trains streak through those same rice fields at speeds approaching 320kph. And the countryside is dotted with satellite dishes on buildings aside which are parked multiple cars, usually made by Japanese manufacturers, but also the occasional BMW, Jeep, Mercedes-Benz, or Land Rover, as well.

Tōhoku has long been characterized as a place of declining population and economic stagnation. It is a region that people are often from, but less frequently move to. As Christopher C. Thompson notes, the history of depopulation in the region has contributed to and been a product of socioeconomic challenges experienced particularly strongly in farm communities since the end of World War II.[21] Jobs can be scarce or limited to low-paying positions in the tertiary sector and there are often insufficient young people to populate schools or local rituals such as the *shishi odori* (鹿踊 deer dance) that Thompson describes in his research from another part of Tōhoku.[22] Indeed, among many Japanese, the region long has been known somewhat disparagingly as the Tibet of Japan, a moniker that indexes inclement weather, beautiful mountains, economic stagnation, and images of "traditional," simple, or backward values, as well as social and thought patterns.[23]

Despite the fact that during the 1960s investments were made in pulp, petroleum refining, and cement-production industries in the region, the area struggled to compete successfully on national or international scales, leaving Tōhoku functioning primarily as a major producer of agricultural products, rather than industrial goods.[24] Many of these images of Tōhoku as a place of economic and population distress were amplified following the earthquake/tsunami/nuclear disaster in 2011, as local residents and the national government struggled to cope with the extraordinary level of destruction and suffering and the difficult process of rebuilding.[25]

Such ideas about Tōhoku—as a place characterized by impediments to economic growth and aged, declining populations—often oversimplify the actual social and economic conditions in the region. William W. Kelly argues that areas of Japan like Tōhoku are complex regions characterized by agricultural production but also tied to urban centers—particularly Tokyo—that have penetrated outlying areas with institutional and ideological structures associated with the metropolitan core.[26] Along with images of underdeveloped regions has arisen what Kelly describes as a "faddish sentimentalism" stimulated by rural nostalgia, often among urbanites, for a countryside that has faded from an empirically evident social and geographical space into the imaginary of historicized longing for a particular Japanese past. Nonetheless, while some conceptualize Tōhoku by looking backward to an idealized agrarian antecedent to contemporary, urbanized Japan, others engage the future through the creation of places of potentiality like wildlife sanctuaries and popular sites for outdoor sports such as hiking, skiing, and camping.[27] One finds resorts in the mountains (hot springs and ski areas), newly constructed shopping malls, and not a few McDonald's and other fast food restaurants like Kentucky Fried Chicken and MOS Burger both in the cities of Tōhoku and in outlying areas along routes that connect those cities, although the further one moves away from the main transportation lines, the less likely it becomes to find these types of restaurants and stores.[28] As Kelly notes, the Tōhoku of the early twenty-first century remains somewhat enigmatic in its blending of agricultural imagery and identity with an industrial and increasingly post-industrial political economy.[29]

This contrast is evident in Kanegasaki where, alongside rice fields, there is an industrial park that includes a manufacturing facility for export models (left-hand drive) of the Toyota Prius C, a semiconductor factory, and a pharmaceutical company. Neighboring towns have manufacturing facilities for Citizen watches and offices for companies such as Hitachi, as well as stations for the bullet train and, as noted above, exits off the expressway that runs through the northern part of Japan tying the area not only to metropolitan regions like Tokyo and Osaka but also to international economic and cultural hubs. There are shopping malls and movie theaters, exercise centers and art museums. Indeed, postmodernity's version of the Tibet of Japan is a place highly interconnected with national and global cultural and industrial flows both through transportation and communication networks.[30] Like in other parts of Japan, WiFi is easy to find in coffee shops or stores, the vast majority of people of all ages are connected to the web through their cell phones and smart phones, and many engage in domestic or international interactions via applications such as Skype and FaceTime, creating and negotiating—virtually—multigenerational and transnational family and business spaces.[31]

Despite these features of the social, economic, and political landscape in the region, Tōhoku has experienced annual net losses in migration since the 1970s, although return migration—sometimes referred to as the U-Turn pattern, a term coined by Kuroda Tashio in the 1970s—has also been a common feature of a demographic landscape with a significant non-metropolitan oriented proportion of migrants.[32] By the 1990s, the term "U-turn" had come to be widely associated in the Japanese media with turnaround migration where people who had moved to metropolitan areas for education or work eventually chose to return to their natal homes or simply move out to the countryside to escape the stress and crowding of large cities. This pattern is accompanied by the L-turn, in which someone who grew up in an urban area moves, perhaps with a U-turning spouse, to a region perceived as rural.[33] The growth of these terms used in both academic literature and the popular media underscore a simple fact that modern Japan is a mobile society in which people often move from one social and geographical landscape to a different type of space and may live in a variety of locations and cultural contexts over the course of a lifetime.

A fairly common reason for moving/returning to an area like Tōhoku after living in an urban area like Tokyo for several years is the need to care for aging parents or accompany a spouse who needs to provide care or simply wants to be closer to aging parents after many years apart.[34] In some cases, although the numbers are relatively small, people have moved from cities to the countryside motivated by back-to-the land sentiments aimed at pursuing healthier lifestyles or to learn organic farming practices.[35] Indeed, settlements have been developed where groups of people have migrated from the cities with common interests in traditional and organic farming techniques,[36] and there have been entrepreneurial efforts to establish traditional and organic farming practices in a variety of communities not only in Tōhoku but in other parts of Japan, as well as the creation of educational programs to promote awareness among urbanites about preservation and development of ideas and practices related to sustainable lifestyles through opportunities to work and learn via participation in the practice of organic farming as helpers for full-time farmers.[37]

One such program I have observed in Niigata Prefecture (adjacent to Tōhoku) is known as Panorama Farm (PF). This is a fairly new business aimed at helping local farmers deal with the high costs of rice farming as well as providing labor for rice farming by supporting opportunities to bring urban adults and children to Niigata to experience farm life through work, often for a weekend. One of the ways PF helps farmers is by purchasing rice production equipment—which, including machines such as rice combines, can involve an expense equivalent to at least $125,000 and represents a cost that can take more than 10 years to recoup if a farmer has one hectare of rice paddy (many farms are smaller than this and the average size of a farm in Japan, excluding those that involve livestock, is 1.5 hectares[38]), leaving no income as a result of labor from rice production for a long period of time. As an alternative to each farm family owning its own equipment, PF purchases the equipment and manages production on over 150 hectares of rice paddies that are owned by local families. The families can buy into the company or lease the land to the company, but the number of shareholders is quite limited, with most of the capital coming from the two men who started PF. Returns on leased land are small, but farm families often have a strong connection to the land because it was inherited from their ancestors, which generates an impetus to continue working the land. For some, at least, passing on the land to the next generation in good condition—meaning that the land is productive—is a moral imperative that is taken quite seriously and can motivate land-holders to continue farming even if it is not particularly profitable and requires considerable work.[39] The business and labor assistance available through PF offers an alternative to the labor involved with farming and an incentive to keep land in one's family rather than selling to corporate farms, which is becoming increasingly common in Japan.

While PF manages rice production for members, it also has the aim of using organic farming techniques as much as possible. By using organic methods, the owners hope to create a luxury item in the form of premium-quality rice, which then can support the high production costs associated with locally grown rice in Japan, which is usually considerably more expensive than imported rice. PF also provides a corporate environment—which contrasts with the typical family farm—where younger people can work and gain experience in farming practices or access mentoring to help set up farming-related businesses of their own; in some ways, it provides an entrepreneurship mentoring program in that PF is partially intended to provide younger farmers with the knowledge and experience necessary to operate their family farms more as businesses. In part, PF represents an entrepreneurial response to the Trans-Pacific Partnership Agreement, which poses a threat to Japanese rice farmers due to its potential to open the doors to importing increased amounts of less expensive—and what is perceived as lower quality—rice. It also should be placed within the context of agricultural reforms pursued by the Abe Administration, in which controls on national agricultural cooperative associations over local cooperatives and farmers were relaxed somewhat and which has opened the door for novel businesses like PF focused on organic farming to emerge.[40] This allows for businesses like PF to develop new agricultural products, in this case using organic farming techniques, that might have been more difficult given the political climate in the past.[41]

SMALL BUSINESSES, ENTREPRENEURIALISM, AND ENTREPRENEURIAL ECOSYSTEMS

Examples like PF represent not only entrepreneurial endeavors from a business perspective but also novel and creative approaches to addressing issues such as depopulation and economic stagnation in agricultural areas by developing programs that are either overtly or tacitly focused on promoting the construction of an entrepreneurial ecosystem. One way of thinking about entrepreneurial ecosystems is that they are constituted via a group of interconnected actors located in a socio-geographical community and who are interested in creating a context of sustainable development by encouraging and supporting the creation of sustainable ventures.[42] Entrepreneurial activities and ecosystems also represent contexts through which individuals can construct a sense of existential meaning at a personal level, which brings me to one of the central themes of this book: an exploration of the ways in which personal identities are intertwined with the creation of small businesses and embedded in political and economic processes related to the creation of entrepreneurial ecosystems.[43] One of the key reasons that I focus here on entrepreneurialism is because it is a useful lens through which to see how the countryside of Japan, as both social and geographical space, is being reshaped by political and economic processes and policies such as the Japanese Ministry of Economy, Trade, and Industry (METI) emphasis on the creation of small-to-medium-sized businesses as important in community revitalization efforts. The entrepreneurial identity is not simply an innate property of an individual but is something that develops in relation to social, political, and economic context, which is a point that will become clear as I move through the examples discussed later in the book.

Context is, of course, shaped by overt activities, such as information and policies produced by government agencies, such as METI, which publishes a wide array of reports and statistical data on the state of the Japanese economy including annual white papers on the conditions and growth of small and medium enterprises that are accessed and used by local politicians, bureaucrats, and business leaders in places like Niigata or Tōhoku. And, of course, governmental agencies play a significant role in defining how enterprises are defined and how entrepreneurial activity is encouraged and supported. From the perspective of the Japanese government, small-and-medium enterprises (SMEs) are defined in the service and retail industries as having a stated capital of 50 million yen or less and 100-or-fewer employees (service) or 50-or-fewer employees (retail). METI refers to very small businesses as micro-businesses, and this is the type of business on which I will focus throughout the book, although the pharmacy and healthcare corporation I will discuss in chapter 4 is currently growing beyond the definition of a micro-business. A small enterprise is defined as a business operator whose number of regular employees is typically 20 or fewer (5 or fewer in the case of a business operator whose business is situated in the retail or service industries). METI refers to small enterprises as micro-businesses in order to articulate that not only companies but also sole proprietorships are included in its discussion of small/medium business trends.[44]

Between 2012 and 2014, there was a national decrease of about 91,000 in micro-businesses, which was largely due to a decrease in sole proprietorships. During the same period, there were approximately 285,000 business startups and 457,000 business closures. The numbers of businesses in retail trade, manufacturing, and construction have decreased significantly while during the same period there has been an increase in the medical, healthcare, and welfare sector, as well as the education/learning support sector.[45] An important reason for the decrease in micro-businesses is related to the broader problem of population-aging facing Japan. The aging of self-employed business owners has accelerated, with self-employed business owners in their 70s representing the largest segment at about 800,000. According to the 2012 employment status survey conducted by the Ministry of Internal Affairs and Communications (MIC), the most commonly cited reason for retirement from self-employed business was illness and old age (40.4%), followed by concerns or anxiety over the future (12.3%).[46]

Region and population size have an influence on the types of micro-businesses one finds in Japan. Examining the quantity of business establishments in various municipalities shows that in terms of the number of small-sized business establishments per 1,000 residents, there are more in large cities for business types such as information and communications, professional and technical services, wholesale trade, real estate, and medical, health care, and welfare industries. However, micro-businesses focused on construction, retail trade, and personal-care industries such as barber shops and laundries are more common in rural areas, and this is the pattern that I have observed in my research in Tōhoku, which certainly contributes to the fact that most of my entrepreneurial interlocutors are those who have developed retail businesses. Interestingly, small businesses in rural areas tend to last longer than in large cities and it appears that countryside areas in general tend to have small businesses that manage to operate over long periods of time and micro-businesses in rural areas tend to account for higher percentages of total wages and numbers of employees than in urban areas. In short, there is a significant divide between the nature and importance of micro-businesses between regions defined as rural and urban within Japan.

One of the more interesting aspects of the 2016 White Paper on SMEs is its brief discussion of micro-businesses and working environments for women.[47] The report notes that women tend to choose smaller businesses when they look for work after a break for childbirth and child-rearing, rather than looking for work in a larger company. Women also are likely to work for longer periods for small businesses with fewer than five employees. These points suggest that micro-businesses may offer flexible options for both recruitment and working environments for some women. This possibility is supported in my own research, where micro-businesses often employ women part-time with very flexible hours and (as will become evident in the case of Kanegasaki Creamery in chapter 5) some female business owners prefer to hire female employees.

Understanding the political climate that shapes the creation of small businesses and influences the nature of entrepreneurialism is an important element in thinking about the creation of entrepreneurial ecosystems and the expression of identity among entrepreneurs. In 2014, the Japanese government promulgated The Basic Act for Promoting Small Enterprises, which presents four measures aimed at promoting the growth of small businesses and has influenced individuals at the local level interested in entrepreneurialism. Article 6 of the act spells out the basic policies/priorities the government established for small businesses as follows:[48]

- Promoting business management that should be implemented for future demand: Creating and discovering demand for micro businesses by more proactively taking advantage of their conventional face-to-face relationships with customers.
- Promoting business renovation: Developing and creating businesses by providing diverse and new human resources with opportunities for success in the workplace.
- Facilitating business activities contributing to regional economies: Increasing the public awareness of certain regions to create brands so as to invigorate regional economies.
- Developing a system for supporting micro-businesses through region-wide collective efforts: Providing detailed measures to address challenges that business operators are facing in running their businesses.

The plan prioritizes providing support for and promotion of the creation of business startups that will have spillover effects on local communities, which is tied to taking advantage of local/regional characteristics and is intended to play a role in stabilizing regional economies. There is also an important component of the Act that emphasizes building sustainable business, rather than specifically focusing on growth of SMEs, although growth is certainly encouraged. And one of the key features of the Act is the emphasis on creating small businesses that are able to react to social and demographic change, which is particularly important in rural areas, but is relevant to the country as a whole given the general population decline currently occurring in Japan.

The METI White Paper includes case studies of startups that made use of well-developed business plans, an approach the government is encouraging as a way to create sustainable small businesses and anticipate conditions in changing business climates like depopulating rural areas. In fact, the 2016 White Paper notes that only about 50% of small-business owners developed any sort of business plan, which may in part be due to the fact that many of these micro-businesses are family centered and thus kin-based in terms of both employment and financial support, leading to informal arrangements and informal business plans in the place of consciously developed and articulated plans.

The conceptualization of small-business startups and support for local communities can be seen in other government policies and plans. A good example is a government campaign called *chihō sōsei* (地方創生), whose term literally means region or countryside creation. The campaign was developed in 2014, following the beginning of Prime Minister Shinzo Abe's second term and is designed to mitigate the effects of an over-concentration of population and economic activity in the Tokyo area. Japan has long struggled with an intense concentration of education, government, business, and cultural products in the Tokyo area, and this continues to represent a significant concern, particularly given the fact that the region is prone to major earthquakes. In order to shift economic activities and population to other areas and to revitalize rural areas, the government developed a set of programs aimed at promoting local and rural organizations as well as small businesses.[49] There is a large array of programs and goals under this framework, including areas devoted to professional development and strategies for developing human resources and subsidies to promote regional development.[50]

More specific to the Tōhoku region and to recent events are a series of policies aimed at recovery and revitalization of the areas devastated by the earthquake/tsunami/nuclear disasters of 2011. A variety of programs have helped encourage startups or restarts along coastal areas of Miyagi and Iwate prefectures, which were hit particularly bad by the disaster. Within a year of the disaster, there were many small business startups, particularly restaurants and other services such as barbers, in the areas along the coast, often to take advantage of the influx of construction workers there to help with the reconstruction. In some cases, people returned to restart businesses they lost in the disaster, while others moved into the area from other parts of Japan to start new businesses—a few locals told me that they looked at this somewhat negatively because it appeared as though outsiders were taking advantage of the situation. Most of these programs have been focused on the coastal areas that were hit by the tsunami, the closest of which is more than an hour by car from the area where I do my research, although they certainly have had an influence more generally throughout the Tōhoku region, just as the triple disaster has shaped life and businesses in northern Japan in general over the past eight years.

Small-business creation, entrepreneurship, and the generation of entrepreneurial ecosystems, of course, are not simply about government policies and business plans. For many who start micro-businesses, ambitions are at least equally related to personal desires and feelings of fulfillment through one's work and in one's life.[51] Indeed, several of the cases of local-business owners I discuss in this book focus on the lives of individuals who, after spending several years working in corporate Japan and living in a major city, decided to leave secure employment situations in order to start businesses in a small town in Tōhoku. What emerges is a complex intersection of personal identities, concern with community, and the politics of population that are expressed not only in terms of revitalization of rural areas, but also as an effort to create a new social and geographical space that does not fit neatly into traditional images of rurality.

Conceptualizing Rurality

The nature of twenty-first-century rurality is difficult to characterize analytically, a problem that has led to a variety of terminologies being used to express a contrast between social and geographical spaces in terms of oppositional binaries such as agricultural/industrial, traditional/modern, rustic/cosmopolitan, periphery/center that are used to represent geographical, economic, cultural, and political frames of individual and collective experience not only in Japan but also more generally throughout the world. The idea of peripheral and center has often been used in discussions of the social, political, economic, and geographical landscapes of Japan both within Japan and from the perspectives of scholars studying Japan from outside, and it has played an important role in Japanese history in relation to the conceptualization of areas like Tōhoku as being on the periphery.[52] And this idea remains one way in which scholars have imagined contemporary Japanese life, although here I hope to show that this is a problematic way of thinking about Japan in the twenty-first century.[53]

As Manfred Kühn notes, peripheralization is a concept that references a sensibility that social relations have spatial implications not only related to geography but also to ideas viewed as being in some way removed from the metropolitan and cosmopolitan. In many cases, the idea of the periphery also indexes perceived temporal inequalities—inequalities in economic status, education access, social status, and overall quality of life—that reflect and generate significant differences related to lived experience between areas deemed peripheral and central.[54] The periphery, as both an analytical category and popular descriptive trope, may often rather vaguely contain representations that suggest notions of marginality as characteristic of peripheral regions as places and peoples left behind but also as places harboring traditions viewed as culturally and socially authentic, as was noted above in reference to Tōhoku. In many respects when used either analytically or more generally, the idea of peripherality tends to index assumptions about differential access to and unequal distribution of power that can lead to variations in spatial and economic development.[55]

The peripheral/marginal and central/core contrasts, of course, even if presented as binary oppositions, exist along sliding scales in which peripheries may become centers over time and areas deemed as centers also are contexts of inequality and marginalization that may be expressed along racial or socioeconomic lines (or both), as is often the case in American cities like Detroit and that may lead to open rebellion when conditions of marginalization become intolerable.[56] Indeed, because both peripheries and centers are composed of social actors with agency, not only do the relationships between peripheries and centers change over time but individuals and groups may also intentionally attempt to reconstruct and reconceptualize these relationships or reinvent the socio-spatial composition of either context or the perceived relationships between contexts. Of course, it is not necessarily the case that actors in rural areas will attempt to reconfigure their immediate socio-spatial surroundings into archetypal centers; instead, as we will see in the narratives and ethnographic observations I discuss in this book, people may create socio-spatial environments that do not fit neatly into the binaries of urban/rural, peripheral/central, agricultural/industrial, or modern/traditional.

This process of reinventing the nature of rurality and questions related to the meaningfulness of the notion of the periphery in Japan are central in my thinking as I move through the remainder of this book. I see this process as a locus of hybridization that can involve not only some of the more typical examples associated with globalization such as intermarriages and international trade but also that is constructed through the creation of hybrid spaces or material hybridities—that often reflect hybrid identities—which are themselves depolarized manifestations of temporal and spatial frames of experience.[57] These processes are not engines of globalized homogenization as was argued by many in the 1990s such as George Ritzer,[58] although this idea has been challenged by several scholars in recent years as many have come to think more about the interrelation between global and local flows,[59] but are instead loci of interspatial and intersocial borrowing, reconfiguring, and fusion generated through access to local and global sources, often creating new and different types of spaces and identities that cannot be easily classified in terms of categories such as rustic and cosmopolitan or agricultural and industrial.

COSMOPOLITAN RURALITIES IN NORTHERN JAPAN

Rural Japan has been the focus of considerable research by anthropologists and other social scientists since the 1930s, beginning with John F. Embree's ethnography *Suye Mura: A Japanese Village.*[60] Numerous studies of rural life in Japan have followed Embree's work, including Richard K. Beardsley, John W. Hall, and Robert E. Ward's *Village* Japan, Robert J. Smith's *Kurusu: The Price of Progress in a Japanese Village, 1951-1975,* Dore's *Shinohata: A Portrait of a Japanese Village,* Gail L. Bernstein's *Haruko's World: A Japanese Farm Woman and Her Community,* and Norbeck's *Takashima: A Japanese Fishing Community,*[61] as well as more recent works like my own *The Practice of Concern: Ritual, Well-Being, and Aging in Rural Japan* and Wood's *Ogata Mura: Sowing Dissent and Reclaiming Identity in a Japanese Farming Village.*[62] The list is long and the depth of ethnographic writing that has been produced related to lifeways in regions viewed as rural Japan from the 1930's until the present is impressive.

Perhaps part of the reason for this highly developed research literature on rural life in Japan is related to a general fascination among scholars after World War II with processes of modernization and the reconfiguring of Japan as an urban, industrial society with a broadly defined middle class, as exemplified in Vogel's study of urban white-collar families in Tokyo in the late 1950s.[63] This literature describes a fairly rapid transition during the postwar period from rural areas traversed by "wash-board corrugated" roads more easily navigated on a scooter described by Dore,[64] to a countryside crisscrossed with limited access highways and elevated *shinkansen* (新幹線 bullet train) tracks, and well-developed surface-road systems that people use to purchase goods at large shopping malls, often in neighboring towns or somewhat distant cities such as Sendai.[65]

Research related to changing patterns of life in the Japanese countryside, of course, must be contextualized in the political, economic, and social flows of the nation-state and global economy. It is difficult to characterize towns such as Kanegasaki in terms of binaries like agricultural and industrial. On first glance, these places may look decidedly agricultural with their wide expanses of open farmland—used not only for planting rice but also in Kanegasaki for dairy farms set amidst rolling hills where corn is grown in fields that abut large barns housing dairy cows. But, as noted earlier in the book, nestled into the hills adjacent to that farmland is a Toyota factory that produces the Prius C, as well as pharmaceutical and semiconductor production facilities.

To ride the *shinkansen* north from Tokyo into Tōhoku is to be confronted not with a transition from urban/industrial to rural/agricultural Japan but to glide through a pastiche of urban and rural spatialities intertwined in a latticework of variously populated areas linked through limited-access highways, rail lines, and communications networks that are set amidst checkerboard rice fields, red and yellow McDonald's restaurants, 7-Eleven convenience stores, high-rise hotels, and shopping malls with large parking lots that accommodate the automobile-centered lifestyle of the Japanese countryside. Kelly's nuanced description of contemporary rural social patterns in Japan and his notion of regionality as a way of rethinking life in agricultural Japan provides a productive way to contemplate the relationship between rural and urban spaces. Kelly describes an ongoing process of metropolitanization of rural lifeways that has generated patterns of living in which highly mechanized farming no longer takes significant amounts of people's time, which, in turn, means that for many it no longer represents the primary social framework through which life is organized and experienced. Instead, as Kelly wrote in 1990, patterns of work, school, and family life in the Japanese countryside have become largely "indistinguishable from those of...relatives and acquaintances who have moved to metropolitan Tokyo," and this observation seems even more evident in the Tōhoku region of 2018.[66]

People comfortably traverse regional, national, and international borders and it is common for residents of Tōhoku to have had living experiences in other parts of Japan, as well as in other parts of the world. Today's middle-aged, college graduates in towns like Kanegasaki or Ōshū grew up at a time when study abroad was becoming more common, and even those who did not attend college may well have visited other countries for recreation or for experiences related to work—study trips for farmers have been organized for many decades in this part of Japan, meaning that it is not unusual to find a dairy farmer working his farm on the outskirts of Kanegasaki who has also spent time in Europe or the U.S. studying agricultural practices. Indeed, Hogan found in her study of globalization in rural Japan and Australia that 25 percent of participants indicated they had travelled abroad for business, pleasure, or study, and the majority of farmers and small businesspeople, teachers, and public servants felt that international connections formed an important part of their work and many of her participants noted the importance of imported commodities in daily life.[67] The emergence of regionalized social spaces and behaviors is related to a general standardization of many aspects of life patterns that has occurred throughout Japan as different parts of the country have become synchronized and integrated with metropolitan centers and reflect a mainstream or middle-class consciousness (*chūryū ishiki* 中流意識) continually expressed and reconstructed in various forms of media that are available throughout the country via the Internet and through television broadcasts.

This process of metropolitanization is itself situated within a post-modern demographic context of negative population growth or a situation of late-stage demographic transition where birthrates are low and death rates are high, leading to a long-term decline in population that is showing itself visibly in the Japanese countryside. This produces short-term problems related to a decrease in the working population and increase in elderly population that can become a drain on the economy as there are fewer workers paying into government programs like the long-term care program I will discuss briefly in chapter 4 and more people placing demands on those programs as they age.[68] In Japan, another byproduct of this has also been a proliferation of empty, sometimes collapsing buildings and abandoned grave sites that have become readily evident over the past 15 years in areas like Kanegasaki and Ōshū as older people have died without resident offspring to reside in or continue caring for the family property.[69]

As I have argued in this chapter, contemporary Japan is perhaps best understood in terms of ongoing processes of socio-spatial depolarization of periphery and center combined with growing interconnectedness among different types of social and geographical communities, making it difficult from an analytical perspective to differentiate the rustic from the cosmopolitan in many places. However, the fact remains that many Japanese, including most of those with whom I have spoken in Kanegasaki and other parts of Tōhoku, at least to some extent, characterize the region as rustic/rural/agricultural and contrast that to regions like cosmopolitan/urban/industrial Tokyo. In other words, despite the empirical complexity of characterizing the region I encounter as an anthropologist, the notion of a binary relationship is often reproduced in local discourses about socio-spatial differences and is particularly evident in the use of terms like *inaka* 田舎, which is used by both locals and outsiders to describe rustic/rural regions and people and which can imply a feeling of agricultural lifeways that contrast with the lifeways of more densely populated areas and unambiguously urban spaces like Tokyo, despite the fact that one certainly finds urban and industrial areas within the context of regions described as *inaka,* as noted above.

I raise this point because it is important to recognize that Japanese themselves often draw a fairly clear distinction between what is viewed as spatially and conceptually rural/agricultural as opposed to urban/

industrial, even if the meaning in some ways shifts in relation to context and analytically the spatio-social dimensions of the relationship are not always readily evident in the expressions of depolarization that have occurred in the region over the past several decades. This process is not unique to Japan, and several scholars have attempted to address the blurriness of rural and urban regions in other parts of the world that have undergone processes related to and generating spatio-social depolarization. For example, in examining changes in the Benelux region of Europe, Gulinck and Dortmans use the term "remnant rurality" as a way to characterize regions removed from urban centers, but within which there may also be patches of urbanity and well-developed infrastructure, such as high-speed rail and limited-access highways, that link together all parts of a region and connect that region to larger political and economic structures.[70] From an analytical perspective, I am unconvinced that the notion of "remnant" rurality adequately expresses reconstructed contexts associated with spatio-social depolarization because the idea indexes images of rurality as something of and from the past that is, in a sense, dematerializing in the face of modernization rather than being a social process that is continually reconstructed by locals to reflect desires and hopes for life now and in the future. Human agency is left out of the picture as is a sense of the ways in which people regularly redefine the metaphors they use to represent their own patterns of life.

Another term that has been helpful in thinking about contemporary life outside of unambiguously urban areas is neo-rural. Unfortunately, neo-rurality has been defined inconsistently in academic literature, where it can refer to back-to-the-land movements and the associated reconstruction of eco-political territory as a geographical and epistemological challenge to contemporary urban spaces and capitalist exploitation of the land.[71] Although to some extent this conceptualization of neo-rurality occurs in Japan, a broader definition is useful as I am thinking about the term here. Elsewhere, I have defined neo-rurality as referring to socio-spatial regions that: 1) are culturally and socially viewed by locals (and outsiders) as unambiguously rural in contrast to urban or suburban spaces, 2) continue to carry ecosystems such as agricultural plains or forested mountains as unbuilt surface features of the land while also having highly built areas with dense populations, 3) have engaged in strategic practices associated with building economic and social sustainability while attempting to retain value structures and ideas associated with images and discourses of the rustic, and 4) are linked to larger regions, including the global social imaginary, through infrastructure such as transportation and communications networks, as well as other flows like the dissemination of cultural commodities associated with the cosmopolitan.[72]

When applied to the context of northern Japan, this definition is intended to incorporate the attitudes of people living in Tōhoku, that often represent the region as an aesthetic landscape that reflects the pastoral and a social context that displays value structures distinct from that of the urban and industrial parts of the country.[73] However, people in the region also recognize that their experiences of the spatial and social manifestation of what I am calling neo-rural Japan are linked to the expression and movement of global ideas, products, and people. Indeed, people in parts of Iwate, for example, are regularly reminded of their linkages to the global economy and global cultural flows by examples such as the success of native son and Major League Baseball phenom Shohei Ohtani who has become a star with the Los Angeles Angels in the U.S. after several years playing professional baseball in Japan. Ohtani grew up and played little league and high-school baseball in Iwate and his career has been followed closely by locals, some of whom have even travelled to the U.S. to watch him play.

When we look at this part of Japan, at least, we see a region that retains a significant agricultural element and is perceived by many as unambiguously rural but also represents a context that displays an entanglement of local, national, and global flows that challenge the idea of peripherality and index the ongoing processes of depolarization of urban and rural that neo-rural people experience. The experiences of this process have created a social context that has become a locus of innovation as governments work to address the problem of negative population growth and a variety of long-term economic and social concerns present, particularly in relation to the continued aging of the population and the associated increases in need for healthcare services.[74] It has also become a locus for entrepreneurial activity as individuals have recognized and exploited opportunities that have emerged as local residents resituate their social and spatial environment as a depolarized space that is difficult to characterize as obviously peripheral or central, rustic or cosmopolitan.

RESEARCH APPROACH

This book is the product of several years of ethnographic research in the southern part of Iwate Prefecture, starting with the pilot study I conducted for my dissertation in 1994. Although the data are drawn from my fieldwork over the years, I believe that the years I spent in the computer industry prior to becoming an anthropologist have also shaped my interests and ideas. Employment at both a small software company on Long Island and one of the largest computer companies in the world in the 1980s—Digital Equipment Corporation (DEC)—clearly stimulated an interest in trying to understand the nature of entrepreneurial activity. DEC, in particular, was associated with a culture of innovation that led to many publications focused on its organization or corporate culture and the relationship of that culture to entrepreneurial and innovative activities.[75] These experiences, although not analyzed systematically, clearly have shaped my thinking about the relationship between business, culture, and entrepreneurial activities.

When it comes to the locale I focus on here, it is important to recognize that Iwate is a diverse place and my fieldwork represents observations from a small corner of the prefecture situated in the plains between the two large mountain ranges that traverse the region. The central part of Iwate, where the prefectural capital city of Morioka is located, is historically and to some extent culturally distinct from the south, having been part of a different feudal domain from the southern towns and cities until the late nineteenth century, evidence of which remains in dialect and other cultural differences found in northern and southern parts of the prefecture. Lifeways also vary in relation to coastal regions in which fishing and tourism have been dominant industries and in the city of Kesenuma that is located in Miyagi Prefecture but borders with Iwate and was Japan's busiest port for processing bonito and swordfish prior to the 2011 disaster. It is important for the reader to recognize this diversity and understand that the area of Iwate about which I write—although I believe has many similarities with other parts of the region as a whole (not just within the prefecture)—is also part of a culturally, economically, and historically complex place.

My research in my early career as an ethnographer was focused on concepts of health and illness, rather than small businesses, but very early on I noted the entrepreneurial efforts of locals to strengthen the economy and address the population problems that were clearly on the horizon and are now widely evident. Methods used to accomplish this have included local government support for small businesses and other activities, such as the creation of a historical museum in the center of the hamlet where I lived for 1.5 years in 1995/6 that I will discuss in chapter 6, and policies aimed at promoting the town and making features that might reduce out-migration and potentially attract in-migrants. For example, the town of Kanegasaki, where I lived during my dissertation work and to which I have returned annually ever since, had publicized itself as a *shōgai kyōiku sengen no machi* (生涯教育宣言の町) or (to paraphrase) a "town supporting the development of lifelong learning" and, to that end, had created a network of community centers throughout the town designed as spaces in which to engage in lifelong learning. These centers are, in actuality, simply the standard *kōminkan* (公民館) or community centers that one finds throughout municipalities in Japan, but Kanegasaki in the 1980s engaged in a rebranding effort through which the names of these facilities were changed to emphasize the idea and practice of lifelong learning as a way to try to build a distinctive identity for the town.[76] Political leaders also made use of the presence of a two-year agricultural college in the western end of the town and a sister-city relationship with Amherst, Massachusetts as a way to emphasize the educational orientation of the community and tap into images of similarities to Amherst as a rural locus of higher education.

The ethnographic fieldwork that forms the empirical foundation for this book has taken place in two communities, Kanegasaki and Ōshū (previously known as Mizusawa), which as noted earlier are neighboring municipalities of about 16,000 and 120,000, respectively. The modern city of Ōshū came into existence in 2006, with the amalgamation of several smaller municipalities in the Isawa region of Iwate Prefecture, including the cities of Esashi and Mizusawa, and the towns of Isawa, Maesawa, and Koromogawa. This practice of amalgamation of municipalities to increase administrative efficiency has been a common feature of the political landscape in neo-rural Japan for some time,[77] and it is particularly interesting to have observed this process in the area of my fieldwork because Kanegasaki has steadfastly resisted amalgamation with either of its neighbors, despite repeated overtures from both of its neighboring cities (Mizusawa/Ōshū to the south and Kitakami to the north) and, as the mayor of the town explained to me on one occasion, the ongoing threat of fiscal punishment from the national government.

As noted above, the Tōhoku region has been the focus of ethnographic research for some time, starting with the work of Jackson Bailey in the village of Tanohata in the 1950s.[78] L. Keith Brown first conducted fieldwork in Mizusawa in 1961 and he has observed the processes of social, political, and economic change in the region for several decades as well as translating a local history that provides a great deal of information related to social and economic change in Mizusawa following World War II.[79] Brown's contemporaries in the anthropology of Japan, David Plath and Robert Smith, both visited Mizusawa and collected data there and David Plath's student, Christopher S. Thompson, did his dissertation fieldwork in the nearby town of Tōwa. More recently, my own student, Benjamin

Cox, conducted his dissertation fieldwork in Ōshū, focusing on childhood socialization, religious ideology, and education.[80] In short, the region has been widely studied ethnographically by foreign anthropologists, but it also has been the focus of research among many Japanese scholars, most notably archaeologists interested in the area due both to its importance as a border between feudal states in the Tokugawa Period (and earlier) and the history of the Ezo or the indigenous people of the region and there has been increased interest, even in inland areas like Kanegasaki with large industrial parks, following the earthquake/tsunami in 2011.[81]

I first visited the area in 1988 and have returned regularly for research purposes since 1994, with long stays in 1995/6 (Kanegasaki) and 1998 (Ōshū). These long-term periods in the area for fieldwork have been followed by visits lasting usually between two weeks and two months most years since that time during the summers. This has allowed me to observe the process of economic and population change including the closing of many local businesses and the shuttering of numerous houses, as well as the more recent emergence of a small group of entrepreneurial individuals who have decided to start businesses in the area, usually after having lived in another part of Japan such as Tokyo for several years.

Although my initial fieldwork in Kanegasaki represented something akin to the traditional village-focused project, with the exception of two summers, this project is largely not the product of a single long-term stay at my field site. Instead, I have brought together field notes and interview data collected over the past three decades, mining the data for information related to small business and the changing economic and demographic climate of the area where I have spent my research time. To live in rural Japan is to interact with local small business owners and family businesses on a regular basis, although the frequency of these interactions has declined a great deal since I first arrived in the area. The growth of strip malls and chain convenience stores like 7-Eleven and Family Mart, as well as large grocery and department stores, has deeply influenced the ability of small-business owners to operate and has caused the closing of many family-run shops.

Although I will draw on data that I have collected since the mid-1990s, the interview data that form the core of the book and are found in the case-studies discussed in chapters 3 through 7 have been conducted during over the past eight years and in many cases have involved several interviews and conversations with the same individuals over that period of time. Indeed, this study is the product of both systematic and informal observation of daily life in the region that has occurred not only over the past eight years, but also over the past 25 years. It also incorporates awareness of and limited involvement in the businesses run by my own family in the Japanese dairy industry. This has given me a somewhat different perspective from my position as ethnographer and has allowed me to experience participant observation not only as an observer of a small business but also as one who has a personal and emotional investment in the success of one such business. In addition, some of the small-business owners I will write about here are among my closest friends, while others are people whose businesses I have frequented regularly and whom I have interviewed in a more formal manner with the specific goal of learning the ins and outs of their experiences as small-business owners in neo-rural Japan.

I should emphasize that this book focuses on the experiences of a small number of individuals and, thus, should not be taken as representative of broader social patterns related to small-business ownership and entrepreneurial activity in rural Japan. However, the examples here are not cases that lack parallels outside of Kanegaski, Iwate, or the Tōhoku region. I have observed similar entrepreneurial activities and experiences in Niigata and, although the data here focus on a small region of northern Japan, this is part of a larger project in which my research assistant and I collected interview data related to the experiences of small-business owners in Tokyo and Hiroshima. The data collected from other parts of Japan have been useful in contextualizing the examples I discuss here and recognizing that many themes are not particularly unusual. Furthermore, the demographic patterns related to population aging and out-migration from areas like Kanegasaki and Ōshū are happening throughout Japan, so I think it reasonable to conclude that similar social and economic behaviors are occurring elsewhere in rural Japan and research by anthropologists such as Susanne Klien also tend to confirm this conclusion.[82] Generalization, of course, is not the aim of ethnography; the goal is detailed description and analysis of ideas and experiences of a specific group of people and my intent here is to deeply explore the lives and experiences of small-business owners in one region of neo-rural Japan. I make no claims that this is necessarily representative of Japan nor that this represents the experiences of entrepreneurs in other contexts outside of Japan. However, I do think that the examples discussed here are instructive about the Japanese experience and useful for those interested in comparative research.

Long Engagements

I have endeavored to construct this book in a way that will reveal the complex interplay of demographic and economic change as it shapes interpretive frames that people use to think about their world. To some extent, the model for this book is a much earlier contribution to the anthropology of Japan—David Plath's *Long Engagements: Maturity in Modern Japan*.[83] Plath used narratives of the aging process to illustrate the experience of adulthood among modern Japanese in the 1970s and paired those narratives with discussions of novels that reflect similar themes to those Plath pulled from the experiences of his informants. Plath's work shows the creativity that goes into the process of human maturation and the fact that people generate pathways through which they self-realize the values expressed within a particular cultural context. Plath's approach made use of personal narratives and novels as a way of exploring what he refers to as "standard pathways of Japanese culture," that were built by individuals against a backdrop of Japanese values, social organization and history, while also showing the ambiguities and problems those individuals must resolve as they go through life along with others in the peer groups Plath refers to as convoys.[84]

My approach here is similar, although I will not employ fictional literature and I am less concerned with standard pathways of life-course construction than I am with somewhat non-standard pathways that the individuals I discuss here have created. Central in my emphasis on entrepreneurialism is a fascination with the ways in which people engage creativity as a way to navigate and negotiate the aging process and manage their social, economic, and political surroundings as they move through the life-course. By looking at the narratives of several entrepreneurs building their lives within the cosmopolitanizing social and geographical space of neo-rural Japan, my aim is to bring the reader into contact, at least, with rhythms of life that link people into webs of experience—the hopes and dashed hopes, goals and failures, loves and losses—that make us human and that in the context discussed here contribute to the formation of a distinctive social and geographical space in which the meaning of periphery and center has become increasingly depolarized and recast as a socio-geographical milieu that can be characterized as a locus of hybridity in the form of a cosmopolitan rurality.

Notes

1. When Japanese read the works of Basho, they often need to consult translations into modern Japanese. This poem represents a feeling that the place or figure of the house may remain the same, but the feeling and atmosphere of the house will change as new people come to live in it over time.
2. Léon Walras, D.A. Walker, and J. van Daal, *Walras: Elements of Theoretical Economics: Or, the Theory of Social Wealth*, trans. Donald A. Walker and Jan van Daal (Cambridge: Cambridge University Press, 2014).
3. Carole Howorth, Sue Tempest, and Christine Coupland, "Rethinking Entrepreneurship Methodology and Definitions of the Entrepreneur," *Journal of Small Business and Enterprise Development* 12, no. 1 (2005).
4. Murray A Sperber, "The College Coach as Entrepreneur," *Academe* 73, no. 4 (1987); 持田昇一, "地域をフィールドとした社会起業新論 [Social Entrepreneurship " 開発工学 *[Development Engineering]* 35, no. 2 (2016).
5. David A. Ley, "The Effective Gm: Leader or Entrepreneur?," *Cornell Hotel and Restaurant Administration Quarterly* 21, no. 3 (1980); Paul D Hannon, "Why Is the Entrepreneurial University Important?," *Journal of Innovation Management* 1, no. 2 (2013).
6. Hannon.
7. Wayne H. Stewart et al., "A Proclivity for Entrepreneurship: A Comparison of Entrepreneurs, Small Business Owners, and Corporate Managers," *Journal of Business Venturing* 14, no. 2 (1999/03/01/ 1999), http://dx.doi.org/https://doi.org/10.1016/S0883-9026(97)00070-0.
8. Pierre Bourdieu, *Outline of a Theory of Practice*, trans. Richard Nice (Cambridge: Cambridge University Press, 1977).
9. Edward Norbeck, *Takashima: A Japanese Fishing Community* (Salt Lake City: University of Utah Press, 1954).
10. Ibid.
11. Ronald Dore, *Shinohata: A Portrait of a Japanese Village* (Berkeley: University of California Press, 1993); Ronald Dore, *City Life in Japan: A Study of a Tokyo Ward* (Berkeley: University of California Press, 1958).
12. Theodore C. Bestor, *Neighborhood Tokyo* (Stanford: Stanford University Press, 1989).

13. John W. Traphagan, *Taming Oblivion: Aging Bodies and the Fear of Senility in Japan* (Albany: State University of New York Press, 2000).
14. Karen Nakamura, *Deaf in Japan: Signing and the Politics of Identity* (Ithaca: Cornell University Press, 2006); Karen Nakamura, *A Disability of the Soul: An Ethnography of Schizophrenia and Mental Illness in Contemporary Japan* (Ithaca: Cornell University Press, 2013).
15. Donald C. Wood, *Ogata-Mura: Sowing Dissent and Reclaiming Identity in a Japanese Farming Village* (New York: Berghahn Books, 2012).
16. Scott Clark, *Japan: A View from the Bath* (Honolulu: University of Hawaii Press, 1994).
17. Dore, *Shinohata: A Portrait of a Japanese Village.*
18. Robert Desjarlais and C. Jason Throop, "Phenomenological Approaches in Anthropology," *Annual Review of Anthropology* 40 (2011), http://www.jstor.org.ezproxy.lib.utexas.edu/stable/41287721.
19. The term *inaka* is routinely used by locals at my field site to describe areas that are perceived as being rural. However, the term *dentōteki* is something of a technical term. I have heard local residents in Kanegasaki use this term fairly often, although this usually has been in the context of discussions related to local history or archaeology.
20. Ahmed Saleem, "Japan's Alternative Farming Approaches: Farmer-Distributor-Consumer Linkages," *Ambio* 24, no. 6 (1995), http://www.jstor.org/stable/4314371.
21. Jackson Bailey, *Ordinary People, Extraordinary Lives: Political and Economic Change in a Tohoku Village* (Honolulu: University of Hawaii Press, 1991); Traphagan; Christopher S. Thompson, "Depopulation in Regional Japan: Population Politics in Tōwa-Chō," in *Demographic Change and the Family in Japan's Aging Society*, ed. John Traphagan and John Knight (Albany: State University of New York Press, 2003); Christopher S. Thompson, "Preserving the Ochiai Deer Dance: Tradition and Continuity in a Tōhoku Hamlet," in *Wearing Cultural Styles in Japan: Concepts of Tradition and Modernity in Practice*, ed. Christopher S. Thompson and John W. Traphagan (Albany: State University of New York Press, 2006).
22. Thompson, "Preserving the Ochiai Deer Dance: Tradition and Continuity in a Tōhoku Hamlet," in *Wearing Cultural Styles in Japan: Concepts of Tradition and Modernity in Practice*; Christopher S. Thompson, "The Ochiai Deer Dance: A Traditional Dance in a Modern World," *The Journal of Popular Culture* 38, no. 1 (2004/08/01 2004), accessed 2019/01/10, http://dx.doi.org/10.1111/j.0022-3840.2004.00103.x.

23. Sabastian Boret, *Japanese Tree Burial: Ecology, Kinship, and the Culture of Death* (London: Routledge, 2014).
24. Ibid.
25. Tom Gill, Brigitte Steger, and David H. Slater, eds., *Japan Copes with Calamity: Ethnographies of the Earthquake, Tsunami and Nuclear Disasters of March 2011* (Oxford: Peter Lang, 2013).
26. William W. Kelly, "Rice Revolutions and Farm Families in Tōhoku: Why Is Farming Culturally Central and Economically Marginal?," in *Wearing Cultural Styles in Japan: Concepts of Tradition and Modernity in Practice*, ed. Christopher S. Thompson and John W. Traphagan (Albany: State University of New York Press, 2006); William W. Kelly, "Regional Japan: The Price of Prosperity and the Benefits of Dependency," *Daedalus* 119, no. 3 (1990).
27. Boret, 39.
28. John W. Traphagan and L. Keith Brown, "Fast Food and Intergenerational Commensality in Japan: New Styles and Old Patterns," *Ethnology* 41, no. 2 (2002), http://dx.doi.org/10.2307/4153002.
29. William W. Kelly and Merry I. White, "Students, Slackers, Singles, Seniors, and Strangers Transforming a Family-Nation," in *Beyond Japan*, The Dynamics of East Asian Regionalism (Ithaca: Cornell University Press, 2006), 47.
30. It's worth noting that many people I know in northern Japan were as shocked by the election of Donald Trump as were many Americans. People living in the region are tied to both national and international news sources and very aware of goings on in other parts of the world.
31. Chiho Sunakawa, "Virtual *Ie*: A Three-Generational Household Mediated by Webcam Interactions," *Journal of Pragmatics* 69 (2014).
32. Tashio Kuroda 黒田俊夫, 日本人口の転換構造 [The Structure of the Japanese Population in Transition], 古今書院, 1979; Kao-Lee Liaw, "Interprefectural Migration and Its Effects on Prefectural Populations in Japan: An Analysis Based on the 1980 Census," *The Canadian Geographer* 36, no. 4 (1992); Peter Matanle and Anthony Rausch, *Japan's Shrinking Regions in the 21st Century: Contermporary Responses to Depopulation and Socioeconomic Decline* (Amherst, NY: Cambria Press, 2011).
33. Nakamura.
34. John Knight and John W. Traphagan, eds., *Demographic Change and the Family in Japan's Aging Society* (Albany: State University of New York Press, 2003).

35. Nancy Rosenberger, "Making an Ant's Forehead of Difference: Organic Agriculture as an Alternative Lifestyle in Japan," in *Capturing Contemporary Japan: Differentiation and Uncertainty*, ed. Satsuki Kawano, Glenda S. Roberts, and Susan Orpett Long. (Honolulu: University of Hawaii Press, 2014).
36. John Knight, "Organic Farming Settlers in Kumano," in *Farmers and Village Life in Twentieth-Century Japan*, ed. Ann Waswo and Nishida Yoshiaki (London: RoutledgeCurzon, 2003).
37. Takako Takano, "Exploring the Values of Rural Communities through Place-Based Education in Niigata Prefecture," in *Educating for Sustainability in Japan: Fostering Resilient Communities after the Triple Disaster*, ed. Jane Singer et al. (New York: Routledge, 2017).
38. For a good discussion of rice farming and the Trans-Pacific Partnership (TPP) see "Farming in Japan: Fieldwork" published in *The Economist* online (13 April 2013), accessed 19 January 2017, http://www.economist.com/news/asia/21576154-fewer-bigger-plots-and-fewer-part-time-farmers-agriculture-could-compete-field-work.
39. John W. Traphagan, *Taming Oblivion : Aging Bodies and the Fear of Senility in Japan, Suny Series in Japan in Transition* (Albany: State University of New York Press, 2000).
40. Patricia L Maclachlan and Kay Shimizu, "Japanese Farmers in Flux: The Domestic Sources of Agricultural Reform," *Asian Survey* 56, no. 3 (2016).
41. Takano, in *Educating for Sustainability in Japan: Fostering Resilient Communities after the Triple Disaster.*
42. Erik Stam, "Entrepreneurial Ecosystems and Regional Policy: A Sympathetic Critique," *European Planning Studies* 23, no. 9 (2015/09/02 2015), http://dx.doi.org/10.1080/09654313.2015.1061484.
43. John W. Traphagan, "Entrepreneurs in Rural Japan: Gender, Blockage, and the Pursuit of Existential Meaning," *Asian Anthropology* 16, no. 2 (2017/04/03 2017), http://dx.doi.org/10.1080/1683478X.2017.1281534.
44. 経済産業省, 平成*27*年度 ものつ#くり基盤技術の振興施策 *(*概要*)*東京.：経済産業省 *[2016 White Paper on Small Enterprises in Japan (Summary)* (Tokyo: Ministry of Economy, Trade, and Industry, 2016).
45. Ibid.
46. Ibid.
47. Ibid.
48. Ibid.
49. 石田正昭, 農村版コミュニティ・ビジネスのすすめ: 地域再活性化と *Ja* の役割 *[Advising Rural Communities and Business Recommen-*

dations: Regional Revitalization and the Role of Ja] (東京: 家の光協会 [Home Light Association], 2008); 川村保, "販売力強化へ向けて農協販売事業をどう改革するか (特集 農協を立て直す)--(Ja は農業者の所得増大にどう取り組むか) [How to Reform the Agricultural Cooperative Sales Business to Strengthen Sales Power]," 農業と経済 *[Agriculture and Economy]* 82, no. 8 (2016).

50. See http://www.kantei.go.jp/jp/singi/sousei/index.html.
51. Traphagan, "Entrepreneurs in Rural Japan: Gender, Blockage, and the Pursuit of Existential Meaning."
52. Michele Mason, *Dominant Narratives of Colonial Hokkaido and Imperial Japan: Envisioning the Periphery and the Modern Nation-State* (New York: Springer, 2012).
53. cf. Donald Denoon et al., eds., *Multicultural Japan: Palaeolithic to Postmodern* (Cambridge University Press, 2001); Yusuke Yamashita, "How Does the Restoration of Tōhoku Society Begin? Center and Periphery in the Great East Japan Earthquake," *International Journal of Japanese Sociology* 21, no. 1 (2012).
54. Manfred Kühn, "Peripheralization: Theoretical Concepts Explaining Socio-Spatial Inequalities," *European Planning Studies* 23, no. 2 (2015/02/01 2015), http://dx.doi.org/10.1080/09654313.2013.862518; Haroon Jamal and Amir Jahan Khan, "The Changing Profile of Regional Inequality," *The Pakistan Development Review* 42, no. 2 (2003), http://www.jstor.org.ezproxy.lib.utexas.edu/stable/41260530.
55. Kühn.
56. Heather Ann Thompson, *Whose Detroit? Politics, Labor, and Race, in a Modern American City*, 1 ed. (Ithaca: Cornell University Press, 2001).
57. Marwan M. Kraidy, "The Trails and Tales of Hybridity," in *Hybridity: the Cultural Logic of Globalization*, ed. Marwan M. Kraidy, (Philadelphia: Temple University Press, 2005).
58. George Ritzer, "Mcdonaldization," *The Blackwell Encyclopedia of Sociology* (1993).
59. Dannie Kjeldgaard and Søren Askegaard, "The Glocalization of Youth Culture: The Global Youth Segment as Structures of Common Difference," *Journal of Consumer Research* 33, no. 2 (2006); Diana Crane, "Culture and Globalization: Theoretical Models and Emerging Trends," in *Global Culture*, ed. Diana Crane, Nobuko Kawashima, and Ken'ichi Kawasaki (New York: Routledge, 2016).
60. J.F. Embree, *Suye Mura: A Japanese Village, by John F. Embree* (Chicago: University of Chicago Press, 1939).

61. Norbeck; Richard K. Beardsley, John W. Hall, and Robert E. Ward, *Village Japan* (Chicago: University of Chicago Press, 1959); Robert J. Smith, *Kurusu: The Price of Progress in a Japanese Village, 1951-1975* (Stanford: Stanford University Press, 1978); Gail L. Bernstein, *Haruko's World: A Japanese Farm Woman and Her Community* (Stanford: Stanford University Press, 1983); Dore, *Shinohata: A Portrait of a Japanese Village.*
62. John W. Traphagan, *The Practice of Concern: Ritual, Well-Being, and Aging in Rural Japan, Carolina Academic Press Ethnographic Studies in Medical Anthropology Series* (Durham, N.C.: Carolina Academic Press, 2004); Wood.
63. Ezra F. Vogel, *Japan's New Middle Class: The Salary Man and His Family in a Tokyo Suburb* (Berkeley: University of California Press, 1971).
64. Dore, *Shinohata: A Portrait of a Japanese Village.*
65. Traphagan and Brown.
66. Kelly, "Regional Japan: The Price of Prosperity and the Benefits of Dependency."
67. Jackie Hogan, "Constructing the Global in Two Rural Communities in Australia and Japan," *Journal of Sociology* 40, no. 1 (2004/03/01 2004), accessed 2019/01/16, http://dx.doi.org/10.1177/1440783304040451.
68. John B. Hall, "Negative Population Growth: Why We Must, and How We Could, Achieve It," *Population and Environment* 18, no. 1 (1996), http://www.jstor.org.ezproxy.lib.utexas.edu/stable/27503504; John W. Traphagan, "East Asia's Population Problem," *Georgetown Journal of International Affairs* 15, no. 2 (2014), http://www.jstor.org.ezproxy.lib.utexas.edu/stable/43773623.
69. John W. Traphagan, "Empty Houses, Abandoned Graves: Negative Population Growth and New Ideas in Neorural Japan," *Brown Journal of World Affairs* 24, no. 2 (2018).
70. Hubert Gulinck and Carl Dortmans, "Neo-Rurality: The Benelux as a Workshop for New Ideas About Threatened Rural Areas," *Built Environment (1978–)* 23, no. 1 (1997), http://www.jstor.org/stable/23287850.
71. Joan Nogué, "Neo-Ruralism in the European Context: Origins and Evolution," in *The New Ruralism: An Epistemology of Transformed Space*, ed. Joan Ramon Resina and William Viestenz (Madrid: Iberoamericana Vervuert, 2012); Joan Ramon Resina, "The Modern Rural," in *The New Ruralism: An Epistemology of Transformed Space*, ed. Joan Ramon Resina and William Viestenz (Madrid: Iberoamericana Vervuert, 2012).
72. Traphagan.

73. Pere Salabert, "A Semi-Peircean Essay on "New Ruralism" by Means of Nature," in *The New Ruralism: An Epistemology of Transformed Space*, ed. Joan Ramon Resina and William Viestenz (Madrid: Iberoamericana Vervuert, 2012).
74. Phua Kai Lit, "The Japanese Experience with Population Ageing and the Financing of Social Security, Health and Other Social Services for the Elderly: Lessons for Other Nations," *Asian Journal of Social Science* 34, no. 4 (2006), http://www.jstor.org.ezproxy.lib.utexas.edu/stable/23654550.
75. Edgar H. Schein, *Dec Is Dead, Long Live Dec: The Lasting Legacy of Digital Equipment Corporation* (San Francisco: Berrett-Koehler Publishers, 2004).
76. Traphagan, *Taming Oblivion: Aging Bodies and the Fear of Senility in Japan.*
77. Christopher S. Thompson, "Population Decline, Municipal Amalgamation, and the Politics of Folk Performance Preservation in Northeast Japan," in *The Demographic Challenge: A Handbook About Japan*, ed. Florian Coulmas et al. (Leiden: Brill, 2008).
78. Bailey.
79. L. Keith Brown, *Shinjō: The Chronicle of a Japanese Village* (Pittsburgh: University Center for International Studies, University of Pittsburgh, 1979).
80. Benjamin Davis Cox, "Gods without Faces: Childhood, Religion, and Imagination in Contemporary Japan" (University of Texas at Austin, 2018).
81. 工藤雅樹, "考古学から見た古代蝦夷 [Ancient Ezo from an Archaeological Viewpoint]," 日本考古学 *[Journal of the Japanese Archaeological Association]* 1, no. 1 (1994); 清水希容子 and 松原宏, "東日本大震災後の東北製造業の回復と産業立地政策 [Tōhoku's Industrial Recovery and Industrial Location Policies after the Great East Japan Earthquake]," *E-Journal GEO* 9, no. 2 (2014).
82. Susanne Klien, "Entrepreneurial Selves, Governmentality and Lifestyle Migrants in Rural Japan," *Asian Anthropology* 18, no. 2 (2019), http://dx.doi.org/10.1080/1683478X.2019.1572946.
83. David W. Plath, *Long Engagements: Maturity in Modern Japan* (Stanford: Stanford University Press, 1980).
84. Ibid.

Chapter 2

Business, Depopulation, and Return Migration

> The region is defined not by uniformity, but by wide variations in climate, topography, demography, language, and culture, to name a few. Tōhoku has always been divided, diverse, and changing....[1]

It would be difficult to discuss contemporary neo-rurality in Japan without devoting space to the process of depopulation occurring in areas outside of the cities, as these areas represent the leading edge of an issue that is being faced by the country as a whole. In 2018, Japan's population decline accelerated to approximately 500,000/year and the rate of population decline will continue to increase in the near term. This loss of population, combined with migration into cities, has contributed to a growth in the number of abandoned houses in the country that has been estimated to be 8 million as of 2019, with a large proportion of those being in areas deemed rural. In many ways, the situation facing many of the parts of Japan that are either rural or neo-rural is encapsulated in the juxtaposition of two institutions I visited in Niigata Prefecture in 2014 as part of a trip my students in a summer program at Waseda University in Tokyo took to learn more about rural lifeways. The first of these was an elementary school in a mountain farming village. The school at one time had 125 students and was the thriving center of community life; as of 2014, it had nine students (across six grades) and five of these were actually transfer students from larger schools who had been placed in this small school because they were struggling socially or academically; thus, the school board and parents agreed to move them to a smaller environment that they believed would be more comfortable and allow the student to perform better. There were actually more staff working in the school than students, due to government regulations on staffing for schools. The second institution I visited was a nursing home located in the valley overlooked by the school's village in the mountains. Fully occupied at the time, the nursing home had 70 residents and a list with 350 people on it waiting for a spot to open. This contrast provides a window into the demographic challenges facing people living in neo-rural Japan. Indeed, there are few children, causing an increasing number of schools to have insufficient students to operate fully and in some cases these schools are forced to close. I have encountered similar situations in Kanegasaki, in which the elementary school that both my children attended had been designed for about 250 students but had a population of about 70. The principal commented to me at one point that while she appreciated having my kids in the school because they brought an international experience to the students, she also appreciated the additional numbers they added to the student population. The lack of children translates into fewer young adults who can care for the elderly, work the rice fields or vegetable gardens, or simply keep up houses and farmland so that they do not collapse from disuse or turn into weeds from years of being left fallow. In fact, most farming in contemporary Japan is done by people over the age of 60, but as these people are aging, their ability to continue operating family farms is diminishing, which is part of the reason there is considerable fallow land in many areas.[2]

Figures 1 and 2 (at the end of this chapter) show population changes for areas viewed as typically rural and urban between 1920 and 2016. Figure 1 includes the six prefectures that comprise the Tōhoku region, and figure

2 includes Tokyo and Chiba (which is a part of the Tokyo metroplex). Through the 1950's most of Japan experienced a trend towards increased population, although the war obviously had a profound influence on population in Tokyo. However, as one can see in figure 2, after roughly 1955 while the populations of Tokyo and Chiba (and other major urban areas) continued to grow, those of rural areas begin to decline. The exception in the Tōhoku region (figure 1) is Miyagi Prefecture, which is where Sendai is located—the largest city in Tōhoku and one that draws population from surrounding areas. Throughout the 1970s and 1980s, the populations of prefectures in Tōhoku were fairly stable, but by the mid-1990s, one can see the beginnings of a pattern of negative population growth that has continued into the present.

Interestingly, Tokyo, while fairly stable from the 1970s through the 1990s, started to experience significant growth again in 2000 and this certainly related to an important component of negative population growth in rural and neo-rural areas in the form of out-migration. This is evident in figure 3, which shows net migration for Tōhoku, Tokyo, and Chiba for the years 2015 and 2016. Unsurprisingly, Tokyo and Chiba show positive net migration while all of the Tōhoku prefectures other than Miyagi display negative net migration. This pattern, when combined with low fertility rates, has generated the environment of rural and neo-rural depopulation that characterizes the demographic landscape in Tōhoku and in most other areas set apart from major population centers that form something like a centripetal force that draws in migrants for work and education.

Demographic Patterns in Iwate Prefecture

In comparison to many other municipalities in Iwate Prefecture, Kanegasaki has managed to fare well in maintaining its population. Like other parts of the prefecture, in Kanegasaki (although there are some areas of new housing development) empty buildings are a common sight and the business district of the town consists of numerous vacant storefronts that once housed liquor stores, barber shops, dry cleaners, and small appliance and electronics stores. However, it is likely that vacancies would be considerably more evident were it not for the industrial park in the western part of the town that provides employment for locals, particularly on the assembly line for the Toyota Prius C at a facility that can produce approximately 25,000 cars per month. This facility has provided a significant number of largely manufacturing jobs for locals, as managerial positions are often held by individuals who move to the factory for a few years from corporate offices in another part of Japan and then move on to another facility. It seems likely that the industrial park has played a significant role in helping Kanegaski to maintain its population over the past two decades, which has remained fairly stable at between 15,000 and 16,000 since I first started research in the mid-1990s. However, with 30% of the population over the age of 65 as of 2019, it is unlikely that the town will be able to maintain that population level for much longer. Indeed, as of early 2019, Kanegasaki had 15,654 people compared with 16,325 in 2010. Through week 44 of the 2018 fiscal year in Japan, there were a total of a total of 67 live births and 131 deaths in Kanegasaki, while 363 people moved in and 330 moved out of the town, leaving a net population decrease of 31.[3] The fact that deaths are roughly double live births indicates that the population will continue to decrease, as it did between 2010 and 2015, during which time the town had a net population growth of - 416.[4]

For comparative purposes, table 1 shows rates of population change for Japan as a whole and several prefectures between 2010 and 2015, with the six Tōhoku prefectures highlighted. With the expected exception of Miyagi, each of these prefectures has experienced a negative rate of population change and these are higher than most other prefectures in the country. This trend is likely to continue for some time and, based on current government population forecasts, should accelerate in the coming years. Indeed, as noted above, the entire country is experiencing negative population growth, and current government projections indicate a population of about 42 million Japanese by 2110, down from the current

126.5 million if one assumes consistent fertility patterns over the next 100 years.[5] Clearly, unless there is some intervening factor such as changes in immigration policies or a sharp increase in fertility rates, regions like Tōhoku are poised to lose significant proportions of their populations over the next several decades.

The aging of the population as a result of out-migration of young people and lower fertility is having a visible influence on the lifeways of people in Kanegasaki and surrounding towns, with a variety of cultural traditions being lost. On February of 2017, *The Japan Times* reported that the annual "deer dance" in Kanegasaki (which I mentioned in chapter 1), which is a harvest ritual in which dancers dress in costume and play drums, would be shelved due to health issues of the 61-year-old leader of the group.[6] The newspaper reported in the same article that about 60 similar events in various rural areas had been shelved as a result of declining and aging populations in recent years. When it comes to ritual performances, this pattern has become quite common, with festivals disappearing as localities have insufficient population to maintain traditions. It should be pointed out that this is not really a new phenomenon. In Kanegasaki, the fire prevention festival that has taken place in the center of town since the 1920's was on the verge of collapse when I lived there in the mid-1990s due to a shortage of children to ride the floats that are pulled through the center of town. It was explained to me by local community leaders that at one time there were six of these floats and by the 1990s there was only one left. The demise of rituals and festivals like this is a product of not only low fertility but also out-migration from rural areas, leaving few people in the early years of adulthood to participate in local events and to shoulder the physical work that often accompanies putting on a festival. That said, it would be a mistake to paint too bleak a picture; Kanegasaki holds other festivals that are well-attended, particularly by younger people in the town. A good example of this is the annual summer festival, which not only provides entertainment but also promotes local produce such as asparagus.

ECONOMIC PATTERNS IN IWATE

Festivals can be an important source of income for local businesses in Japan, because participants often purchase food and drink while observing the ritual performances. Larger festivals, in particular, have the potential to draw in tourists from surrounding areas (and very large festivals draw national and international tourists as well), which of course feeds the local economy.[7] Ōshū, for example, holds a large fire-prevention festival in April that draws in thousands of people who come from other towns in Iwate to enjoy reveling and watch the procession of floats carrying young people dressed in traditional costume who play drums and shamisen. Festivals in smaller towns like Kanegasaki, by contrast, normally bring in only a few participants who live outside of the town.

On the surface the economic climate in Iwate appears to be good (see figure 4). As of 2016, the annual unemployment rate was 2.4%, which has followed a steady decline since 2009, when the unemployment rate was 5.4%.[8] This rate is slightly lower than the 2.5% unemployment rate for the entire Tōhoku region as of 2018. Following the economic crisis of 2008, real and nominal growth rates have increased for the prefecture, reaching a high of about 4.9% in 2013; however, in 2014 the real and nominal economic growth rates dropped significantly to 1.0% and 2.5% respectively.[9] Since 2000, Iwate has experienced an average nominal growth rate of -.69% and an average real growth rate of .47% and the per capita income in Iwate is 2,359,000 yen or about 86% of the national average.[10] The recent increase in economic growth for the prefecture is notable, but should be understood in the context of the triple disaster that struck the region in 2011. [11] As the Iwate Prefecture statistical web site notes, the recent economic growth is a product of public investment and private demand related to post-disaster reconstruction, rather than evidence of a long-term shift in the economic situation of the region. This has stimulated opportunities for developing businesses in the region, a process that has been examined in detail by Klien, who explores the influx of volunteers and young, ambitious individuals who have moved from urban areas to initiate revitalization or business projects following the 2011 disaster and she situates this entrepreneurial activity in the context of broader economic and labor trends in Japan.[12] However, despite the movement of entrepreneurs into areas of Tōhoku hit by the disaster, it seems unlikely that economic growth will be sustainable over the long-run, particularly given the ongoing depopulation of the region.

Better Living Through Science

Over the past few decades, there have been a variety of large-scale entrepreneurial projects in the Tōhoku region that engage scientific or technological innovation and research as a means to strengthen local economies, stabilize populations, and potentially attract new residents. The City of Kamaishi, for example, is located on the Pacific Coast of Iwate and was once a major steel producer; its economy collapsed in the late 1980s when the steel mills closed. Following extensive damage from the 2011 disaster, the city has embarked upon a program of creating a comprehensive "eco-model" to support recovery and revitalization through the employment of technologies focused on sustainability, as well as developing social programs such as the creation of video surveillance and communication systems for seniors.[13]

The Kamaishi sustainability project is one among several in the region, the most prominent perhaps being evident the considerable political efforts among residents of southern Tōhoku to attract construction of the International Linear Collider (ILC)—a project involving Japan, the US, and the EU that is associated with CERN (The European Organization for Nuclear Research)—in the Kitakami Mountains that cross Iwate and Miyagi prefectures. In 2013, the Kitkami mountain region was one of two remaining candidate sites, the other being Sefuri in Kyūshū, and at the end of August of that year the ILC Strategy Council announced that the Tōhoku site scored slightly higher in a technical evaluation, while the Sefuri site scored higher in the socio-environmental evaluation[14] It was decided that the Tōhoku site was the better location; however, this did not mean the push from municipalities and organizations in Tōhoku could be discontinued. In fact, as of early 2019, the Japanese national government had yet to make a decision as to whether or not it will host the ILC, despite allocating 260 million yen to the project for FY2018, which represented an increase of about 150 million yen over the previous year's allocation.[15] In August of 2019, it was announced that the Ministry of Education, Sports, Culture, Science and Technology (MEXT) had requested 480 million yen for ILC-related items within its fiscal year 2020 budget and in July of 2019, the Japanese, French, and German governments agreed to start a discussion group, and that added a 50 million yen increase to the budget beyond what was requested in FY 2019.[16] Local newspapers and ILC support organizations have argued that these increases represent a sign that a positive decision will be made in the future.

The size of the ILC project is impressive and in some literature is compared to the International Space Station in terms of scale, financial expense, and importance of the science it will produce.[17] There are a variety of cost estimates associated with the project, with some as high as a total expenditure of about $25 billion from organizations outside of the ILC itself. The ILC organization estimates a cost of about 8 billion 2012 US dollars and another $1.8 billion contributed by the host country for site-specific necessities such as supplying water and electricity.[18] Costs are complex and there have been disagreements about the total expense associated with the project's construction and operation over time, making it difficult to arrive at an accurate assessment of what the total cost of the project is likely to be in the end, but it is clear that it will be expensive for the host country. Proponents in Japan hope that the project will begin construction in 2020 with experiments commencing ten years later, although as of April 2019 it remains unclear if the project will be funded . For my purposes here, I am less interested in the actual impact of the ILC than ways in which the project is being used as an ideational element in efforts to reshape the social and economic environment of southern Tōhoku as an element in the creation of what, if not overtly, at least implicitly is intended to be the cornerstone in the creation of an entrepreneurial ecosystem in the region.

An examination of PR and other literature related to the ILC project that has been used to represent the value of the ILC to local residents and to outsiders provides something of a window into the manipulation and construction of contingent social processes through which people literalize the metaphors by which they construct individual and collective identities. Specifically, PR literature and local media coverage often represent a framework through which locals, and particularly political and scientific leaders in this case, actively represent the ILC project as a way to reshape not only the economic landscape but also the social identity of the region as an international and modern research center that reflects metaphoric allusions to Japan's rural, agricultural milieu and values associated with that context. It is also often represented as a post-disaster revitalization effort, similar to other projects in rural and neo-rural areas that are aimed at creating a sustainable economic and social environment that is hoped will turn the tide of rural depopulation, particularly as a product of out-migration of younger people.[19] And the project as a whole is constructed from an ideational perspective in ways that tend to transform it as a whole into a metaphor not only for revitalization but also for the creation of a cosmopolitan space within a region normally represented as traditional and rural in the Japanese imagination.

Indeed, there is a steady stream of writing that espouses the potential cultural, social, and economic benefits of the project and in many ways the project as a whole has become something of a metaphor for post-3/11 recovery of the region. For example, proponents of the ILC argue that if the project succeeds it will bring an international population of researchers, engineers, support personnel and their families to build and operate the facility and will generate a "multicultural international city" in the region with close to 3,000 people taking up residence in towns through which the project is constructed.[20] While 3,000 people will only have a limited impact on the declining population in the region, leaders of the project have argued that the ILC will stimulate business startups related to the project, thus attracting additional people and, potentially, holding on to more of the native population of younger people. In fact, local proponents of the ILC argue that the project has the potential to facilitate interest and spur motivation among children in the region to pursue interests in science, and local governments have already undertaken initiatives to support the ILC through local educational frameworks, including activities such as symposia and workshops to educate adults on the project and poster competitions in elementary schools to visually represent the ILC project as a way of involving children.[21]

From a national and international perspectives, similar sentiments can be found in justifications for construction of the facility. Of course, the scientific merit of the project is central in virtually all discussions of the ILC, but the potential social, political, and economic impacts of the facility are also prominent. Descriptions of the facility on the CERN website or on websites in Japan supporting the construction often express internationalist sentiments, noting (as mentioned above) that the facility will "bring together" researchers, engineers, their families, and locals into a community supporting the aims of science and the ILC. Indeed, in an interview for the website *Iwate and the ILC*, Professor Suzuki Atsuto, President of Iwate Prefectural University, argued that the significance of the ILC lies not simply in scientific research but also in the potential social consequences of the project: "A diverse society," states Suzuki, "doesn't just mean bringing in people from other cultures. We must *evolve our society* into one where everyone can live in harmony, at every age, without barriers. We hope to keep Iwate's societal development in mind as we move forward."[22] I have added the emphasis here to Suzuki's idea related to actively evolving society to point out the utopian rhetoric that at times is used to describe the benefits and values associated with construction of the facility. This sentiment is similar to comments I have heard from local officials in the city of Ōshū, such as the Mayor, in public settings where the ILC is being either discussed or raised as an example of positive developments that could shape the future of the region.

In reading the literature available online and found at government offices in Iwate and Miyagi Prefectures, it would be easy to assume that there is overwhelming and widespread agreement on the value of the ILC. Politicians seem to be largely strong supporters of the project often on the grounds that it has the potential to be a significant component of revitalization efforts following the 2011 disaster.[23] There are several websites from both government and non-government organizations that publicize and support efforts at gaining approval for construction of the ILC in the Tōhoku region, including a website run by the Morioka Chamber of Commerce and Industry and its subsidiary Iwate Prefecture International Linear Collider Promotion Council that publishes the *Kitakami Times*, an online newspaper devoted to producing updates, stories, and interviews related to (and in support of) the ILC project. In Miyagi Prefecture, Governor Murai Yoshihiro has aggressively led efforts to secure construction of the ILC in the region and in March of 2013 the prefectural assembly adopted a resolution supporting construction of the ILC as a symbol of reconstruction following the 2011 Tōhoku earthquake/tsunami disaster.[24]

However, the ILC is not perceived as an unambiguous good either by locals or at the level of national politics. In 2013 scientists from the Science Council of Japan (SCJ) raised concerns about the ILC, noting the need for strategies related to cost-sharing among member nations and establishment of a clearly developed and articulated vision for managing human resources, and a large number of international residents, related to construction and operation of the facility. And five years later, the SCJ moved beyond the expression of concerns about the ILC and published a draft opinion in which it opposed plans to invite the ILC to Japan on the grounds that the facility's scientific merits were unlikely to justify the enormous construction and maintenance costs.[25] Other voices in opposition to the ILC can be found, such as the news arm of the Japanese

Communist Party (JCP), *Japan Press Weekly* (japan-press.co.jp), which indicated the JCP has voiced opposition to the ILC on the grounds that reconstruction work should focus on "rebuilding people's livelihoods rather than focusing on the questionable economic effects and profits of large industries."[26]

Local residents, who would be most directly affected by the construction and operation of the project, seem to have somewhat mixed reactions. The local newspaper *Iwate Nippo* conducted a public opinion poll and in December of 2017 published the results showing attitudes about the ILC.[27] According to the article, 34.5% of respondents said they were "interested in" the ILC and 29.7% of respondents said they were somewhat interested, which represented an increase of about 1 point over the previous year. Showing something of a bias in favor of the ILC project, the newspaper presented this as an indication of increasing interest among the public, despite the fact that this is unlikely to be statistically significant. In the reported survey, older people showed more interest than younger people, with 68.7% of those in their 60s indicating interest, followed by 65.5% of those in their 40s, 64.7% in their 20s, and 50% in their teens. There was also more interest indicated in inland regions directly affected by the construction as compared to coastal regions that would only be indirectly influenced. According to the survey, 27.8% of the respondents indicated little or no interest in the ILC; the anticipated effect most people expected was an increase in employment and development (35%), followed by internationalization and interaction with other cultures (18.3%); 14.7% of respondents expressed the hope that the project would stop or at least slow depopulation. While close to 30% of the population showing little or no interest is not insignificant in terms of assessing how people view the project, it also does not mean that those same people oppose construction—this sort of ambiguity is common in Japanese surveys, leaving room for people to avoid taking a strong position for or against the object of questioning.

In discussions I have had with individuals living in the area, some have expressed reservations about the project. For example, one individual who lives in the area that will be directly influenced by the ILC project explained:

> People around here think it's a shame to show their ignorance, so they don't want to speak up and ask questions. Three years ago, the PTA in Morioka worried about the danger of an accident with the ILC. They wondered if the ILC could have the same type of nuclear accident as Fukushima. Researchers who are related to the ILC repeat and repeat at public lectures that an accident will never happen in the future. Now is difficult timing, some say [following the nuclear disaster in Fukushima], and some people have asked why nobody has any doubts or questions about the ILC.

Another person with whom I spoke referred to the protest allegory *Matin Brun*, by French author Franck Pavloff, in which the local politics subtly change so that brown becomes the only acceptable color. Eventually books start to be burned that counter the prevailing ideology and those who have other colored dogs are told to put them down, while most individuals continue to feel secure in their cafes and comfortable lifestyles. In the end and too late to change anything, people realize that they have fallen victim to a government demanding conformity.[28] That said, through a variety of discussions concerning the project, most of my research participants have displayed either neutrality or a positive reaction to the possibility of the ILC being located in the region.

Study of the ILC project captures a sense that much more is going on than simply a push to get the ILC located in Tōhoku for economic and population reasons, supporting Anthony Rausch's point that a simple economically based approach to thinking about development is not appropriate in areas like Tōhoku, given the region's "peripheral location far-removed from the industrial and metropolitan centers of Japan..."[29] As should be clear at this point in the book, I do not agree with the characterization of Tōhoku as far removed or on the periphery, but Rausch's discussion of development is helpful in exploring how the creation of projects like the ILC in northern Japan are viewed as much more than economic endeavors. These projects are often intended at least in part as means by which to engage in a gradual restructuring of local identity and consciousness within the context of government support and innovative entrepreneurship.[30]

THE ILC AS ENTREPRENEURIAL ECOSYSTEM ENGINE

The fact that the ILC can be interpreted as an attempt to reconfigure the identity of the southern Tōhoku region represents a locus where the idea of an entrepreneurial ecosystem becomes interesting and relevant to the construction of the ILC and to other efforts being pursued by locals to strengthen, or stabilize, the social and economic environment. First, it is important to recognize that the reconfiguring—the evolving of society, as Suzuki put it—is conceptualized neither as part of a rural periphery nor as an urban center; instead, those pushing for the ILC project are often engaged in a process of reconceptualizing the region as a hub of international scientific research that blends the rural character of the area with linkages to global economic, political, and intellectual flows. In other words, the social context being presented in PR and other literature on the ILC is one in which the ILC operates as a metaphor for a Tōhoku region conceived as part of a socially and spatially de-polarized (global) social imaginary, circumventing the traditional binaries between rural and urban, agricultural and industrial, periphery and center.[31] The Tōhoku envisioned by those leading pursuit of the ILC is not that of the often discussed (in anthropological literature on rural Japan) *furusato* ふるさと symbolically representing romanticized and nostalgic images of rustic rural scenery linked to Japan's imagined agrarian past, although it does have connections to the idea *of furusato tsukuri* ふるさとづくり (hometown-making) that has been encouraged by the national government.[32] Rather, the ILC is constructed as a metaphor for a reconfigured social and physical space that is neither explicitly rustic nor cosmopolitan and that is conceptualized and situated as part of a globally linked frame of existential experience that is perhaps best described as what I will term for the remainder of this book as a cosmopolitan rurality.

It is important to recognize that the attempt to resituate Tōhoku into a more cosmopolitan social frame has been going on for some time. In fact, efforts at internationalization (*kokusaika* 国際化) have been important components of local governmental efforts for at least the past two decades and have formed a vector along which local municipalities have attempted to build "modern" communities by investing in a future that is believed to have the potential to retain and attract younger people.[33] Perhaps what is most interesting about the ILC is that, at least as it is presented in government and NGO-sponsored literature, it has come to form not simply a potential economic boon, but also a symbolic marker of the region as having successfully reconfigured its identity as a modern or even postmodern locale tied in with international flows, and specifically international scientific flows, but one that retains a rural flavor associated with strong feelings of community, natural surroundings, and a healthy lifestyle. In this sense, the ILC project represents an attempt at changing the context of social and economic life in the region and, at least in part, to create an entrepreneurial ecosystem centered around the ILC in which new ideas and enterprises are generated.

In the first part of the twenty-first century, there has been a fair amount of interest from business and academic perspectives in the metaphor of the entrepreneurial ecosystem, which refers to a matrix of activities, policies, and resources that form an environment in which entrepreneurial activity operates.[34] The entrepreneurial ecosystem is sometimes discussed in terms of domains that typically include areas of human activity such as policy-making, financial institutions, infrastructure, social elements, markets, and human capital. The list varies somewhat from one researcher to another but usually includes these types of domains.[35]

Figure 5 shows some of the factors or elements we can think of as contributing to the specific nature of an entrepreneurial ecosystem. I have avoided the notion of domains in part because that suggests a lack of interpenetration among these elements. While we can think of, for example, government and support systems as different domains, this is not really accurate because people constantly move from one domain to the other, creating an ongoing cross-fertilization of ideas and practices—the different areas form something more like clouds than domains. In figure 5, I have identified several fields that influence the formation and structure of an entrepreneurial ecosystem, but these should not be taken as exhaustive. One element here that is different from most attempts at identifying the aspects of entrepreneurial ecosystems is the importance of culture and history.

Indeed, much of the writing on this topic fails to explore how entrepreneurial ecosystems interpenetrate other cultural elements such as religious practices and beliefs in terms of the manner in which the influence the ways in which an entrepreneurial ecosystem operates. Seales provides a good example of how the entrepreneurial is intertwined with other aspects of a cultural context via his work on corporate chaplaincies in the US. These corporate chaplaincies represent an environmental factor related to the religious context in which a business operates can play a significant role in shaping the nature of entrepreneurial ecosystems, particularly in rural parts of the US. Seales explains that corporate chaplains are religious ministers trained in pastoral care that are paid by companies to provide emotional and spiritual support to workers on the jobsite. This is a growing profession—itself one that involves entrepreneurs such as the creators of the Dallas-based company Marketplace Chaplains, founded in 1984 by Ann and Gil Stricklin, which supplies several thousand chaplains who minister to over 500,000 employees in companies throughout the United States.[36] Clearly, this type of enterprise is only likely to work in an environment that is significantly shaped by Christian religious ideologies and in this case largely Protestant worldviews. Its presence in the US, and location in Texas, is a product of a cultural context that supports the creation of an entrepreneurial ecosystem or environment that is favorable to evangelical activities in the workplace. A similar business would be a complete non-starter in Japan, where Christianity is relatively insignificant in the religious landscape and even Buddhism is not generally associated with counseling or pastoral care.[37] In other words, the capacity of a business such as Marketplace Chaplains to grow is dependent upon the overall religious environment in the southern United States (and perhaps the country as a whole), which tends to be dominated by Christian ideologies of one form or another. One can imagine that the company is not particularly successful in places like Long Island, New York, which has a large Jewish population, although this assumption may be wrong.

Another example that raises the importance of cultural variables in shaping the structure and success in efforts to create an entrepreneurial ecosystem can be found in the nature of kinship and family ideologies. Primogenitural stem-family systems, like that historically typical in Japan,[38] by virtue of limiting succession and inheritance to a single, usually co-resident, child have promoted out-migration from rural to urban areas. In contemporary Japan, primogeniture is less significant in terms of succession and inheritance than it was in the past, but there remains a tendency for one child to take the role of successor, which implies eventually co-residing with parents as they grow old.[39] After the successor grows to adulthood and secures a spouse, non-successors function as surplus children who can be economically and socially burdensome should they remain in their natal households, and in Japan it is expected that they will form an independent household. Thus, there tends to be a push out of one's natal household that accompanies the pull of urban life and draws many younger people to move to cities like Tokyo to seek opportunities for education, work, and marriage, leading to the problems of out-migration and depopulation discussed earlier in this chapter.[40] This process also creates a drain on potential entrepreneurial talent that might remain or return to start new businesses but that have only limited family obligations to pull individuals back to the countryside from city life.

However, there is also a modest flow of migrants out of cities in favor of life in the countryside that is often portrayed in the Japanese media as a return to an idealized *furusato*, a "home" where one can escape the stresses associated with urban anomie, Western influences, and industrial dehumanization.[41] In recent years, this has also become increasingly associated with interests in development of organic farming techniques and educational programs designed to attract urban residents to rural areas in part to help in developing an understanding of rural value structures and generate contexts to help in preserving cultural features of some of the more remote rural areas. There has developed some level of urgency to attract residents, or at least find ways to maintain communities, in areas known as *chūsankan chiiki* (中山間地域semi-mountainous regions), where depopulation represents more than an economic problem, forming an existential threat to many communities. As Takano notes, Japanese governmental surveys of semi-mountainous regions in 2010 identified 64,954 communities in depopulating areas, of which 10,091—or 15.5 percent—had more than 50 percent of residents over the age of 65, while 575 communities had no residents under the age of 65. The communities whose residents are all older than 65 are concentrated in mountainous rural areas, and between 1999 and 2004, 191 such communities disappeared and this trend has continued into the present.[42]

While semi-mountainous regions such as those Takano discusses in Niigata are faced with immediate and potentially dire consequences from depopulation in terms of the future of many communities, the basic cocktail of out-migration and population aging in rural and neo-rural Japan has pushed local leaders to develop programs and projects that have the potential to maintain population and provide economic and social opportunities for long-term residents while potentially attracting new residents. This is where projects like the ILC are particularly important, but it is only one of many large and small projects that serve a similar function of helping to create a different sort of region that is characterized as open to and supportive of entrepreneurial activities. It is also worth noting that attempts to generate entrepreneurial ecosystems are not new in Japan. As David B. Friedman noted in the late 1980s, the context of politics and economic policy in Japan during the post-war era led to an environment of governmental support for the creation of small firms and flexible approaches to production, which we might view having been aimed at generating entrepreneurial ecosystems.[43]

As I bring this chapter to a close, I want to emphasize the point that the neo-rural represents not the juxtaposition of binaries such as rustic/cosmopolitan or agricultural/industrial but the reconfiguration of lifeways in order to negotiate and manage the historical contingency of collective existence within the context of a global imaginary in which these types of binaries have lost the depth of meaning they once had in many places. This is being done by transforming projects like ILC into much more than efforts in big science. The ILC's symbolic import lies in its capacity to capture and express a sense of postmodern hope and to tie individual and collective identities to that sensitivity as part of a larger program aimed at turning the region surrounding Kanegaski and Ōshū into an environment or ecosystem supportive of entrepreneurial activities both large and small. In this sense, then, the ILC is a centerpiece project aimed not simply at development but functions as an incubator in the reconfiguring of southern Tōhoku into a node of cosmopolitan rurality—a space that synthesizes images of the traditional with images of the modern within the context of the global. The ILC is not simply a metaphor for modernity nor for tradition, nor is it a metaphor for urbanity or rurality; it represents a conceptual space that overtly attempts to reconfigure these binaries into a new kind of social landscape outside or beyond an oppositional and dialectic configuring of personal and collective lifeways.

In the remaining chapters of this book, my goal is to explore several much smaller entrepreneurial endeavors that are part of this overarching entrepreneurial ecosystem that local leaders hope to develop through the ILC and other programs, both large and small, designed to draw in migrants and retain those residents already living in the region. I will shift now in my discussion from the macro to a more micro-scale of data presentation and analysis as I explore the narratives and experiences of several individuals who have engaged in different forms of entrepreneurialism—and often built their identities around the entrepreneurial endeavor—both as a means to contribute to the community in which they have created businesses and to find existential meaning at the level of their own lives.

Figure 1. Population change (x 1,000) in Tōhoku, 1920–2016.

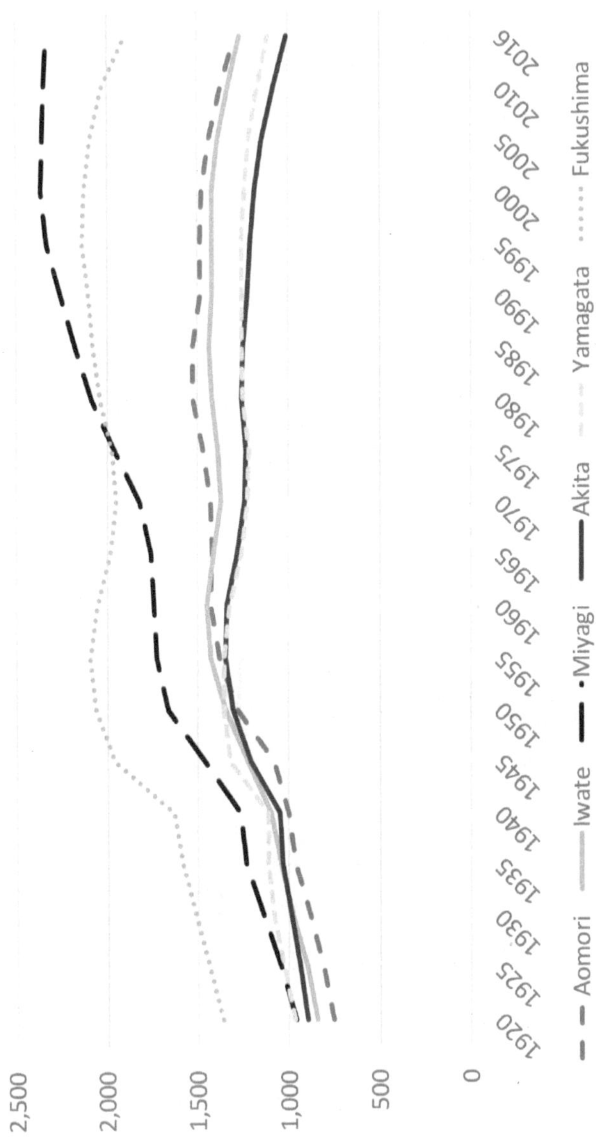

Figure 2. Population Change (x 1,000) in Chiba and Tokyo, 1920–2016.

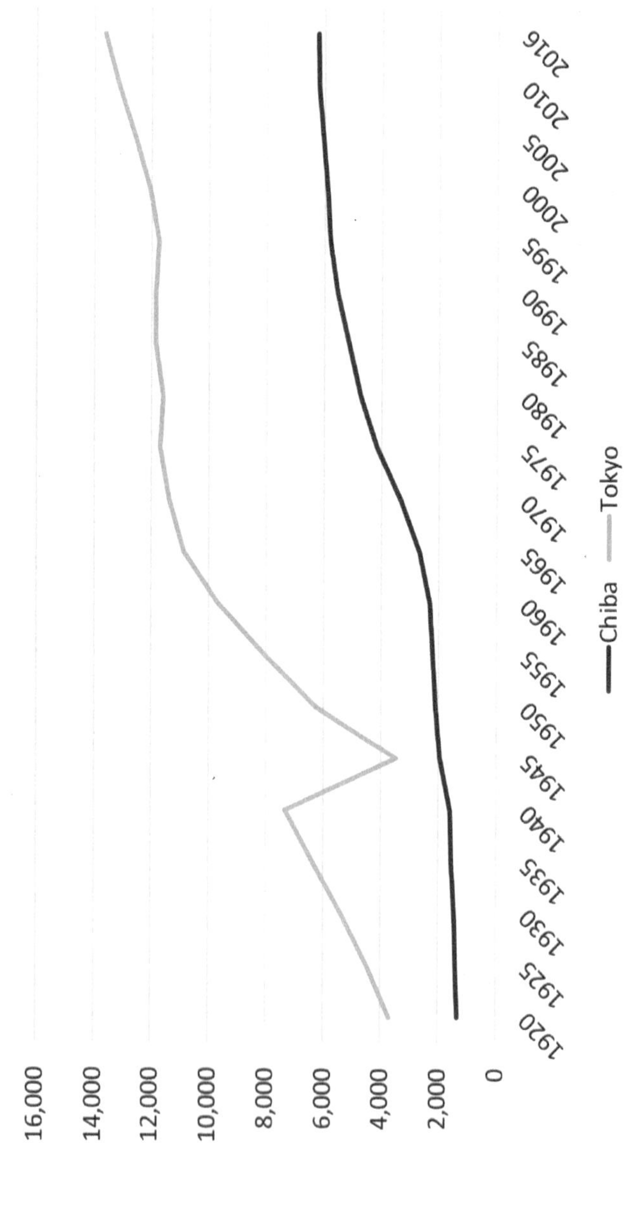

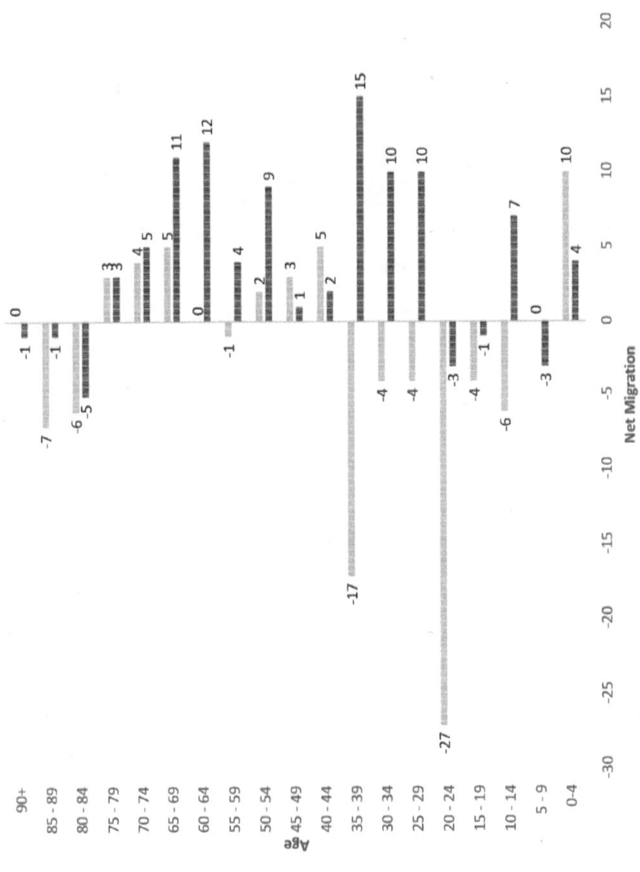

Figure 3. Net migration for Northern Japan, Chiba, and Tokyo, 2015–2016.

Table 1. Population change rates for Japan and selected prefectures, September–October, 2010–2014.

	2010	2011	2012	2013	2014
Japan	-1.7	-1.9	-1.4	-1.4	-1.1
Aomori	-7.4	-9.4	-10.1	-10.5	-10.9
Iwate	-11.6	-6.8	-5.6	-6.8	-7.8
Miyagi	-9.3	1.1	1.9	0.7	-0.4
Akita	-10.3	-11.3	-11.8	-12.7	-13.3
Yamagata	-5.9	-7.5	-8.3	-8.5	-9.0
Fukushima	-20.4	-15.3	-8.8	-6.6	-6.7
Ibaraki	-3.4	-4.2	-3.4	-3.6	-3.3
Tochigi	-3.8	-4.2	-3.0	-2.9	-2.9
Gumma	-3.3	-3.7	-3.9	-3.4	-3.2
Saitama	2.0	1.0	1.7	2.6	2.7
Chiba	0.1	-2.7	0.1	1.2	2.2
Tokyo	3.0	2.7	5.5	6.9	8.7
Niigata	-4.4	-5.8	-6.2	-6.6	-6.9
Toyama	-4.6	-4.4	-5.5	-5.3	-5.0
Nagano	-4.7	-4.7	-4.6	-5.6	-5.5
Gifu	-4.5	-4.4	-4.6	-4.8	-5.3
Shizuoka	-3.6	-3.3	-2.5	-4.1	-3.9
Aichi	1.0	1.7	2.4	2.0	2.6

Figure 4. Economic growth for Iwate Prefecture, 2002–2014.

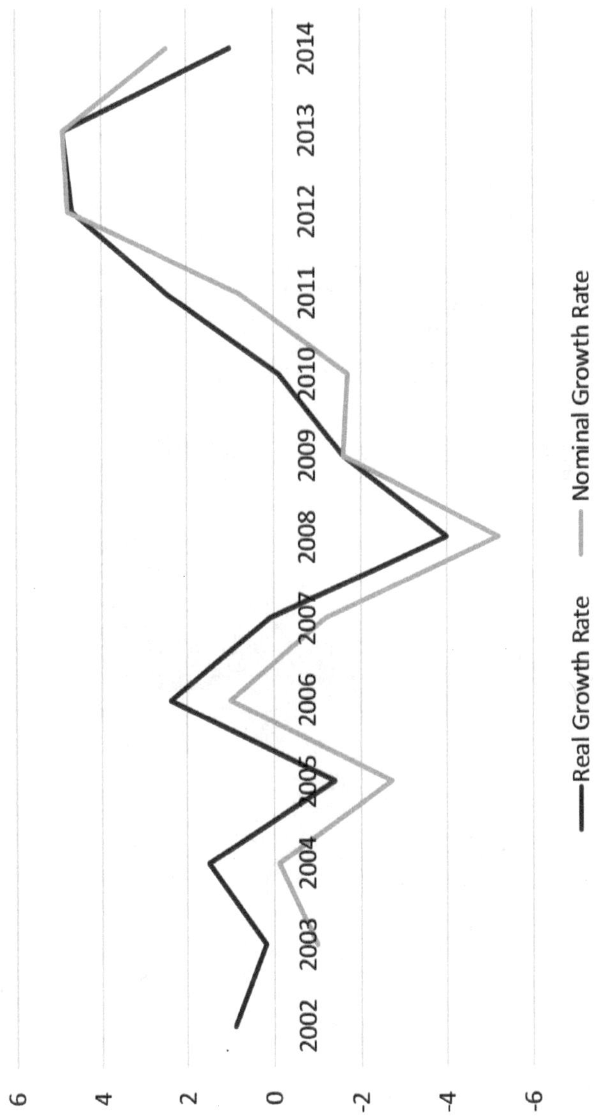

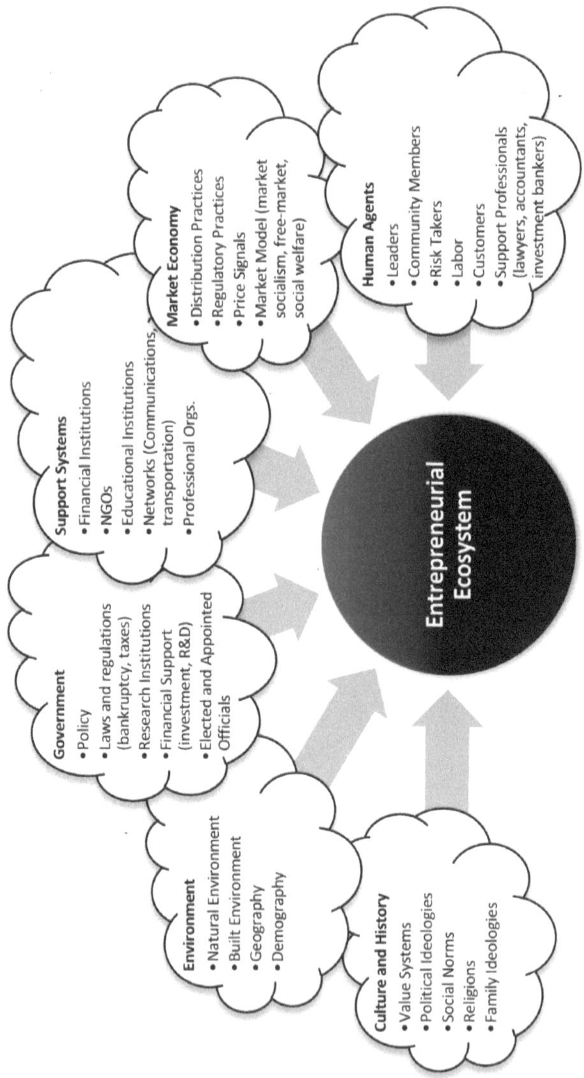

Figure 5. Elements of entrepreneurial ecosystems.

Notes

1. Nathan Hopson, *Ennobling Japan's Savage Northeast: Tōhoku as Postwar Thought, 1945–2011*, vol. 407, *Harvard East Asian Monographs* (Cambridge, Mass.: Harvard University Asia Center, 2017).
2. Fumie Kumagai, "Forty Years of Family Change in Japan: A Society Experiencing Population Aging and Declining Fertility," *Journal of Comparative Family Studies* 41, no. 4 (2010).
3. Town of Kanegasaki, accessed online 3 January 2019, http://www.town.kanegasaki.iwate.jp.
4. Population Census / 2015 Population Census / Preliminary Tabulation Preliminary Counts of the Population and Households, accessed online 3 January 2019, https://www.e-stat.go.jp/en/.
5. Population data are drawn from the Japan Statistical Yearbook, which is produced by the Japanese government: http://www.stat.go.jp/english/data/nenkan/1431-02.htm. Traphagan, "East Asia's Population Problem."
6. Toru Fujioka and Connor Cislo, "Rural Japan's Folk Traditions Fading as Residents Age," *The Japan Times*2017, https://www.japantimes.co.jp/news/2017/02/09/national/rural-japans-folk-traditions-fading-residents-age/#.XLYJZy2ZPOQ.
7. Scott Schnell, *The Rousing Drum: Ritual Practice in a Japanese Community* (Honolulu: University of Hawaii Press, 1999).
8. Iwate Prefecture Policy Area Department, 岩手県時計白書*2018 [Iwate Prefecture Statistical White Paper 2018]*, by 岩手県 政策地域部 (盛岡市 [Morioka]: 岩手県 [Iwate Prefecture], 2018).
9. Real growth rate (RGR) = NGR – inflation
10. Source: http://www.pref.iwate.jp/kokusai/27900/28905/028935.html, accessed 4 January 2019
11. Source: Iwate Prefectural Government, http://www.pref.iwate.jp/kouchoukouhou/27900/28905/028935.html
12. Susanne Klien, "Reinventing Ishinomaki, Reinventing Japan? Creative Networks, Alternative Lifestyles and the Search for Quality of Life in Post-Growth Japan," *Japanese Studies* 36, no. 1 (2016/01/02 2016), http://dx.doi.org/10.1080/10371397.2016.1148555.
13. Source: http://doc.future-city.go.jp/pdf/english/forum/kamaishi.pdf. Accessed, 15 September 2019.

14. ILC戦略会議, "Announcement of the Results of the Ilc Candidate Site Evaluation in Japan," accessed 11 January, 2018. http://ilc-str.jp/topics/2013/08281826/.
15. 岩手日報, "ILC関連に2.6億円18年度政府予算案 [260 Million Yen Allocated for ILC-Related Items in National Budget for Fy2018 – an Almost 152 Million Yen Increase from Fy2017]. ," accessed 9 January, 2018. http://www.iwate-np.co.jp/cgi-bin/news.cgi?ilc=20171223_1.
16. Ibid.
17. Japan Times Editorial Staff, "A Chance to Host Linear Collider," accessed 11 January, 2018. https://www.japantimes.co.jp/opinion/2013/03/05/editorials/a-chance-to-host-linear-collider/#.WleKZSOZNE4.
18. ILC, *Guidelines for Preparation of National Cost Estimates Based on the ILC Tdr Value Estimate* (2013); H. Baer, V. D. Barger, and J. List, "The Collider That Could Save Physics," accessed 18 January, 2018. https://www.scientificamerican.com/article/the-collider-that-could-save-physics/.
19. A. Rausch, *Cultural Commodities in Japanese Rural Revitalization: Tsugaru Nuri Lacquerware and Tsugaru Shamisen* (Leiden: Brill, 2010).
20. 河北新報, "＜東北市長会＞原発事故対応やILC誘致要望 [Tōhoku Mayors Association Nuclear Accident Response and Ilc Invitation Request]," accessed 4 January, 2018. http://www.kahoku.co.jp/tohokunews/201706/20170607_71015.html.
21. 2017 Ichinoseki Linear Collider bulletin, "Kids Try Their Hand at ILC Posters," accessed 11 January, 2018. http://www.city.ichinoseki.iwate.jp/ilc/en/newsletters/ilc_news_vol20.html#box5.
22. Amanda Wayama, "Iwate and the ILC," accessed 3 January, 2018. http://www.iwate-ilc.jp/eng/ktimes/the-ilc-is-not-a-gamble-33/.
23. 河北新報,
24. It is worth noting that in the literature I have read on the ILC from both government office and NGOs in the region, there is little or no mention of the Fukushima nuclear disaster in relation to reconstruction and revitalization.
25. 酒造唯, "「次世代加速器」誘致支持せず　日本学術会議 [Science Council Not to Support Construction of International Linear Collider in Japan]," 毎日新聞 [Mainichi Newspaper], accessed 7 January 2019, 2019. https://mainichi.jp/articles/20181219/k00/00m/040/058000c.
26. Japan Press Weekly, "Scientists Concerned over Japan's Hosting ILC Project," accessed. http://www.japan-press.co.jp/modules/news/index.php?id=6377.

27. 岩手日報, "ILCに関心 64% [Ilc Interest 64%]. ," 岩手日報, 24 December, 2017.
28. Franck Pavloff, *Matin Brun* (Devesset, France: Cheyne, 1998).
29. Anthony Rausch, "Local Identity, Cultural Commodities, and Development in Rural Japan: The Potential as Viewed by Cultural Producers and Local Residents," *International Journal of Japanese Sociology* 14 (2005).
30. Ibid.
31. Mark Altaweel and Andrea Squitieri, "Material Culture Hybridization," in *Revolutionizing a World*, From Small States to Universalism in the Pre-Islamic near East (UCL Press, 2018); Peter de Souza, *The Rural and Peripheral in Regional Development: An Alternative Perspective* (New York: Routledge, 2018).
32. Millie Creighton, "Consuming Rural Japan: The Marketing of Tradition and Nostalgia in the Japanese Travel Industry," *Ethnology* 36, no. 3 (1997); Christopher S. Thompson and John W. Traphagan, eds., *Wearing Cultural Styles in Japan: Concepts of Tradition and Modernity in Practice* (Albany: State University of New York Press, 2006).
33. Tomoko Traphagan, "Negotiating Internationalization in Kitasawa," in *Wearing Cultural Styles in Japan: Concepts of Tradition and Modernity in Practice*, ed. Christopher S. Thompson and John W. Traphagan (Albany: State University of New York Press, 2006).
34. Carmen Freitas and Michael Kitson, "Perceptions of Entrepreneurial Ecosystems in Remote Islands and Core Regions," *Island Studies Journal* 13, no. 1 (2018), http://dx.doi.org/10.24043/isj.44.
35. Ibid.; Daniel Isenberg and Vincent Onyemah, "Fostering Scale up Ecosystems for Regional Economic Growth," *Innovations* 11, no. 1/2 (2016).
36. Chad E. Seales, "Corporate Chaplaincy and the American Workplace," *Religion Compass* 6, no. 3 (2012/03/01 2012), accessed 2019/01/09, http://dx.doi.org/10.1111/j.1749-8171.2012.00340.x. For those interested, the URL for Marketplace Chaplains is https://mchapusa.com.
37. Ian Reader, *Religion in Contemporary Japan* (Honolulu: University of Hawaii Press, 1991).
38. Keith Brown, "The Content of Dozoku Relationships in Japan," *Ethnology* 7, no. 2 (1968), http://dx.doi.org/10.2307/3772742; Akitoshi Shimizu, "Ie and Dozoku: Family and Descent in Japan," *Current Anthropology* 28, no. 4 (1987), http://www.jstor.org/stable/2743443.
39. John W. Traphagan and John Knight, *Demographic Change and the Family in Japan's Aging Society, Suny Series in Japan in Transition* (Albany: State University of New York Press, 2003).

40. G. William Skinner, "Family Systems and Demographic Processes," in *Anthropological Demography: Toward a New Synthesis*, ed. David I. Kertzer and Tom Fricke (Chicago: University of Chicago Press, 1997).
41. Creighton, 240.
42. Takano, in *Educating for Sustainability in Japan: Fostering Resilient Communities after the Triple Disaster.*
43. David B. Friedman, *The Misunderstood Miracle: Industrial Development and Political Change in Japan* (Ithaca: Cornell University Press, 1988).

Chapter 3

A Challenging Business Climate

虎穴に入らずんば虎子を得ず (*koketsu ni irazunba koji wo ezu*)

If you do not enter the tiger's cave, you will not catch its cub.
—Japanese aphorism

In the summer of 2016, my daughter, Sarah, and I hopped in the car to go get her hair cut. It's an easy drive along modern roads from the Western end of Kanegasaki, with its wide expanses of rice fields and dark-green mountains, to the more built-up City of Ōshū. As one drives, the scene shifts from agricultural plains to housing developments, convenience stores, and shopping malls situated at the outskirts of downtown Ōshū. Along the road toward the center of town, Sarah commented on how many empty buildings there seemed to be. I told her a bit about the problems with depopulation and she started counting the buildings that appeared to be empty as we drove through town. Over the course of roughly a kilometer, she counted 15 buildings that looked empty and run down. It is not difficult to tell which buildings are vacant. The empty ones often have weeds growing around the front walkway, the curtains are drawn throughout the day, and there is no evidence of clothes hanging or having been recently hung out to dry—a normal scene in front of Japanese homes. Some are actually boarded up. There also is usually no evidence of a vehicle anywhere on the property, whether car or bicycle. My daughter thought it was sad that so many houses seemed empty, and I would have to agree.

When we arrived at the hair salon, there were no waiting customers and no one else came in while we were there—which was quite a while, since the stylist and business owner, Mr. Suzuki, spent a great deal of time carefully cutting Sarah's hair. Mr. Suzuki told us that business had dropped off and there usually were not many customers as compared to the past. Although this certainly has caused problems for Mr. Suzuki from an economic perspective, like many family businesses in the area, the shop is on the first floor of his residence; therefore, he does not have to pay rent, as he would if his business were located in one of the shopping malls on the outskirts of town. The salon is clean and neat, but it is obvious that Mr. Suzuki has not updated the décor for many years, perhaps due to the limited number of customers he sees. Fortunately, his property has been in his family for generations, so he does not have to worry about a mortgage on the building—he makes enough money to live reasonably, but no more than that.

Mr. Suzuki's shop is roughly three kilometers from the center of town but still within the densely built area of Ōshū, and a car or bicycle is necessary to get to shopping areas along the bypass route that skirts the center of town or the train station in the center of the city, where trains run hourly in each direction—north and south. There is also a station for the bullet train in Ōshū, but it is several kilometers to the east of the local rail line in the center of town and one must take a taxi to transfer between the bullet train and the local line, which is unlike stations in other cities in the region that combine both local and bullet-train lines, making train travel in Ōshū inconvenient if one lacks a car.

If one walks out of the front doors of the station, the first thing evident is a parking lot for taxis. There used to be several taxis waiting in front of the station at scheduled train arrivals, but now there are typically only one or two waiting for potential customers disembarking in Ōshū. The main street is about 500 meters long and has sidewalks over which awnings have been built to protect shoppers from the rain, but now there is not a great deal of need for this, because there are few shops remaining open compared to when I first arrived in Ōshū in the 1980s. In fact, when I walked along Main Street in 2015, I counted a total of 17 empty storefronts along the stretch that leads to the train station. Indeed, when I first visited Ōshū, there were two department stores in the center of town, a Daiei and a Jusco—both national department store chains. Neither remain and the Daiei building was torn down several years ago to make space for a parking lot and a branch office of Iwate Bank. Only a few years ago, there were jewelry stores, a camera shop, restaurants, and two sporting-goods shops, one of which specialized only in baseball equipment. Some of those shops remain, including the baseball store, but even stores that one might expect to prosper have closed, including the Mr. Donut that was about halfway down the road from the train station until about ten years ago.

The station road ends in a T. If one turns to the right, there is a day-care center for the elderly at the corner and then beyond that most of the stores that once thrived along the next 100 meters have closed, including an English-language school that occupied the second floor of one office building. Many of the structures throughout the area display the appearance of decay, having not been painted or updated in decades, with the occasional bedsheet or closed curtains hanging behind windows that were once storefronts. The residences above many of these shops, where owners like Mr. Suzuki typically lived, also look empty in several cases. If one turns to the left at the T, there is a four-story building in which there is a small shopping mall known as Maple that includes clothing stores and a few other shops for goods like stationery supplies. Across from Maple there is an innovative coffee shop that was constructed inside a *kura*

(蔵), which is a timber-and-clay building that traditionally was used to store commodities such as rice, but also was used for keeping valuables. These buildings are often aesthetically pleasing, due to their traditional architectural styling, and I have heard many locals commenting on the novel and innovative use of the building for this purpose, making it an attractive spot to enjoy a cup of coffee or lunch.

Beyond Maple the road opens into an area that was targeted for redevelopment by the Ōshū city government in the 1990s. The goal had been to invest in revitalizing the area as a new business district with attractive shops that would cater to young people. There was a plan to spruce up the sidewalks to make the street aesthetically attractive by using architectural cues from the past and paving the roads with cobblestones along with bringing in interesting shops that would generate a vibrant business atmosphere in the center of town. Little of this plan actually materialized.

Part of what prevented the plan from developing was related to the declining population discussed in the previous chapter; in Ōshū the population declined from about 133,000 in the 2010 census to 119,000 in the 2015 census and this pattern will continue for the foreseeable future. Limitations in developing the downtown area associated with declining population in the center of Ōshū have been exacerbated by the construction of a bypass road around the center of town over thirty years ago that has drawn some stores out of the downtown district to strip malls along the bypass that have large parking lots—the Mr. Donut along the bypass route appears to be doing fine with a regular flow of customers, as are McDonald's, Baskin Robins, and MOS Burger, a family restaurant that serves Italian food, several clothing stores, and a home and garden supply store, to name a few of the businesses, all of which are either national or regional chains. Because this part of Japan has limited public transportation, it is normal for people to drive to most of the places they frequent on a daily basis, although bicycles are common forms of transportation for adults as well, and this makes shopping areas with large parking lots attractive to local consumers who live a highly auto-centered pattern of existence.[1]

The first and, as far as I can tell, only store that actually opened along the street in association with the redevelopment effort is known as Pressé, which is an quaint shop catering to young women and particularly to high-school girls who can ride their bicycles to the store after school. Figures 6 and 7 show the outside of the store including some of the merchandise displayed in the shop window. Inside, the store is cluttered with an eclectic variety of objects encompassing clothing, small toys like Gumby dolls, stationery supplies, umbrellas, and imported snack foods such as Walkers Shortbread cookies. I have been in the store many times over the years and as far as I can remember, I have never encountered another man in the store and all of the employees are women. In fact, the owner has explained that her image in creating the store was to create a place that would appeal to young women and much of the merchandise sold there is intended to capitalize on the cute craze that has been part of Japanese culture for some time although, given the inclusion of clothes and imported goods, there is perhaps something of a more sophisticated feeling to the store than one might find in a Hello Kitty–laden shop at a nearby mall, with quite a few objects representing imported and stylish goods.[2]

The owner of the shop is a woman in her late-50s, who I will refer to as Akiko and who grew up in Ōshū and moved to Tokyo after graduating from Mizusawa High School, which is the top college preparatory high school in the area. Akiko attended a two-year college in Tokyo and stayed in the city after graduation to work at a company as an Office Lady (OL), which typically involves tasks such as administrative work like copying and making tea for guests and male members of the staff.[3] OL positions have normally been viewed as temporary jobs, rather than career-track positions, that a woman will occupy for a few years and then when she marries (often to a man in the same company), she will resign and focus on raising a family. Akiko followed this path, working for the company for about three years during which time she met her husband, who was a fellow employee. Although Akiko's experiences were fairly typical of her generation of women, as will become clear, Akiko's life-course path soon diverged from the expected pattern.

AKIKO'S PATH TO ENTREPRENEUR

Akiko explained her history of work and reasons for starting a business in Ōshū while we sat in the back of her store one afternoon in 1997. At the time, the store was busy and one of her employees handled customers while Akiko spoke with me, but occasionally we were interrupted with a question about merchandise that only Akiko could address. In the years since that conversation, I have visited Akiko in her store several times and observed the changes that have occurred in her business. Compared to 1997, the store is much quieter, with only a few customers who come in on most days—the steady flow of uniformed high-school girls that was typical in 1997 has declined in recent years and Akiko has told me recently that she does not think the store will be able to continue much longer, a point to which I will return shortly.

Akiko's is an experience of U-turn or turnaround-migration that is similar to that of many women who spent several years working in other parts of Japan, particularly Tokyo, eventually returning to their natal town either for family or business reasons, or some combination of the two.[4] Akiko's experience represents a good example of the complex experiences related to mobility that many Japanese her age experienced as the allure of Tokyo as a place where one can "make it" or pursue educational and business interests drew young people out of rural areas and smaller cities—a pattern that, of course, continues into the present. In the narrative that follows, I focus on Akiko's discussion of her return to Iwate after spending several years in Tokyo in pursuit of education and work followed by her experience of marriage, which is a key component in her decision to return to Ōshū.

> At the time of my marriage, I quit my job. My [first] husband was from Kanazawa Prefecture [roughly 300km west of Tokyo along the Japan Sea] so we returned there and he took up work in his father's company selling real estate. We started a normal life in Kanazawa and I lived there for about two years. Although he was the second son, he worked in his family's company.[5] After a while, I realized that there was a problem [in our marriage], so I returned to my natal home in Ōshū for about a year. At that time, I was only 25; I was married very early at only 22.[6] During the time I was in Ōshū I began to think about whether or not there was anything I wanted to do with my future. Then I returned to Tokyo one more time. I managed to get a job working for a company that makes sets for television programs that was run by the sister-in-law of one of my friends.

As we talked, Akiko explained that she divorced her first husband due to a variety of problems, but the most important issue was that, as she put it, "money disappeared." It is important to recognize that divorce at that time in Japan was unusual with the divorce rate in the mid-1980s hovering around 1.3 per 1,000 persons; by comparison this number was roughly 5.0 in the United States during the same period. In other words, divorce was fairly uncommon in Japan and generally viewed negatively when Akiko decided to end her marriage, which may have added stress and difficulty to this course of action, although she did not indicate this directly to me in our conversations.[7]

As Akiko described the issues she had with her husband, she said that the ease at which money seemed to vanish confused her at first, but eventually she came to understand what was happening, which turned out to be very disturbing to her in terms of having trust in her husband, as well as his family. And because they had followed the traditional pattern in which Akiko married-in to her husband's family and, as will become evident in the narrative that follows, her father-in-law appeared to be complicit in her husband's problematic behavior, the dilemma she faced involved more than problems with her marriage partner.[8]

> Well, you know this was his father's company and, well, my ex-husband was using our money and company money for gambling. I would find that every two weeks our money would be gone, then it would reappear. I learned that he was taking company funds to gamble and his father was covering for him by putting money back in the bank. There was a lot of money moving with the real estate transactions.
>
> My husband did *pachinko*, the horse races, and other things. Because our money would run out, he would receive a great deal from his father's company. Since it was his father's company, the people around the company looked the other way. I thought this was quite wrong. When we married, I had no idea, but when I came to understand what was going on I realized that I couldn't trust him. This went on for two years. For the first year, we had a normal life, but then I realized what was going on and decided I had to leave him. Therefore, I divorced him and moved back to Ōshū.
>
> But I felt living in Ōshū was unpleasant. I thought I could do more with my life than being here [the implication here is that it is difficult to pursue a career in places like Ōshū]. I thought I could accomplish something in Tokyo. When I was back in Ōshū, having failed once, the idea that my life was over at this point was intolerable, so I felt I needed to go back to Tokyo.

I asked Akiko what she did after she moved back to Ōshū and she explained that she worked in one of the stores in the Maple shopping mall that I mentioned earlier in this chapter, and which is near her family home in the downtown area, after getting a job through a relative who owned one of the mall's shops. She ultimately decided to return to Tokyo and because her work in Ōshū was related to clothing, she became more interested in finding employment in Tokyo in sales related to apparel. For another six years, Akiko stayed in Tokyo during which time she met her current husband, who also worked in the clothing business.

> In the old days Mizusawa [the former name of Ōshū] had a more lively quality [賑やか *nigiyaka*] to it than now, but the stores were

> closing and they wanted to do something about it. Well, I was getting to be 30 and was becoming worried about my future. I was wondering how long I could continue in the life I had in Tokyo and also was concerned about marriage. Because I had been divorced once, I was extremely worried about remarrying. I wasn't sure it would work out. Thus, I was very hesitant about remarriage and it took close to ten years before I actually remarried. But I was thinking about these things and at the same time this section of town was working on a plan to do something to revive businesses and my father was a committee member in this effort. He asked me if there was anything I might like to do in the form of starting a store. I had never thought of doing anything like this before, but since in my previous job I had contact with various merchandise sources from overseas, I decided to give it a shot. It was pretty easy to decide.

In order to start her business, Akiko borrowed money from the prefectural government with what she described as good terms that allowed her to use a building without a lease and defer paying back the loan she received for five years. Her father helped her in securing the loan, which was actually taken out in his name. The combination of a government small-business loan and her father's willingness to assume the risk of repayment allowed her to get started with a limited version of the store and after that succeeded, she expanded into the current space, using both property and money from her family to support the expanded business. As will become evident in the remainder of the book, this pattern is common for small business startups in areas like Ōshū, where entrepreneurs often use a combination of government programs and parental or family help to secure the capital and space necessary to get started in creating a store or restaurant.

Akiko's experience is an example of the way in which opportunities like the downtown revitalization effort in Ōshū can play an important role in generating return migration. In the course of our conversations, Akiko explained that had she not had the opportunity to start a business in Ōshū, it would have been unlikely that she would have returned from

Tokyo, but when the opportunity arose, she jumped at it and her (now) husband returned with her. However, the return was not without some personal sacrifice, because Akiko's husband could not find work similar to what he was doing in Tokyo. Eventually, he managed to find a job working in a company that manages funerals, which is not insignificant, because funeral work in Japan is often at least somewhat stigmatized, as shown in the 2008 film *Departures* (おくりびと), directed by Yōjirō Takita. The film follows the experiences of a character similar to Akiko's husband, who returns to his home town and is only able to get work in a funeral company, which leads his wife to leave him (and eventually return) due to the embarrassing nature of his work. In contrast to Takita's story, Akiko did not see her husband's work as problematic, and, in fact, she explained that her husband's willingness to return and take a job that was not ideal helped her decide in favor of marriage, because she thought his commitment to her was genuine. I asked her if he returned specifically to be with her, and she laughed, then responded: "Probably. He is very kind. In fact, when he returned with me, it became easier for me to think about marrying again because it seemed that it would work out and I gave thanks for his moving to Ōshū with me."

STRUGGLING TO KEEP THE BUSINESS GOING

In 2016, I was walking with my daughter through a large shopping mall, known as Ezuriko Shopping Center Pal, located in the city of Kitakami, which is about 25km north of Ōshū. The mall is similar to indoor malls in the United States, with a variety of clothing stores, restaurants, and a large anchor department store called Aeon. The mall is situated very close to the major limited-access highway that runs through Tōhoku and is easily accessible by car due to the large parking garage attached to the main mall building. Sarah was looking for some new clothes to take back to the US and we saw a store with some attractive and stylish merchandise, so we wandered in to look around. As we entered, I noticed the sign on the back wall said Pressé and I realized that Akiko must have opened another store. In fact, she was working there when we walked in and after a happy reunion, we chatted about the new shop. Her reasons for opening a new store in Kitakami were related to Ōshū's failing economic situation, which of course is tied to the depopulation happening in the center of town. Akiko explained that the original shop is not doing well and she felt that it was necessary to open another store if she was to continue the business and her career. The Kitkamai branch of the store is significantly different from the one in Ōshū. Although it continues to cater to women, it has an upscale feeling with some fairly conservative business casual clothing and accessories that are more expensive than the merchandise found at the Ōshū branch. The Kitakami store also lacks the cute and eclectic atmosphere and objects for sale found in the original store; it has the feeling of an upscale shop one might find in a standard shopping mall in the US or along a street in Tokyo, which is precisely what Akiko said the store was intended to convey. Unlike the Ōshū Pressé, customers at the Kitakami branch were not high-school girls, but instead were adult women looking for fashionable clothing.

The combination of the two Pressé stores is a good example of how the construction of shopping malls along bypass routes is hollowing out local downtowns—the original store is struggling while the store in the mall is doing well, according to Akiko. The mall is only accessible by car and like malls in the US, the smaller shops rely on the anchor department store that is part of a national chain to bring in shoppers. Ezuriko Shopping Center Pal bills itself as the largest mall in southern Iwate and has a varied range of shops from food stores and restaurants to many clothing stores, stationery stores, luggage shops, a crepe shop, dry cleaner, and branch of Iwate Bank. Basically, it is a one-stop shopping mecca that also has several other malls surrounding it that are easily accessible by car due to adjacent parking lots. This pattern, which is quite similar to what has been observed in other countries like the US, has made it quite difficult for small shops such as the original Pressé to continue operation, due to its location being remote from primary shopping areas and parking representing a considerable challenge (one has to park about a block away from the store and it is difficult to find the parking area for the store). In opening the additional shop, Akiko may have been interested in growing the business, but when we talked, she explained that the primary issue was that the original store was failing and she did not think she could continue her business activities unless she expanded into a mall like Ezuriko.

Akiko's experience starting, and attempting to maintain, a business after returning to Ōshū raises an interesting question related to motivations for starting a business, and becoming an entrepreneur, in neo-rural Japan (or at least southern Iwate): Is the path to entrepreneurialism about creating and growing a business or is it about sustaining a lifestyle? Indeed, this question arose in my mind frequently as I conducted interviews for this book and will recur in most of the narratives I discuss in the following chapters. Of course, it is not necessary that this is a dichotomous choice for those who participated in this study—both reasons may be occurring at the same time in the minds of the people discussed here. But for each of the entrepreneurs discussed in this book, there was a tendency to frame their experiences in terms of something of a choice between profit and personal well-being, with the two being, at least to some degree, conceptualized as being in conflict with each other.

In the case of Akiko, expanding her business was less about becoming and entrepreneur and more about survival and sustainability, both for herself and for her business, as opposed to being about "growing" a business. Considered in terms of Virginia L. Lewis and Neil C. Churchill's five stages of small-business growth, entrepreneurs like Akiko are largely disinterested in stages beyond the third stage—success—at which point the business has reached a point of sustainable profitability.[9] Expansion for Akiko was not about growing her business, but, instead, was a response to the likelihood that the original shop will fail and close at some point over the next few years. In fact, what will become clear as we move through the cases discussed throughout the remainder of this book is that my entrepreneurial interlocutors do not generally see the central goal of business as being growth or turning a profit.

Although part of this orientation may be related to the difficult business climate in this part of Japan, it should not be purely interpreted in this way. The lack of interest in growing a business among my interlocutors also reflects cultural values in Japan that do not necessarily view entrepreneurial activity in a positive light and that favor an atmosphere of sustainability over growth. One the one hand, small-business owners like Akiko represent entrepreneurs in the sense that they are engaged in risk-taking activities both from a financial and from a personal perspective.[10] However, it is important to recognize that in rural Japan the idea of entrepreneurialism can have a negative meaning, in part as a result of perceptions in the context of a transition economy where the approaches associated with entrepreneurial activity can be connected to attempts to skirt government regulation.[11] Although I do not want to diverge into a discussion of the history of social stratification in Japan, it is worth noting that during the Tokugawa Period (1603–1868) the merchant class occupied a fairly low standing. However, as Andrew Gordon notes, while the Tokugawa merchant class occupied a subordinate place in the Confucian status order of the time, samurai and merchant classes operated in "functionally equivalent roles; the former were to run the bureaucratic administration, while the latter managed economic affairs that were of importance to the entire society."[12] In other words, despite their importance functionally in Japanese society at the time, the merchant class experienced relatively low status and entrepreneurial activity was not highly regarded by the elites. In my experience, I have never encountered any survival of this attitude towards merchants in Japan; however, it is conceivable that it has played something of a role in creating a social environment in which entrepreneurial activity centered on growing a business to attain wealth is of less interest than what one may find in places like the US, which lack that sort of past. Admittedly, this comment is speculative. However, Fujimura Shinya argues that Japanese moral ideals associated with the *bushidō* ethic (of the samurai...) suggest "continual and rapid growth doesn't have to be the ultimate goal of economic existence."[13] Although Fujimura's perspective drawing on the notion of *bushidō* is at once romanticized, simplistic, and essentializing, his basic point—that growth (and the consequence of becoming wealthy) is not necessarily a motivation for engaging in business or entrepreneurial activity among Japanese represents a key element in understanding the attitudes of individuals with whom I've spoken about their business activities in Kanegasaki and Ōshū. For Akiko, the goal of starting and sustaining (not necessarily growing) a business was presented to me as being related to generating personal satisfaction, or existential meaning, combined with maintaining an acceptable personal standard of living for herself, her family, and her employees.

It should be noted that other rural entrepreneurs may approach the start and expansion of businesses differently from the individuals I discuss here. For example, Wood describes a new venture created by a businesswoman, Fujita Shiho, in the village he studied in Akita Prefecture (which neighbors Iwate) in which young women from Tokyo known as "Shibuya Gals" participate in rice-planting tours in which they slog through paddies to experience farming. The crop is marketed as "Shibuya-mai" or Shibuya rice and sold over the Internet in packaging that shows the image of Hachikō, the famous dog whose statue stands in front of Shibuya Station in Tokyo. Wood explains that Fujita's motivation for this enterprise was in part related to a desire to change the prevailing image of agriculture as traditional and rural by associating rice with a modern, urban image; however, it is clear that if the product succeeds it has the potential to form a profitable export item from the village to other parts of Japan and, thus, will have positive economic influences both for the area and for Fujita should it succeed and grow.[14] That said, the business owners with whom I've talked in Iwate do not express a similar interest in situating their businesses in larger economic flows for the purpose of growing the business or attaining wealth, although as more than one business owner commented, often somewhat jokingly, these business owners may have little objection to becoming wealthy either.

Neo-Rural In-Migration and Existential Meaning

There is a fairly well-developed body of literature on reasons behind rural in-migration going back to the 1970s in the fields of rural sociology, entrepreneurship behavior, and rural geography.[15] Two general models have been proposed to explain this migration pattern: 1) the demand-driven model which proposes that people move to rural areas due to wage and employment opportunities associated with increased labor demands, and 2) potential residents are pulled to rural areas due to quality-of-life variables such as climate, recreation, cost of living, or a desire to escape urban life, following which labor demand increases and more jobs become available. In other words, the two models indicate that either population follows jobs (1) or jobs follow population (2), although it seems likely that both models may co-exist and operate together in any particular context. Data from Jerry D. Johnson and Raymond Rasker's study of qualitative factors associated with businesses located in rural areas in Montana suggest that factors such as scenic beauty, environmental quality, and rural atmosphere can play a central role in the decisions of companies to locate or remain in rural areas, while factors such as cost of doing business or tax structures were less important to business owners.[16] Additionally, entrepreneurship in rural environments often involves engagement with a socially oriented network of individuals and groups that are characterized by high levels of trust and social cohesion, which may be attractive to potential in-migrants/entrepreneurs from a lifestyle perspective while also aiding in the process of starting a new business as one accesses the social networks and social embeddedness of businesses that are typical of the overall business environment in many rural or neo-rural communities.[17]

Clearly, in Akiko's case the presence of established social networks—including those accessible through her family—contributed to generating a level of trust and confidence that allowed her to comfortably engage in taking a risk associated with starting her business. However, her decision to return involved a complex set of factors including quality-of-life and career issues. Although she was not unhappy living in Tokyo, at the time she was considering following a significantly new path in her life-course as she assessed opportunities related to the overall entrepreneurial climate in Ōshū.

The decision was closely tied to personal interests related to her future and developing a career that she found satisfying. Interestingly, her assessment of the business climate and potential in Ōshū, at least, seems to have proven inadequate, because it is unlikely that she will be able to continue operating the store there, given the loss of population and the failure of the city to more generally develop the part of town in which she located her store.

Put another way, Akiko's decision to engage in starting a business, to become an entrepreneur, had less to do with business or becoming wealthy than it had to do with pursuing her own happiness or well-being. As Neil Thin notes, well-being is a concept that is quite complex from cultural and personal standpoints, but that has not been particularly well developed as a research topic in anthropology.[18] The notion of well-being, of course, is culturally reified—it is difficult to measure or compare the nature of well-being, or happiness, across different cultural settings because the factors that influence definitions and feelings of well-being and happiness are intertwined with expectations and attitudes derived from a particular cultural context. Nonetheless, well-being also exhibits some commonality across cultural settings due to the fact that we share basic features of our humanity and that human societies are intertwined in both space and time.[19] Well-being may be a matter of individual subjectivity, but it is also something that it is reasonable to think concerns most people in some way regardless of social or geographical context. Well-being and happiness also are influenced by national and global institutional and ideational forces that shape how individuals determine what constitutes happiness and how to achieve it in life.[20] This is evident in Akiko's concern over marriage—at some level she seems to feel that marriage and family represent a desirable life-state to pursue; otherwise, she may have chosen to remain single after her divorce, which is not an unusual pattern of adulthood for women in Japan.[21] However, she resists this based upon her own negative experiences in marriage which, in turn, creates a level of existential anxiety and conflict in that she feels she should marry but is hesitant to do so until her husband shows genuine commitment and an ability to be trusted.

Generally, in Japan, the idea of well-being is associated with a concept known as *ikigai* 生きがい, which can be translated as one's purpose in life. The social and personal value in having an *ikigai* is a fairly common cultural trope in Japan and use of the concept as a way of assessing one's quality of life is widespread. To have an *ikigai* is at least suggestive that one has a good quality of life and, thus, that one's experience of living is constructed in terms of positive images related to personal well-being.[22] For example, in my research related to the lives of older people living in Iwate, the concept has frequently come up as a way of describing those who are doing well. One question that I have often asked is what types of things make life satisfying (*manzoku* 満足). The responses often involve the concept of *ikigai* and are typically similar to the comments of one man in his late 60s, Abe Hiroshi, who when I spoke with him was a member of the town assembly and had just been re-elected to his second four-year term in office. In thinking about what brings satisfaction to life he said, "I was somewhat disappointed at the time I retired because I liked my work and thought I was too young to retire, but I have found things to do since and have not had problems with income. My life is satisfying because I am busy; the Town Assembly keeps me busy, as do many other activities in which I'm involved." When I asked about his concerns, he stated that wants to avoid becoming ill and bedridden:

> One needs to have an *ikigai* especially in old age, which will help to keep one healthy physically and avoid becoming bedridden. I'm busy now with work for the Town Assembly and that's good, but I also need to think about my future and what sort of activities I will do when I am finished with this work.

Another many in his sixties explained when I asked him to offer some examples of people living in the neighborhood that he knew who were experiencing a good quality of life:

> Yes, there are people who are doing well, the best example would be those who are active in society and who have an *ikigai*. I think that Inoue Takeshi is doing very well, both from a social point and as an individual. He has been active in a variety of socially oriented groups and activities and his travel is impressive.

Inoue was a man in his early nineties at the time of our conversation who had retired from a position in the government when he was 55 (at that time the mandatory retirement age) and had occupied his retired life by travelling overseas and within Japan. In my own conversations with Mr. Inoue, he often commented proudly that he had been overseas 27 times, and his focus on travel was something he invariably described in terms of *ikigai* which, in turn, he believed contributed significantly to his overall good physical and mental health. The last time we talked, when he was 92, he intimated his deep concerns that a trip to Kyūshū, at the southern end of the Japanese islands, would be his last adventure and, thus, would mean the loss of his *ikigai* leading to an inevitable decline in both his physical and mental health.[23]

Indeed, the lack of an *ikigai* is often linked to having a particularly unhappy old age, characterized by physical and cognitive decline, and ending with being bedridden or even suicide.[24] Those who are perceived as being at greatest risk for this outcome are those who live alone. As Ms. Chiba, who was sixty-five and had devoted several years of her retirement to caring for her bedridden husband put it, "for those who are living alone, they become tired, they do not have any *ikigai*, and they are very pitiful and they decide to commit suicide." The polysemic nature of *ikigai* is important to keep in mind, because the term is used in a variety of ways by Japanese of all ages. A middle-aged woman might describe her *ikigai* as her children, or a hobby such as archery, while a man of the same age might discuss his work as his *ikigai*. The term can be used in a humorous way, so someone who enjoys beer a great deal might describe beer as his *ikigai.*

In his interesting book focused on the topic of *ikigai* and finding meaning in life in Japan, Gordon Mathews explains the term as consisting of two basic components that have both individual and social significance. From a social perspective, having an *ikigai* indicates a commitment to the group to which one belongs, as is clearly evident a conflation of living alone and the likelihood of not having an *ikigai* that has often arisen in conversations I have had with Japanese of many ages. This suggests that group participation of some sort is important to having an *ikigai,* although it is certainly possible and reasonable for individuals to pursue personal interests without belonging to a group, even if the concept often implies participation in an activity that involves group membership and regular social interaction. The term also conveys a more inner aspect in that it refers to engagement in activities associated with self-realization or self-actualization.[25] These notions might seem contrasting from the perspective of Americans, at least, but for Japanese it is often through membership in a group and involvement with the activity or activities associated with that group that one can engage most effectively in self-actualization.

The *ikigai* concept is often presented to the public by government agencies as being an important component of personal well-being and health. For example, a pamphlet that I picked up in Ōshū City Hall and that I also found in various local health and welfare offices had bold letters at the top that stated, "*ikigai* is the source of vigor," following which it encouraged potential readers with, "let's aim at becoming a health millionaire with *ikigai*!" The pamphlet describes various ways in which individuals might find an *ikigai* and offers an interesting list of possibilities, such as study, sports, and house cleaning (I think I'll pass on the last one) and makes the point that it matters less what one does than *that* one picks an activity that one likes. The pamphlet offers advice about how to identify an *ikigai* in four easy steps: 1) search for something one likes, 2) find a friend for mutual encouragement, 3) don't get tired out or impatient (do the activity at your own pace), 4) keep hold of your aims.

Of course, it is difficult to determine the extent to which people living in Ōshū or Kanegasaki buy-in to the ideas presented in the pamphlet—I have never talked to anyone who viewed house cleaning as his or hear *ikigai*—nor is it possible to determine the extent to which people living in the area actually read the pamphlet and others like it. However, it is clear in my work and that of scholars like Matthews that the concept is an important part of Japanese discourses on well-being, and I would argue also is important in how Japanese conceptualize the good person.[26] A good person is someone who is actively engaged in activities that support self-actualization and the creation of personal and community well-being, particularly if they are pursued within contexts that promote social interaction. And these activities are often politically framed in terms of activities that promote not only personal well-being but that contribute to the social whole—meaning one's family and community. Indeed, the pursuit of *ikigai* is often linked to benefits to the social whole by government offices and officials and expressed in terms of the idea that one's efforts in self-actualization also are important contributions to the health and well-being of the community as a whole.[27]

Clearly, for Akiko the decision to return to Iwate was based upon concerns about her own long-term goals and well-being, expressed through the desire to achieve a career with which she was satisfied and also a lifestyle, in terms of her family/husband, that was happy and fulfilling—rather than trying to become an entrepreneur, she was trying to find or develop an *ikigai*. Return-migration was not the only route to this, but when the opportunity arose to not only create a store/career that she found interesting and appealing but also to participate in a program that might benefit the local community in which she grew up, it seemed like an excellent avenue for achieving personal aims and, although she never used the term directly in relation to her work, one can interpret her goals within the broad framework of developing an *ikigai.* Akiko's goals are primarily related to finding existential meaning or a purpose in life; she was not motivated by a desire to become an entrepreneur *per se.* Rather that was something of an afterthought or byproduct of trying to establish a life path through which she could find satisfaction and meaning.

As Holthus and Manzenreiter have noted, there is a fundamental interpersonal dimension of happiness in Japan in which elements of relatedness and connectedness through social networks play central roles in shaping the ways in which notions of happiness and well-being are conceptualized and constructed by Japanese.[28] In Akiko's case, personal well-being is generated through the pursuit of personal agency in the form of creating her own business; the ability to control and manage her life and career—and to secure a path of well-being—played the primary role in the decision to start Pressé, rather than a desire to obtain wealth. Additionally, there is evident in Akiko's experience an interconnection between agency and larger social contexts, in the form of governmental institutions, that provided the opportunity for Akiko to pursue her business activities. Had the opportunity to create the store lacked governmental and familial support—in other words, had there been significant limitations on financial and personal risk—it is doubtful that Akiko would have returned to Ōshū to start her business. When it comes to Akiko's goals as an entrepreneur, much more important than the business itself or attaining wealth, we find a complex set of motivations in which happiness and well-being are constructed through frames of relatedness (connections to her father and husband), community (government support), and the larger social networks in which both her store and her life are embedded.[29]

This emphasis on existential meaning and personal happiness is one of the key themes that arises in the conversations I have had with entrepreneurs in neo-rural Japan. In the next chapter, I turn to the case of Keiko who, along with her husband, has built something of a healthcare empire in Ōshū, following the promulgation of the national long-term care insurance program in 2000, expanding both the scope and size of the pharmacy that has been in her family for several generations. Like Akiko, Keiko's goal was not specifically to become an entrepreneur, but family and other conditions led her to become what I refer to as a reluctant entrepreneur.

Figure 6. The Pressé shop as it appeared in the summer of 2018.

Note: The building behind the shop is an example of a *kura*.

Figure 7. Looking at goods displayed in the window at Pressé.

NOTES

1. David W. Plath, "My-Car-Isma: Motorizing the Showa Self," *Daedalus* (1990).
2. cf. Manami Okazaki and Geoff Johnson, *Kawaii!: Japan's Culture of Cute* (New York: Prestel, 2013).
3. Y. Ogasawara, *Office Ladies and Salaried Men: Power, Gender, and Work in Japanese Companies* (Berkeley: University of California Press, 1998).
4. Anthony J. Fielding and Yoshitaka Ishikawa, "Migration and the Life Course in Contemporary Japan," *Geographical Review of Japan* 76, no. 12 (2003), http://dx.doi.org/10.4157/grj.76.12_882.
5. The standard pattern is for the eldest son to work in the family company and eventually become head of both household and company; however, it is not unusual for another child to take on this role or simply to represent an additional family member working for the company. See Traphagan, "Entrepreneurs in Rural Japan: Gender, Blockage, and the Pursuit of Existential Meaning."
6. The average age of first marriage in Japan for women has been around 29 for many years.
7. cf. Fumie Kumagai, *Family Issues on Marriage, Divorce, and Older Adults in Japan: With Special Attention to Regional Variations* (Springer Singapore, 2014).
8. See Hendry for a good discussion of marriage patterns in Japan. Joy Hendry, *Marriage in Changing Japan: Community & Society* (Routledge, 2010).
9. Virginia L. Lewis and Neil C. Churchill, "The Five Stages of Small Business Growth," (1983).
10. Traphagan, "Entrepreneurs in Rural Japan: Gender, Blockage, and the Pursuit of Existential Meaning."
11. Wood, 21.
12. Andrew Gordon, *A Modern History of Japan: From Tokugawa Times to the Present* (New York: Oxford University, 2003), 38.
13. Shinya Fujimura, "The Samurai Ethics: A Paradigm for Corporate Behavior," *Kennedy School Review* 11 (2010): 212.
14. Wood, 211.
15. Jerry D. Johnson and Raymond Rasker, "The Role of Economic and Quality of Life Values in Rural Business Location," *Journal of Rural*

Studies 11, no. 4 (1995/10/01/ 1995): 406, http://dx.doi.org/https://doi.org/10.1016/0743-0167(95)00029-1.

16. Ibid., 414.
17. Artur Steiner and Jane Atterton, "Exploring the Contribution of Rural Enterprises to Local Resilience," *Journal of Rural Studies* 40 (2015/08/01/ 2015): 34, http://dx.doi.org/https://doi.org/10.1016/j.jrurstud.2015.05.004.
18. Neil Thin, "Why Anthropology Can Ill Afford to Ignore Well-Being," in *Happiness: Well-Being in Anthropological Perspective*, ed. Gordon Mathews and Carolina Izquidero (New York: Berghahn Books, 2009).
19. Gordon Mathews and Carolina Izquierdo, "Anthropology, Happiness and Well-Being," *Pursuits of happiness: Well-being in Anthropological Perspective (1–19). New York: Berghahn Books* (2009).
20. Ofra Goldstein-Gidoni, "Being Happy as a Woman: The Promise of Happiness for Middle-Class Housewives in Japan," in *Life Course, Happiness and Well-Being in Japan* (Routledge, 2017).
21. Nancy Rosenberger, "Rethinking Emerging Adulthood in Japan: Perspectives from Long-Term Single Women," *Child Development Perspectives* 1, no. 2 (2007).
22. John W. Traphagan, "Being a Good Rôjin: Senility, Power, and Self-Actualization in Japan," in *Thinking About Dementia: Culture, Loss, and the Anthropology of Senility*, ed. Annette Leibing and Lawrence Cohen (New Brunswick, NJ: Rutgers University Press, 2006).
23. John W. Traphagan, "Moral Discourse and Old-Age Disability in Japan," in *Disability in Local and Global Worlds*, ed. Benedicte Ingstad and Susan Reynolds Whyte (Berkeley: University of California Press, 2007).
24. Gordon Mathews, *What Makes Life Worth Living? How Japanese and Americans Make Sense of Their Worlds* (University of California Press, 1996).
25. (Mathews 1996:17)
26. Traphagan, "Being a Good Rôjin: Senility, Power, and Self-Actualization in Japan," in *Thinking About Dementia: Culture, Loss, and the Anthropology of Senility.*
27. Traphagan, *Taming Oblivion : Aging Bodies and the Fear of Senility in Japan.*
28. Barbara Holthus and Wolfram Manzenreiter, "Conclusion: Happiness as a Balancing Act between Agency and Social Structure," in *Happiness and the Good Life in Japan*, ed. Wolfram Manzenreiter and Barbara Holthus (London: Routledge, 2017), 245.
29. Ibid., 249.

Keiko: I was a salaryman[1] and I didn't want to return. I was working in a pharmaceutical company. That work was better. I didn't want to come home and take over the business. I wanted to stay doing that work in that company.

JT: Why?

Keiko: Why? When you work for yourself, you can't take much vacation time. You work 365 days a year. You can't travel. And there are anxieties [不安 *fuan*]. You have to worry about how the company is doing and about your employees. If things don't go well, it's not just a problem for you; it's a problem for them [one's employees] as well. Also, when we returned our income went down. But since we can live with family, it's ok [financially, because they live in the same compound with her parents, albeit in a separate and fairly new domicile]. It was very difficult.

As our conversation continued, Keiko and Kazuo made it clear that the decision to return to Ōshū was not an easy one, particularly from a financial perspective. They were doing better financially when they both worked in large companies in the Tokyo suburbs as opposed to trying to run a business in Ōshū. But, at least for Keiko's husband, the work in Tokyo was unfulfilling and placed him in a position where it was likely that he would be forced to spend long periods of time away from his family. Kazuo, in separate conversations, intimated to me that his children are what he values most in life. In fact, having been friends for many years and having raised children during the same period, I have seen that he is a dedicated father who has spent a great deal of time helping to raise their three children, and Keiko confirms this.[2] However, while their business has allowed him to be more involved in raising their children than he would have had they stayed in their corporate jobs, it also has placed constraints on Keiko's life, which she discussed when I asked her about some of the challenges she has faced in running the business.

Keiko: The store and our home are together, right?[3] Everything is mixed up. While I'm working in the store, I have to take care

> of the kids and family. I have to say "good-bye" to them in the morning. I have to, while working, also be attentive to family needs. If I worked at a normal company, I wouldn't have to do this. Also, because it's a family company, I'm always on call.

Although she struggles with the responsibilities of being an employer at times and misses the relative freedom that she associates with work in a large company, Keiko has devoted a great deal of time, energy, and money to expanding the pharmacy into a set of businesses that are focused on providing healthcare-related products and services. It will be instructive to devote some space here to exploring the details related to the nature of the company the Yoshidas have built over the last twenty years.

BLENDING EASTERN AND WESTERN MEDICAL APPROACHES

The front page of the website for the Yoshida's business looks quite different from that which one might expect of a similar page for an American family-run (or corporate) pharmacy, which often have images of pills, medical supplies, and medical professionals designed to create an feeling that customers are engaging the medical profession and accessing its expertise, power, potential to cure illness, and in some cases masculine authority.[4] On the Yoshida Pharmacy site, there are no images of powerful medical professionals in white lab coats with stethoscopes hanging around their necks. Instead, the frontpage show images of crumbled plants and some twigs in small white dishes. Under these images, the site states in large characters: "I want to be youthful and healthy forever [いつまでも若々しく健康でありたい]", following which the site lists what the business will do to ensure that this happens for its clients by supporting the health of individuals from the perspective of the pharmacist through the offering of advice and counselling. In fact, counselling services are a central feature of the Yoshida Pharmacy's activities and include not only provision of advice about the use of western biomedical products but also the use of *kampō-yaku* 漢方薬 or the Japanese take on Chinese herbal medicine. Unlike in the United States, where East Asian medical ideas and practices form something of a parallel approach to Western-style biomedicine, in Japan *kampō-yaku,* along with acupuncture and acupressure, is largely integrated into the modern healthcare system and is regularly accessed by individuals along with Western biomedicine.[5] In general, people, including many medical professionals, do not see a contradiction between Western and Eastern approaches to medicine; instead, they tend to see the two as complementary.

Yoshida Pharmacy provides consulting in both Western medicine and East Asian medicine, but according to Kazuo the focus of most of the counselling that they perform is related to East Asian medicine. As one enters the store, to the right there is a large area devoted to different types of herbal medicines and a sitting area that is regularly used by pharmacy employees (usually Kazuo and Keiko) to discuss health-related concerns of customers who enter the store and also to provide advice about how to address those concerns. Kazuo may suggest either Western or Eastern medical approaches depending on the individual and also the nature of the ailment about which he is consulting. Sometimes a recommendation is based on what Kazuo sees as working well. At one time, I observed him discussing acne problems with a customer and he suggested an herbal approach to the problem because, he stated, *kampō-yaku* is more effective than Western medicines such as creams, indicating that often the choice of one approach over the other is pragmatic rather than ideological in nature. To the left of the main entrance is the more traditional pharmaceutical area of the store, to which people bring prescriptions from their doctors to be filled at the pharmacy. In general, there is a fairly steady flow of customers at Yoshida Pharmacy throughout the business day, which begins at 8:00am and ends at 6:00pm, although as Keiko commented, if customers see anyone inside outside of business hours, they will usually knock on the door and will be served.

The emphasis on East Asian medicine and health consulting differentiates Yoshida Pharmacy from other pharmaceutical businesses in the area, particularly the large chain drug stores, such as Tsuruha Drug, which is similar to a Walgreen's or CVS in the US. It provides not only over-the-counter and prescription drugs but also has products for beauty care and supplies like toilet paper that Yoshida Pharmacy does not carry. Chain stores like Tsuruha Drug, that are located along bypass routes around the center of town and have large parking areas, have driven many family-owned stores out of business and Yoshida Pharmacy has in part managed to survive by focusing its business activities on East Asian medicine and providing services and equipment related to eldercare, as I will discuss shortly.

The results of The Yoshida's business approach can be seen clearly in the nature of their services that have expanded to other areas of health care beyond pharmaceuticals and their focus on the downtown area of the city. For example, the Yoshida Day Service Center is situated in the middle of Ōshū about a block away from the pharmacy and is typical of day service centers throughout the region, with large tables at which elder clients sit and participate in various activities throughout the days that they attend. The facility is small, occupying space that was once the location of a clothing store that went out of business a few years ago. On one of the days I visited the day service center, people were making paper objects to use for the annual Tanabata (七夕 Star Festival) celebration; on other days one might see people playing games or doing crafts such as making mosaics out of painted, dried macaroni. There are also some interesting features that distinguish Yoshida Day Service Center from many others. First, the placing of the business in downtown Ōshū was a conscious decision on the part of the Yoshidas that runs contrary to the approach taken by many businesses in the area, which usually involves leaving the downtown area in order to continue operation in locations that are easily accessible by automobile. Because many similar facilities had been built on the outskirts of the city, the Yoshidas decided that it would be better to place the business in the center of town where, in fact, the population is predominately people over the age of 65 and many of the residents in that age group do not drive, which has led some municipalities in neo-rural areas to develop transportation services for older people.[6] The thinking was that clients would be able to attend with friends and be able to get there with the assistance of family but not necessarily requiring the use of a car. Both of these approaches are responses to issues that have been identified by health care professionals in the area, particularly the unwillingness of many older people to attend facilities if they do not feel their immediate friends—normally from their neighborhood—are also attending at the same time.[7] The facility also has limited space to allow bedridden individuals to visit for the day after being picked up at their homes by Center personnel; the maximum capacity is 12 people which is insufficient to meet the actual needs of the bedridden population living in the downtown area.

The Yoshida Day Service Center benefits from the long-term care insurance program (*kaigo hoken* 介護保険, which I will refer to as LTCI here, and which I will discuss below) in that clients use the program to pay for services, but the facility itself was not built with the assistance of government funds. All of the money to renovate the clothing-store space into a day-service center came from the Yoshida's healthcare business; thus, while the amount of risk involved with starting the business was mitigated by the LTCI program, there was also risk related to taking out loans in order to complete the reconstruction of the space.

Political Policy and Healthcare Entrepreneurialism

Yoshida Pharmacy has a fairly long history in the town, having been founded in 1919. During most of its history it has been run as a small family business, but in 1999 the Yoshidas shifted from a family-orientation (sole proprietorship) to a corporate structure organized as a limited company (株式会社 *kabushikigaisha*). The timing of this is important because it comes just one year ahead of the promulgation of Japan's national and government-run long-term care insurance program. While the pharmacy remains their core business, Keiko and Kazuo have invested both time and money expanding into new areas such as the Day Service Center, largely as an outgrowth of the mandatory public long-term care social insurance program that was passed into law in 1997 and became effective in 2000.[8] As John Creighton Campbell and Naoki Ikegami note, the program is a comprehensive social insurance program that initiated an important shift from prior approaches to public insurance related to eldercare in that provision of many services were shifted from being services assigned and often provided by the government to services that older people and their families privately contract, which was intended in part to allow older people to select services that they prefer and to change the image of those using these services from patients to service customers, which it was hoped would remove the stigma associated with elder-care services in Japan.[9]

In many respects, the period following 2000 can be described as having stimulated an environment of eldercare entrepreneurship characterized by the creation of a variety of new services and facilities designed to address the rapidly growing needs of an elder population (defined as those over the age of 65) that currently represents about 27 percent of the Japanese total and is expected to grow to more than 40 percent of the population by 2050.[10] As the population of people over the age of 65 has expanded, so has the need for both public and private services aimed at providing care for elders encountering anything from limited problems with activities of daily living to advanced forms of dementia. And this has stimulated an expansion of eldercare-related businesses throughout the country.

Indeed, these demographic and policy trends are important political actions that have created an environment, particularly in rural and neo-rural areas, that is well situated for entrepreneurial activities centered on healthcare and other services that address the needs of older segments of the population, and the LTCI program in particular has been something of a catalyst for the emergence of this entrepreneurial environment. As noted above, the LTCI program in Japan is mandatory; all people over the age of 40 are required by law to contribute premiums to the program and access to benefits is administered by the municipal governments in which people reside. Approximately 50 percent of the costs associated with long-term care insurance benefits are covered by national, prefectural, and municipal governments through taxes. The remaining 50 percent is covered through insurance premiums that all insured are required to pay from the age of 40. In the event that one becomes bedridden, develops senile dementia, or becomes frail and needs assistance with activities of daily living, it is necessary to receive official recognition of one's condition from the local municipal government in order to access the *kaigo hoken* system. The insured normally contributes a 10 percent co-payment for services received and the municipal government provides the remainder of the cost, although there is some gradation based upon income level—those on public assistance only pay 2 percent, for example. A key element of the program that has implications for entrepreneurial activity is that funds can be used to purchase either public or private welfare and medical services, a fact that is a significant shift away from pre-2000 policy in which covered services were almost completely provided by either government organizations or welfare organizations that were under close government supervision.[11] This has created a context in which business people have been encouraged to take risks in creating novel and experimental approaches to providing eldercare.

Another factor that has contributed to encouraging entrepreneurial activity is an increase in diagnoses of Alzheimer-type dementia (AD) since the 1970s.[12] Several studies in the early part of the twenty-first century have shown that the ratio of AD to vascular dementia (VaD) in Japan tended to differ from ratios reported in other industrial societies, with VaD being more frequently diagnosed than AD. This research noted that over a period of about twenty years the relative frequency of AD to VaD may have increased, suggesting changes in approaches to diagnosis of dementia-type disease. In their work in a rural area of Niigata Prefecture in Japan, for example, Nakamura et al. found AD was by far the most common diagnosis at 4.0% while VaD was only diagnosed for 1.2% of the dementia cases they surveyed.[13] In another study in rural Japan, Yamada et al. found prevalence rates of 3.8% for all types of dementia (2.1% for AD, 1.0% for VaD, and 0.7% for other types).[14]

The increase in dementia diagnoses and the rise of AD intersects with the creation of programs related to long-term care not only in terms of care provision but also in terms of policy and has contributed to the creation of a context receptive to healthcare entrepreneurialism. Additionally, for most of the postwar era in Japan, long-term care facilities have been in relatively short supply even while a variety of policies have been developed to cope with a growing aged population.[15] Nursing homes have typically had long waiting lists and the expectation of several years' wait to enter—a considerable portion of long-term care provision has taken place in hospitals—and alternate care approaches such as assisted living facilities were rare throughout most of the 1990s and into the early twenty-first century.[16] Throughout the post-war era, policies related to eldercare have strongly privileged in-home care as opposed to institutional care of both bedridden elders and those suffering from dementia. The widespread assumption in Japanese society has been that the best place to care for older people is at home and the best provider is either a daughter-in-law or a daughter.[17] Although the LTCI program continues to be largely oriented around the emphasis on in-home care, it has also opened the door to alternative approaches to care around which enterprising individuals and companies can develop services.[18] In fact, the emergence of the LTCI program has stimulated the development of innovative approaches to long-term care that range from day-care centers for elders to resident homes that cater specifically to individuals suffering from dementia.[19] Health care entrepreneurs have been particularly active in neo-rural and rural areas, where the proportion of elderly in the population is normally well above the national average, creating a particularly strong need for services and a fertile environment for entrepreneurs to develop businesses. One of these, located amidst rice fields at the border between Kanegasaki and Ōshū, is known as Welfare Foundation Sakura, an organization that consists of several different facilities that are part of a complex of buildings that provide different types of services for the elderly.

Services at Sakura include a day service center similar to the one run by the Yoshida's company, although somewhat larger, two group homes for elders with dementia each of which can support up to nine residents, and a hotel for the elderly designed for short-term stays that give in-home care givers a break from the daily grind of caring for a relative with dementia or who is bedridden. Sakura has focused its business model on designing facilities aimed at addressing the needs of elders suffering from dementia and supporting their families, which fits a need due to the fact that facilities aimed specifically at individuals with AD have been in relatively short supply in Japan in part due to the fact that some nursing homes and day care centers have historically refused AD patients due to difficulties associated with providing care.[20] Sakura is one of several similar facilities run by private corporations that include group homes and day-care centers which have started up over the past 15 years in Iwate and other parts of Japan.

The original group home, known as Astro, was opened in April of 2000 and is among the first such homes to have been constructed in Iwate Prefecture. It contributed to a trend in the area towards the formation of private group homes, particularly for those with AD, and today there are several similar group homes located in other parts of the city, as well as in adjacent towns. The second group home, known as Martha, was opened in 2002. The growth of these group homes and other similar facilities and programs, occurred largely after the promulgation of the LTCI program in 2000. In fact, as of 2000, there were only 369 group homes nationally and 70 within Iwate Prefecture. By July of 2006, the numbers had increased dramatically; nationally there were 8052 group homes for elders and within Iwate there were 860, representing approximately 10.6% of the group homes nationally.[21] In other words, new governmental policies opened the door for organizations such as Sakura (which was founded before the LTCI program) to expand their services significantly.

Indeed, when Sakura was founded in 1997 it functioned like virtually all of the welfare foundations throughout Japan—it was under the direct administrative supervision of the government. In 2000, foundations like Sakura were essentially privatized, although the initial process of privatization can be traced back to the 1980s,[22] shifting to a framework in which, rather than operating under direct supervision, organizations like Sakura contract with the government to provide long-term care services. In terms of management structure, the Foundation operates like a for-profit company; however, it must organize its services within the scope of social welfare law and from an administrative perspective is considered a non-profit foundation because it is part of the *shakai fukushi hōjin* (社会福祉法人,Social Welfare Foundation) and is, thus, not required to pay business taxes. The system is complex. For example, organizations such as Sakura that belong to the Social Non-Profit Service Foundation are permitted to charge for-profit rates in order to assist or continue some types of services. The Care Hotel that is part of Sakura caters to disabled elderly, particularly those with dementia, and because it designed to provide services for profit, Sakura must pay taxes on profits that part of the business. In short, the current system has created a blurring of the lines between non-profit and for-profit corporations and entrepreneurial organizations like Sakura straddle that line in ways that have allowed them to grow significantly over a fairly short period of time in the early part of the twenty-first century.

While the LTCI program has stimulated a considerable expansion in services and facilities for eldercare, there remains a shortage of both—at Sakura, for example, there is normally a list of five or more people who can expect a wait of between two and three years before a spot opens in one of the group homes. Other facilities typically have similar or much longer waiting lists. For example, in her interesting documentary *Everyday is Alzheimer's*, which follows the film-maker's experiences caring for her mother who is suffering from AD, Yuka Sekiguchi notes that when she finally decides a nursing home is the best option for her mother, the waiting list has over 150 people on it and a waiting time of several years.

A Changing Entrepreneurial Climate

Keiko works with the director of Sakura as well as many other facilities within the area and this has contributed to the expansion of the pharmacy business to include a range of products and services directly related to eldercare, although the pharmacy remains the primary source of revenue for the Yoshidas' company. Kazuo also plays an important role as a leader in the healthcare environment of the city beyond his work as president of the Yoshidas' company, because he is a member of the government board that determines levels of need related to services provided through the LTCI program. In the remainder of this chapter, I will focus on the ideas the Yoshidas have discussed with me in relation to their experiences in running and expanding their business. I will return to this point later in the chapter, but it is important to understand the expansion of the Yoshidas' business within the context of a political and demographic climate in which the services that the Yoshidas provide are in need and the existence of the LTCI program has not only supported but also stimulated the expansion of eldercare-related business. Recognizing the potential of the changing legal environment related to healthcare at the turn of the century, the Yoshidas—along with other local entrepreneurs such as the creator of Sakura—have ridden the wave of privatization as a means of expanding their business, and this process has been at the center of their emergence as healthcare entrepreneurs in Ōshū. Like with Akiko discussed in the previous chapter, the Yoshidas entrance into the world of entrepreneurialism has been less motivated by the pursuit of wealth than it has been by the desire to provide a service for the community, even if that service does not prove to be particularly profitable, as we can see in this conversation I had with the couple over coffee one day.

JT: How is your business going these days?

KEIKO: It's difficult [厳しい*kibishii*]. Particularly the nursing care portion.

KAZUO: Things are moving fast here. About ten years ahead of the rest of the country. There is a lot of competition because this area has so many old people. That makes it difficult.

JT: But you see so many empty houses and business around here. It would seem that the demand for healthcare services is dropping.

KEIKO: Yes, this is a big issue. Lots of empty houses and stores. The population is declining.

KAZUO: But the number of old people is rising, even while the overall population is dropping. And when they die, there won't be anyone left. Everyone [meaning young people] goes to Tokyo.

JT: Won't things get better or at least level-off in terms of the business?

KAZUO: No, it will get worse as the old people die off.

JT: Keiko, the other day we were talking and you mentioned that it can be difficult balancing all of the responsibilities related to both family and your business. You said you miss being a "salaryman" for a large company.

KEIKO: Yes, it can be difficult. People come around all the time, even when we are closed, and phone calls come, people come by any time. They say, "Is it ok?" Meaning to open up for something. It's a pain. But I like the work and I like doing the work for everyone's purpose and for the purpose of the future, the city...

JT: It's like that at another shop I know, too. People come by after-hours routinely. The owner there says it's a troublesome [めんどくさい].

KEIKO: No, don't say troublesome. Say it's appreciated [ありがたいです]! [As Keiko said this she laughed somewhat sarcastically.]

JT: So, what motivates you to expand the business?

KEIKO: Me? Well, what I want to do is be helpful to others.

JT: If you don't think about others, what would you like to be doing?

KEIKO: I would work at a regular company. A pharmaceutical company.

At this point, our conversation shifted somewhat as I asked her more about her own relationship to the family business and she expanded on her motivations behind expanding the business. I asked Keiko if she is the successor (後継ぎ *atotsugi*) in her household, which generally means in a business family that one takes over not only the headship of the family but also becomes the head of the business. Often, as noted earlier in the book and as I will discuss in greater detail in chapter 6, this role has historically been associated with the eldest son, but in contemporary Japan it may fall on any child who is willing or able to take on the responsibility in both the family and the business, and as is the case for Keiko, it may even be divided among two children—her brother handles the household side of the headship while she handles the business side.

KEIKO: Yes, I'm the successor. But my parents never really put any pressure on me about that. They said it would be fine to quit the business. It was my husband who wanted to come back and take over—not me. My brother is also in the pharmacy business. He works in a hospital and lives with my parents. We live in the building next door. I was raised in this house with this business. I like doing the work of the business. I like meeting with customers and selling things. So, I like the work, but [laughs] I didn't want to come back. The problem was that I wanted to stay in the corporate world. I don't mind living here, although it's a bit cold. I just didn't want to be the person in charge of running the family business.

Some of things I don't like about running the family business are related to barriers that exist being a woman in this industry. The main issue is in working with doctors. My husband really needs to do that. The doctors don't want to talk to me because I'm a woman. I can talk to them about specific issues related to prescriptions. But I cannot talk with them about business matters or sales [*eigyō* 営業]. that has to be left to my husband. They won't talk to me about those sorts of things.

JT: What do you think about that?

KEIKO: I think women should be able to do whatever they want, although it doesn't bother me all that much. It's a man's world. Men do business type things. They go out to drink in the evenings and I can't participate in that. I don't really want to either.

JT: Are there any particular problems or obstacles you've encountered related to running the business?

KEIKO: The biggest issue is fear. Not making any mistakes and making sure that all of the information is correct when we dispense the drugs. There is a system for this and big pharmacy companies have machines to check to make sure there are no mistakes. But with a small company like this, we can't really do that. We don't have the money. We use the computer to track things, but we can't afford the type of equipment to track and check to avoid mistakes that you find with the chain stores. So, making sure there are no errors is a lot of work. Also, when we talk about problems like high blood pressure, we have to ask questions about the lives of our customers. We make pamphlets to help with providing information, but we have to make these ourselves. If it is a big company, these are already made. For us it is a major production to make sure we have all of the information correct and have the right pamphlets.

People living alone have doctors and nurses go to them to provide care. We have to do the same. Old people can't drive, can't afford a taxi, etc. So, we have to go to them and it takes a lot of time and effort. We are a small company. And I have to balance this with also taking care of family. My kids always had a lot of things missing from their backpacks when they went to school. I was always forgetting things [laughs]. Another thing is that there is the sense that nursing care as women's work [as opposed to business]. It's the image. But I don't do that, so I have to balance that as well. It's too bad, because women have very good ideas. If women work hard, I think we can make really good ideas and plans. Women can contribute a lot to making a good city.

JT: What do you think about the future of your company?

KEIKO: I want to separate the nursing care portion from the drug portion. I'm not a pro in the nursing care section. I can't do the types of things, like putting someone in a bath or changing a diaper, that someone with expertise can do. I'm an expert in pharmacy, as is my husband. He and I can do that portion fine, but I don't think we really have the expertise for the nursing care portion in the future.

JT: Do you think you might sell that part?

KEIKO: No, we will hire someone to manage it and we will be the head over the entire operation. But we will make it into a separate company.

JT: I guess you can get income from both.

KEIKO: Well, maybe. But the income from the nursing care portion of the business is very low. It requires a lot of manpower but doesn't pay off much in terms of profit. I don't like the idea of using robots for nursing care, so we can't go in that direction. But if the pharmacy brings in 10,000 yen, the nursing care portion brings in only 3,000.

JT: Then why don't you quit the nursing care business?

KEIKO: It's heavy.

JT: Heavy? Do you mean that it's an obligation?

KEIKO: Sort of like that. We want to do things that help others live well. My husband is very strong on that point. He really wants to do that. He is concerned with the needs of others. It's not as big a deal for me. Actually, it's my husband who wants to keep the nursing care portion going.

JT: So, your husband wants to do things that help others.

KEIKO: Yes.

JT: Do you consult with your husband about things related to the company, such as the future?

KEIKO: Yes, we do. We have meetings.

JT: With your husband?

KEIKO: No with the board of directors. There are six of them. We have discussions with them. There is a team. It's not just the two of us.

JT: I thought it was a family company.

KEIKO: It's not a family company. Yoshida is only the name. My husband is the President, but there are six people involved with running the company.

JT: What is your title?

KEIKO: Managing Director [専務 *senmu*].

JT: But this is your company?

KEIKO: No, I am an employee. I work for the company as an employee. The decisions are made by the committee, not by me.

JT: Since the company is from your family, why aren't you the president?

KEIKO: Well, my husband is. It has to do with ideology [理念 *rinen*]—the basic idea of how things are. The ideology is that men do this. It's a cultural thing.

JT: Did you consider being president, Keiko?

KEIKO: No, we did not think about it at all [both said this at the same time]. It's just natural that the man would be the president. We gave it no thought.

JT: What will you do for the future of the company in terms of who takes over?

KAZUO: Hmm. We really don't know.

JT: What about your kids?

KAZUO: Well, it's still too early to be sure about that. They are still in school.

JT: Would you be disappointed if the company shuts down?

KEIKO: Well, if it did soon, I would, but not if I'm 70 or 80. In that case, it's just the way it is, and there is a good chance that is what will happen. In the short term the number of elderly people will continue to grow. Hospitals are expensive and the elderly don't have enough money, so people will be looked after at home and they will need the kinds of services we provide. I think over the next 10 or 15 years the need for home care will grow considerably. But then after that as the current bubble of older people begins to die, our business will die with them.

JT: We have talked quite a bit about your business and some of the challenges you face. For you, what is the purpose of having a business?

KEIKO: For people [人のために *hito no tame ni*]. [She answered very quickly, taking no time to think about it].

JT: What about making money?

KEIKO: Making money?

JT: If you asked an American, maybe the answer would be for making money or to get rich.

KEIKO: I used to think that. The purpose of the business was to make money so that I could enjoy myself. Have some fun. But as I've thought about it, if the business fails and there is no money, it will be a problem financially for sure. But if I think why am I working? Why am I doing this? It has to be to help others. Of course, I want to have fun. But I have to think that I am doing it for the benefit of others. That is comforting.

JT: It's okay to not get rich?

KEIKO: I want to get rich! [laughter]. But, there is a conflict there. I want to have a nice life and have a fun life, but I also think it's important to help others.

ENTREPRENEURIAL MOTIVATION AND ECOSYSTEM DIFFERENTIATION

A great deal of research related to entrepreneurial motivation and intention has been published since David C. McClelland's work in the 1960s on achievement and entrepreneurship stimulated interest in the causes behind individuals choosing to follow entrepreneurial paths.[23] Literature on the topic has tended to show that entrepreneurs tend to be goal oriented and look for opportunities to attain personal and financial rewards.[24] These rewards can take the form of having freedom to pursue one's own interests (freedom from having a boss) and having control over one's future. In general, entrepreneurial motivations tend to fall into two broad frameworks: socially oriented reasons and personally oriented reasons. Motivations such as economic gain, desire for achievement, independence, social status, and personal development fall on the personal side of the spectrum, while motivations such as contribution to the community or helping others tend to fall on the social side of the spectrum.[25] Of course, these are not mutually exclusive and, in fact some motivations, such as the desire to innovate and create something new that others enjoy or need may coincide with desires such as increasing personal status or wealth and interests in helping the community. Perhaps the motivations of many entrepreneurs fall into the shaded area in the diagram in figure 8 and to some extent all of these motivations can overlap within the identity of an individual entrepreneur, but certainly some are more motivated by specific goals, such as economic gain, while others may be more motivated by goals such as helping the community.

Dilani Jayawarna, et al. make the important point that entrepreneurial motivations should be understood within the context of other factors that contribute to both enabling and constraining human agency.[26] Life-course contexts related to where one is situated in the process of aging as well as emotional and intellectual experiences can contribute significantly to the desire and ability to engage in entrepreneurial activities. Family and household represent one context that can impact desires related to starting a business, as can one's satisfaction with career and perceptions about factors such as structural limitations on the ability to advance (as we will see in chapter 5). Entrepreneurialism is embedded in an ongoing biographical process in which people analyze and interpret their own life-courses and experiences in relation to those of others around them and the social conditions that influence their lives. Class, ethnicity, gender, and age are parts of individual biographies that have a significant influence on both the motivation to become an entrepreneur and the sense that one might succeed in doing so.[27] And it is important to recognize that a one-size-fits-all approach to thinking about and understanding motivations behind entrepreneurialism is problematic at best. In much of the literature, for example, there has been only a limited recognition that men and women might pursue entrepreneurship for different reasons; however, Jodyanne Jane Kirkwood's findings suggest that women and men conceptualize the meaning of the term 'entrepreneur' itself differently and women may be less willing to apply the term to themselves than men. In Kirkwood's study, women tended to be more inclined to consider the needs of family when thinking about becoming an entrepreneur, whereas men appeared to be motivated by desires to prove something to other men or to their families. Men also may be motivated by dissatisfaction with their work, while women, at least in her study, were less likely to be motivated by work dissatisfaction, although structural obstacles to rising into positions of power and authority do play a role in reasons behind becoming entrepreneurs for some women.[28]

In the case of the Yoshidas, the motivations behind entering into entrepreneurial activity are closely tied to family for both of them. Kazuo was interested in leaving his work in a large corporation because it necessarily involved unacceptable limitations on his ability to be involved with the raising of his children. And although Keiko did not wish to leave her work in a large company, her position within her natal family, as well as her relationship with her husband, are the key factors in redirecting her life-course into the world of entrepreneurialism. This is, in fact, an important point that is widely missed in the literature on motivations to become an entrepreneur. Keiko did not, in fact, wish to become an entrepreneur; rather, the family context—the combination of her husband's desires and the fact that she was in the position to take over the family pharmacy business—led her, reluctantly, into the path of entrepreneurialism. In fact, taking over the family business presented several negatives for Keiko, including a reduction in income and restrictions on her ability to control her life the way she wished. This is in direct contrast to the notion that desires for freedom and personal control motivate entrepreneurialism.

Keiko feels that she has lost freedom and personal control as a result of becoming an entrepreneur, because her life revolves around and is significantly limited by her business activities and responsibilities. She has often mentioned in other conversations the desire to travel while at the same time lamenting the impossibility of doing so given the demands of her company. Rather than feeling freed to manage her life-course the way she wants, Keiko feels constrained within the context of the "household occupation" or private enterprise through which although one individual will function as head, all members of the household are expected to be involved in and responsible for running the family enterprise.[29] Although Kazuo is actually the head of the business, because the company is an outgrowth of Keiko's family enterprise, she does not simply play a role in the household occupation but is of central importance in the business. In short, rather than being motivated to become an entrepreneur *per se*, Keiko became an entrepreneur in order to make the best of a situation—taking over the family business and leaving her corporate career—that was not actually her preference. She clearly indicates that attaining wealth was not a significant motivation in expanding the business, although at one time she did think along those lines. Instead, she sees her work as an entrepreneur as being focused on the needs of others, including her family, her employees, and the community in which her business is located. But it appears that none of these factors were on her mind when she was working in the corporate world, and she came to think in this way as a result of following the interests of her husband and taking on responsibilities related to her family business.

Along with this was a recognition that there were specific needs in the community that her business could meet, particularly if they expanded the scope and range of services available. As a result, she and Kazuo embarked on developing the company into one that specifically focuses on nursing-care services and products, which complements much of the consulting that they do in the pharmacy. The entire expansion, however, was predicated on the generation of at least the seeds of an entrepreneurial ecosystem that emerged as a result of the promulgation of the LTCI program in 2000. Without government policy shifts designed to promote privatization of many nursing-care services, it is unlikely that the Yoshidas would have found themselves in an economic and political climate suited to expanding their business; many of the services that they provide were largely managed and provided by the government 20 years ago.

In the narratives of the Yoshidas, we can see a combination of factors related to their entry into entrepreneurial activity that do not imply an overt desire to become entrepreneurs: 1) an economic and political climate conducive to entrepreneurialism in relation to healthcare and 2) a demographic environment that provided very specific potential clients in the form of older people and their caregivers. Given the context associated with factors 1 and 2, there was also 3) an interest in developing a business focused on helping others and the community. What is not central in their narrative is the desire or motivation to become entrepreneurs per se; instead, their actions and identities as entrepreneurs arise as a byproduct of Kazuo's desire to work in an environment that allows involvement with raising his family and Keiko's willingness to go along with his desires, as well as the convenient proximity of Keiko's family business. Keiko, in particular, is a reluctant entrepreneur, deeply involved in running and expanding her business in response to the needs of the larger community ecosystem, as well as the needs of her conjugal and extended family. She also is motivated by something of an "if you can't beat 'em, join 'em" attitude in which she has decided that given her situation she will make the most of it. She enjoys her work but does not really find pleasure in running the business and trying to balance that with her responsibilities within her family. She would prefer to work in a company as a typical white-collar worker, as she did before her family returned to Ōshū.

From an analytical perspective, the example of the Yoshidas provides a way to think about entrepreneurialism as a byproduct of opportunity associated with a local social and political environment well situated for certain types of entrepreneurial activities, but not necessarily generated through articulated motivations of individuals to become entrepreneurs. If we think back to the case of Akiko in the previous chapter, she also did not really work from a specific motivation to become an entrepreneur. Instead, she responded to perceived needs in the community and her own life and an opportunity generated by the local government to develop a store. And in Akiko's case, unlike that of the Yoshidas, the expansion of her business was not a result of a desire to "grow" anything or, for that matter, even necessarily to create something new; it was a product of her desire to survive in a climate that is not particularly conducive to entrepreneurial activities of the sort in which she is engaged—building a retail business.

Politics and Entrepreneurial Ecosystems

Dane Stangler and Jordan Bell-Masterson have noted that the methods and desires associated with creating entrepreneurial ecosystems vary from one community to the next: "In some places, the desired outcome is simply more: more entrepreneurs, more companies, and more jobs. Other communities design their ecosystem efforts around a particular type of company or type of job. Some regions, moreover, see the 'entrepreneurial ecosystem' as a marketing effort, and focus on a particular type of individual they hope to attract to their area. For other cities, the only thing that matters is the 'exit'—initial public offerings and acquisitions."[30] They identify four factors to measure the vibrancy of an entrepreneurial ecosystem:

- Density—Number of new and young firms per 1,000 people and the share of employment in those new and young firms.

- Fluidity—Population flux and labor market reallocation along with number of high-growth firms.
- Connectivity—Program connectivity, spinoff rate, dealmaker networks.
- Diversity—Multiple economic specializations, mobility, and immigrants.

Stangler and Bell-Masterson identify some important components related to entrepreneurial ecosystems, but one of the things that we see in the cases of the Yoshidas and Akiko is that the same broadly defined social context or ecosystem may be quite different in terms of entrepreneurial potential depending upon the type of business one develops. In one sense, there really is no such thing as *an* entrepreneurial ecosystem; rather, there are socio-political ecosystems that may be more or less conducive to certain types of entrepreneurial activities. We might then argue that Ōshū does not actually have an entrepreneurial ecosystem, but this would not be quite right, in my view.

Erik Stam, drawing on the work of Brad Feld[31] defines an entrepreneurial ecosystem as "an interdependent set of actors that is governed in such a way that it enables entrepreneurial action"[32] and places entrepreneurs as key agents in contexts that either enable or constrain entrepreneurial activity. Government plays a role in getting the "framework conditions right," these conditions being elements such as education, taxation, employment protections legislation, etc., that enable entrepreneurship to thrive. Evidence for the efficacy of government on the supply of entrepreneurs is not clear, but it has been shown that government can influence the different ways in which entrepreneurs develop their businesses.[33]

However, as is evident the two cases I have discussed in this and the preceding chapters, the ability of the government to influence the ways entrepreneurs develop their businesses is significantly impacted by the demographic conditions in which attempts are being made to develop innovative businesses. In Ōshū, like most of rural and neo-rural Japan, the demographic climate is conducive to entrepreneurial activity directed at businesses in the healthcare sector, and the political climate has reinforced this through policies like the LTCI program. The two are intertwined, in part because the policy-aspect of the overall ecosystem is focused on addressing the problems associated with a rapidly aging population. However, that same demographic variable—an aging population—has generated a challenging environment for entrepreneurs like Akiko that makes it difficult to sustain their businesses. There are simply not enough young people—the people towards whom her business was initially directed—to maintain the business over the long-run, despite the fact that creation of her first store relied heavily upon government support.

In part what is interesting here is the fact that the same demographic conditions are both working for and against entrepreneurial activity and government intervention has not been able to counteract the negative elements of those conditions in relation to small-business startups like Pressé. This provides a good example of how government intervention has significant limitations in its capacity to generate an entrepreneurial ecosystem and represents support for Philip E. Auerswald's argument that the potential for entrepreneurship to succeed is context-dependent.[34] To this I would add that the same context may respond variably to attempts by local governments to generate an entrepreneurial ecosystem, depending on the type of entrepreneurial activity being generated as it relates to other variables such as demographics. In other words, an entrepreneurial ecosystem is not simply a context that supports and promotes entrepreneurial activity; it is a context that supports and promotes certain kinds of entrepreneurial activity depending on other features of the context such as demographics, geography, local values, or approaches to policy.

The fact that one type of business will do better does not necessarily mean that there is some sort of failure in creating an entrepreneurial ecosystem. Rather, some types of entrepreneurial ecosystems are characterized by niche emergence that is contingent upon other elements of the overall ecosystem, such as the age structure of the resident population.[35] By niche emergence, I mean the partitioning of a socio-political and socio-economic ecosystem such that certain types of entrepreneurial activities are more likely to produce successful businesses than others. The resources and conditions evident in a particular entrepreneurial context limit the potential for certain types of niches to emerge within the overall social ecosystem of which entrepreneurial activity is a subcomponent. In addition, the presence of particular conditions of social, economic, and political variables can function as an autocatalytic feedback system in which there is a positive or negative feedback flow that influences the capacity of certain types of entrepreneurial activities to operate effectively. In the examples from this and the previous chapters, we can clearly see how demographic characteristics in the form of the age structure and overall aging nature of the population have the potential to either limit or encourage certain types of entrepreneurial activities, regardless of attempts by government to generate an entrepreneurial ecosystem.

I will return to this point in the last chapter. At this point, I want to turn to examples of two different types of entrepreneurs, in comparison with Akiko and the Yoshidas, both of whom have developed businesses in the form of small restaurants. As will become clear in the next two chapters, these businesses appear to be less susceptible to niche emergence limits as compared to the examples I have discussed in this and the previous chapter.

Figure 8. Motivations for enterpreneurial behavior.

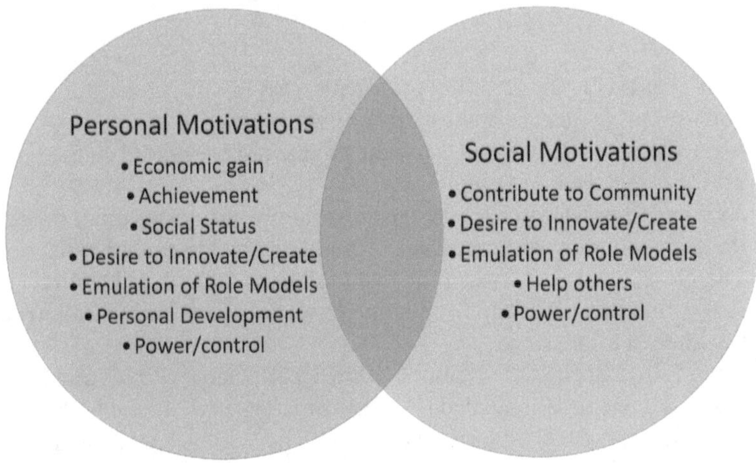

NOTES

1. Note that this is the term my informant used in our conversation, so I will use this to be consistent with her own expression of identity.
2. We actually met as baseball dads when our sons both played on the same Little League team in Ōshū.
3. As noted in previous chapters, Japanese family businesses often occupy the same building or compound of buildings as the family residence. Therefore, the lines between the two tend to be difficult to identify. For Keiko, for example, a trip from home to work is a ten-meter walk from her kitchen to the store.
4. Bisan Salhi, "Beyond the Doctor's White Coat: Science, Ritual, and Healing in American Biomedicine," *Understanding and Applying Medical Anthropology* (2016); Maura C Flannery, "The White Coat: A Symbol of Science and Medicine as a Male Pursuit," *Thyroid* 11, no. 10 (2001).
5. Although somewhat dated, Lock's (1984) work related to East Asian medicine in Japan remains a useful representation of how medical concepts are conceptualized in contemporary Japanese society. F. Yu et al., "Traditional Chinese Medicine and Kampo: A Review from the Distant Past for the Future," *Journal of International Medical Research* 34, no. 3 (2006/05/01 2006), accessed 2019/01/24, http://dx.doi.org/10.1177/147323000603400301; Margaret M. Lock, *East Asian Medicine in Urban Japan: Varieties of Medical Experience* (University of California Press, 1984).
6. 太田幸司 and 山本信次, "農山村地域における多様な主体の協働による市町村交通サービスの在り方: 岩手県雫石町 「あねっこバス」 を事例として," 林業経済研究 54, no. 3 (2008).
7. John W. Traphagan, "Culture and Long-Term Care: The Bath as Social Service in Japan," *Care Management Journals* 5, no. 1 (2004); 奥山純子 et al., "地方自治体における高齢者福祉施設の配置計画: 生活圏を意識した計画の実態 (都市計画) [Placement Planning of Welfare Facilities for the Elderly in Local Governments: Actual Conditions of Planning for Living Areas (Urban Planning)]," 日本建築学会技術報告集 11, no. 22 (2005).
8. Noriko Tsukada and Yasuhiko Saito, "Factors That Affect Older Japanese People's Reluctance to Use Home Help Care and Adult Day Care Services," *Journal of Cross-Cultural Gerontology* 21, no. 3/4 (2006), http://dx.doi.org/10.1007/s10823-006-9028-9.

9. John Creighton Campbell and Naoki Ikegami, "Long-Term Care Insurance Comes to Japan: A Major Departure for Japan, This New Program Aims to Be a Comprehensive Solution to the Problem of Caring for Frail Older People," *Health Affairs* 19, no. 3 (2000); Misa Izuhara, "Social Inequality under a New Social Contract: Long-Term Care in Japan," *Social Policy & Administration* 37, no. 4 (2003).
10. 奥山純子 et al., "介護サービス基盤の圏域設置計画とその整備手法: 地方自治体における高齢者福祉施設の配置計画その 2 (都市計画) [Planning and Setting of Nursing Care Service Base Area:S Placement Planning of Welfare Facilities for the Elderly in Local Governments Part 2 (Urban Planning)]," 日本建築学会技術報告集 *[The Architectural Institute of Japan Journal of Technology and Design]* 12, no. 24 (2006).
11. Naoki Ikegami, "Public Long-Term Care Insurance in Japan," *Journal of the American Medical Association* 278, no. 16 (1997); Naoki Ikegami, Keita Yamauchi, and Yukari Yamada, "The Long Term Care Insurance Law in Japan: Impact on Institutional Care Facilities," *International Journal of Geriatric Psychiatry* 18, no. 3 (2003): 217, http://dx.doi.org/10.1002/gps.818.
12. Masahiro Shigeta, "Epidemiology: Rapid Increase in Alzheimer's Disease Prevalence in Japan," *Psychogeriatrics* 4, no. 4 (2004): 118.
13. Shiori Nakamura et al., "Prevalence and Predominance of Alzheimer Type Dementia in Rural Japan," *Psychogeriatrics* 3, no. 3 (2003): 97.
14. Tatsuo Yamada et al., "Prevalence of Alzheimer's Disease, Vascular Dementia and Dementia with Lewy Bodies in a Japanese Population," *Psychiatry and Clinical Neurosciences* 55, no. 1 (2001): 21.
15. John Creighton Campbell, *How Policies Change: The Japanese Government and the Aging Society* (Princeton: Princeton University Press, 2014).
16. Yashuhito Kinoshita and Christie W. Kiefer, *Refuge of the Honored: Social Organization in a Japanese Retirement Community* (Berkeley: University of California Press, 1993).
17. Akiko Hashimoto, *The Gift of Generations: Japanese and American Perspectives on Aging and the Social Contract* (Cambridge: Cambridge University Press, 1996).
18. Eiji Yano, Kazue Yamaoka, and Nanako Tamiya, "Use of Home Health Services Covered by New Public Long-Term Care Insurance in Japan: Impact of the Presence and Kinship of Family Caregivers," *International Journal for Quality in Health Care* 14, no. 4 (2002), accessed 1/24/2019, http://dx.doi.org/10.1093/intqhc/14.4.295.
19. 奥山純子 et al., "介護サービス基盤の圏域設置計画とその整備手法: 地方自治体における高齢者福祉施設の配置計画 その 2 (都市計画)

[Planning and Setting of Nursing Care Service Base Area: Placement Planning of Welfare Facilities for the Elderly in Local Governments Part 2 (Urban Planning)]."

20. John W. Traphagan and Tomoko Nagasawa, "Group Homes for Elders with Dementia in Japan," *Care Management Journals* 9, no. 2 (2008).
21. Ibid.
22. Yuko Suda, "Devolution and Privatization Proceed and Centralized System Maintained: A Twisted Reality Faced by Japanese Nonprofit Organizations," *Nonprofit and Voluntary Sector Quarterly* 35, no. 3 (2006): 430.
23. David C. McClelland, *Achieving Society*, vol. 92051 (New York: Simon and Schuster, 1967); Alan Carsrud and Malin Brännback, "Entrepreneurial Motivations: What Do We Still Need to Know?," *Journal of Small Business Management* 49, no. 1 (2011).
24. Donald F Kuratko, Jeffrey S Hornsby, and Douglas W Naffziger, "An Examination of Owner's Goals in Sustaining Entrepreneurship," *Journal of Small Business Management* 35, no. 1 (1997).
25. Dilani Jayawarna, Julia Rouse, and John Kitching, "Entrepreneur Motivations and Life Course," *International Small Business Journal* 31, no. 1 (2013/02/01 2011): 35, accessed 2019/01/30, http://dx.doi.org/10.1177/0266242611401444.
26. Ibid.
27. Harriet Bradley, *Fractured Identities: Changing Patterns of Inequality* (Cambridge: Polity Press, 1996).
28. Jodyanne Jane Kirkwood, "One Size Doesn't Fit All: Gender Differences in Motivations for Becoming and Entrepreneur" (University of Otago, 2004).
29. Takei S. Lebra, *Japanese Women: Constraint and Fulfillment* (Honolulu: University of Hawaii Press, 1985), 217.
30. Dane Stangler and Jordan Bell-Masterson, "Measuring an Entrepreneurial Ecosystem," *Kauffman Foundation Research Series on City, Metro, and Regional Entrepreneurship* 16 (2015): 1.
31. Brad Feld, *Startup Communities: Building and Entrepreneurial Ecosystem in Your City* (New York: Wiley, 2012).
32. Erik Stam, *The Dutch Entrepreneurial Ecosystem* (Utrecht, Netherlands: Birch Research, 2014), 1.
33. William J. Baumol, "Entrepreneurship: Productive, Unproductive, and Destructive," *Journal of Political Economy* 98, no. 5 (1990).

34. Philip E Auerswald, *Enabling Entrepreneurial Ecosystems: Insights from Ecology to Inform Effective Entrepreneurship Policy* (Kaufman Foundation, 2015), https://papers.ssrn.com/sol3/papers.cfm?abstract_id=2673843.
35. Roberto Cazzolla Gatti et al., "Niche Emergence as an Autocatalytic Process in the Evolution of Ecosystems," *Journal of Theoretical Biology* 454 (2018/10/07/ 2018), http://dx.doi.org/https://doi.org/10.1016/j.jtbi.2018.05.038.

Chapter 5

The Gelato Shop at the End of the Universe

> How do you know you're having fun if there's no one watching you have it?
>
> —Douglas Adams

As one drives west from the center of Kanegasaki, the tableau of stores and restaurants along the bypass route quickly fades into broad expanses of emerald rice fields dotted with farmhouses and barns. Some of these are modern buildings with ceramic siding, solar panels, a satellite dish on the roof, and an SUV or pickup truck parked in the driveway. Sheets and clothes hang in front of many houses, drying from the daily load of laundry. And tidy gardens take up much of the front yard of each property, producing fresh vegetables planted in carefully arranged rows stippled with a splash of colorful flowers in the summer. Adjacent to many of these farmhouses it is not unusual to find the collapsing remains of buildings that once housed families or livestock, seeming to echo the haunting laughter of children who have grown and moved away and the exhausted dreams of ancestors whose farms are no longer operating.

About 10km from National Route 4, there is a small sign on the right-hand side of the road rendered in impressionistic hues of green, yellow, and blue that direct one to turn right onto a tiny road that looks as though it leads nowhere in particular. After less than a kilometer driving along this "*tambo* road," one of the ubiquitous car-wide paths that border rice paddies, there emerges a long, paved road bordered in parts by the decaying remains of once-productive dairy farms. But if you open the car windows on a summer's day, the pungent aromas of hay and cow manure and the occasional whiff of diesel fumes from a tractor punctuate the fact that there are still working farms in the area. Indeed, the rice paddies, many of which are fallow, quickly morph into working hay and corn fields and after a while there is a large hay field to the left, in the middle of which stands a lonely cherry tree. Across from the cherry tree, a compound of buildings rises against a canvas of evergreens—there is an old farmhouse, an empty barn with a bright blue metal roof, two storage buildings, and a glistening yellow building with a storefront situated directly between the road and the farmhouse. The yellow building seems as incongruous with its surroundings as the cherry tree, constructed in a style that looks somewhat reminiscent of a cottage from the countryside of Holland (see figure 9). Typical of new construction in the area, the building is faced with ceramic surfacing made to look like stone and stucco and the inside is modern and bright, illuminated by large windows beckoning the sunlight to reflect off of the clean, white interior walls.

The shop, which I will call Kanegasaki Creamery, is the only restaurant or store for several kilometers in any direction. The closest businesses are a Family Mart convenience store 4.2km away and an *onsen* (hot spring) resort about 3km in the opposite direction and nestled into the base of a small mountain overlooking rice fields and a water-control station. In other words, the shop sits in an unlikely location for a store of any kind, surrounded by open fields and dairy farms—it is not a business district, nor even a place one would imagine building a restaurant or any other kind of business. The first floor of the shop is devoted to a business run by Mariko, a woman in her mid-fifties who was raised in the farmhouse behind the store along with her two sisters. The family moved to the area after World War II, along with several other dairy farmers, as part of a resettlement program in which colonists who had been settled in Manchuria during the empire period, often without the option of refusing, were repatriated and given farm land to begin a new life.[1] The house behind the store was built by Mariko's father and grandfather, as were most of the other buildings on the farm, and Mariko lives in that house with her mother, who is in her mid-80s and helps with the business, particularly with cleaning the seating area before opening in the mornings.

Mariko's concept for the shop was developed around plans to use local dairy products, particularly the milk produced by the dairy cows on her family farm, as a foundation for creating a business that was not specifically focused on farming. This idea brought Mariko to learn the crafts of making cheese and gelato, which are the main products she sells at Kanegasaki Creamery. However, easy access to dairy products was only part of the impetus to build her store amidst hay fields on the outskirts of town. Mariko also wanted to find ways to incorporate the rural beauty of the area into the business as an attraction along with the interest that might be generated by connecting the shop with a working dairy farm. Unfortunately, circumstances changed and the dairy part of the business was forced to shut down following the sudden death of her father. This caused Mariko to begin purchasing milk from the local branch of the agricultural cooperative, which is part of JA or the organization of regional co-ops throughout Japan that provide help with production, packaging, transportation, and marketing of agricultural products and also provide financial services to farmers and often have a significant, and not always positive, influence over the lives of farmers.[2]

Dressmaker Turned Entrepreneur

After graduating from one of the more prestigious college-preparatory high schools in the region, Mariko attended a fashion design and tailoring school in Tokyo and was employed by a dressmaking company for her first of several jobs in Tokyo that included employment in department stores fitting men's clothing. After about 20 years in Tokyo, Mariko started to think about returning to the countryside, which she explained to me as being a result of coming to appreciate the lifestyle in rural areas and the natural beauty of the Tōhoku region. She also was attracted to the fact that the pace of life seems much slower, as compared to the city, although her own life running her business is anything but slow-paced. This is because in addition to running the business she makes all of the gelato and cheese herself and often works through much of the night to ensure that she has sufficient stock for the shop to last throughout the day, particularly on hot summer days when there are often long lines of customers.

It is important to recognize that Mariko's ability to enter into entrepreneurship was, like Akiko and Keiko discussed in previous chapters, closely related to her family situation. In the case of Mariko, she has never married nor had children, thus she was not in any way encumbered by the needs of a husband or the responsibilities of raising children. Like many women her age, she had remained single throughout her career in Tokyo and, in fact, had no plans on marriage, preferring the single life.[3] In conversations related to her lifestyle, Mariko has explained to me that at one time she wanted to marry and have children, but this changed as she grew older. When she first returned to Kanegasaki, in her mid-40s, several people visited her parents in order to discuss the possibility of introducing her to local men who were single and roughly her age, but she resisted this and has stated clearly that she has no desire to marry at this point in her life. In contrast to some research that has been done focusing on the lives of middle-aged women in Japan, Mariko does not appear to experience feelings of social isolation that have been described in relation to some in mid-life or post-retirement who remain single.[4] This may be related to the fact that Mariko lives with her mother, has friends from high school living in the area with whom she socializes occasionally, and also has constant interaction with her customers, which she has indicated she enjoys and sees as an important part of her life and business. Mariko's resistance to offers of arranging a marriage introduction also may be connected to the fact that she has a somewhat low opinion of men. On more than one occasion she has told me that she does not find men to be terribly bright and, as a result, has made a conscious decision to avoid employing men in her business. This perspective is likely at least partially a product of problems she has had with male employees in the past, including one individual who, prior to the family shutting down the dairy farm portion of the business, accidentally flooded the automated milking system with tap water, which created quite a bit of work to purge and sanitize the system. But it is also related to the fact that she does not have any desire for males to play an important role in either her personal life or her business.

Like both Akiko and Keiko, starting and running a business was not something Mariko envisioned earlier in her life and she explained that she returned to Kanegasaki not to start a business but to learn the art of cheese making, which had interested her for some years. Eventually, as she considered what to do with her life in Kanegasaki, she started to think about making use of milk from the family dairy farm to create a product that would fit into the general business and social environment of the town, which has branded itself as an agricultural area focusing not on rice, but on dairy products and asparagus. Furthermore, located at the western end of town, only a few kilometers from Mariko's shop, is the Iwate Prefectural Agricultural College, which is a junior college (mentioned in chapter 1) that specializes in agricultural and horticultural management and animal husbandry. The college also operates the Iwate Flower Center, a botanical garden complex that attracts visitors to the area and supports student tours of the various flower gardens and green houses, while providing an educational and research facility for the college.

The presence of the agricultural college is an important part of Kanegasaki's overall representation of itself as a sophisticated agricultural area and this characterization contributed to Mariko's thinking about starting a cheese and gelato shop. I have had the opportunity to talk with her about her business and her role in the community on several occasions and it is clear that in some ways she is an accidental entrepreneur in that she did not plan on starting a business even when she returned to Kanegasaki to learn cheese-making. Rather, the path to becoming an innovator and business owner was more a byproduct of her return and the need to find a career as well as a way to sustain herself financially. However, as is evident in the excerpt from one of our conversations below, Mariko's entrance into entrepreneurialism was also related to feelings of limitations in the extent to which she could control her life and manage her career in Tokyo.

As noted above, like Keiko and Akiko, Mariko had a career in the Tokyo area that she left to return to Iwate, but in many ways the similarities end on that point. Mariko is somewhat different from the other female entrepreneurs I have discussed in this book in that she is drawn to the countryside in part as a result of tiring of life in Tokyo. Mariko returned to Kanegasaki not in order to start a business, like Akiko, nor to assume the role of running a family business like Keiko, although there are some similarities in that she was following in the family dairy business and her role in the farm/business is quite similar to Keiko's role in the family pharmacy. But the draw to return seems for Mariko to have been most closely connected to wanting to live in the countryside as opposed to the city. She was attracted by the natural landscape and what she perceived to be a slower pace of life and decided to start a business both to make a living and to take advantage of her surroundings.

> **JT**: Why were you interested in starting a business?
>
> **Mariko**: I didn't intend to start a business. Ah... how do I say this... I didn't have a feeling to create a business at that time I moved home. Well...[long pause]...I wanted to make cheese. That's all. Basically, I wasn't really thinking that I was starting a business and wasn't thinking about selling products; I was only thinking that I needed to do my best so that things would go well. I liked

> my job in Tokyo, but I felt there was a ceiling for working woman to get a promotion in a company, especially in a big company like a department store. I thought that if I wanted to get a promotion, probably it's better to work in a smaller company or start my own business. But starting in business is tough. However, I enjoy it because I can manage my business as I want. Especially as a woman...well, women don't think on the basis of statistics or theory. A woman follows her own feeling—this is right or wrong, this is good or bad, this is going well or not, etc.—compared with men. It's comfortable for me to conduct my business through my feelings as a woman and with the help of female part-time workers. Women can share the sense or feeling of things and are not required to explain their actions using statistics. It's comfortable.

At one level, Mariko left Tokyo in order to be her own boss and make her own decisions. Particularly interesting in this part of her narrative is that she sees the decision-making process related to business as being highly gendered. Men, she thinks, act on the basis of, as she put it, "statistics" while women act on the basis of feelings which in this case implies a sense of intuition. Becoming an entrepreneur for Mariko is at least partially motivated by a desire for control or power over how the business in which she works operates. As I discussed in the previous chapter, motivations for entrepreneurialism often are tied to interests in enabling personal agency through managing and controlling the context in which one pursues a career. In Mariko's case, this is evident in the fact that her identity as an entrepreneur is intertwined with her ideas about how gender influences they ways in which people make decisions and run a business. In other words, Mariko's entrepreneurial life is embedded in the self-reflective biographical process through which she thinks about and constructs her identity as a businesswoman and her role in employing others in her business. Central in her motivations to run the business is her desire to have control over the path over her own life.

BUSINESS AND FAMILY

Another aspect of Mariko's experience as an entrepreneur, one that is similar to those of the Yoshidas and Akiko, is that it is embedded within the context of family, which is often an aspect of small-business startups in rural and neo-rural parts of Japan, although it is certainly not uncommon in urban areas. Hamabata, among others, has shown the interconnectedness of Japanese business families and economic activity. "[T]he internal activities of the family," writes Hamabata, "are intimately related to the position of the family within the economy and the polity, and the way those two realms are organized is intimately related to the internal activities of the family...".[5] The nature of the Japanese family, at least the traditional household structure known as the *ie* (家)or stem family, is somewhat difficult to parse in terms of whether it functions primarily as an economic unit or a social/kinship unit, because the basic structure involves paired vertical relationships in which one individual typically functions not only as the head of the household, but also as the head of the family enterprise. As L. Keith Brown shows in his work on the extended family framework known as *dōzoku* (同族), this structure can be multiplied many times as branches are formed off of a main household and those branches are sometimes set up in businesses that are related to the business of the main household in which successors of household headships in each branch also function as heads of parts of the overall business enterprise.[6] These enterprises may form parts of a single company or they may form separate companies that are closely linked together at a social and not simply business level, because the bonds of doing business are not only economic; they are also socially constructed in relation to expectations associated with kinship bonds. In other words, the head of branch lineage X may be the first cousin of the head of branch lineage Y and they are linked together in terms of both kinship and business ties through the main household, which is the locus of considerable power and represents the starting point, through the originating ancestor, of the entire kinship/business structure.[7]

In terms of the ideological structure of the *ie* it is typically the eldest son who takes on the role of household and enterprise head, but both social and demographic trends in contemporary Japanese society have made this less common than it was in the past, although there have long been exceptions within families and also among certain types of family businesses, such as inns, which have in some cases followed lines of matrilineal descent and succession rather than patrilineal.[8] Also, variations on the basic ideology of patrilineal descent has been a normal part of Japanese family structure in part because not all couples produce male heirs. One common response to the lack of a male heir has been for a household to adopt an adult male (known as a *mukoyōshi* 婿養子) who marries a daughter from that household and takes her family name. This continues to happen in some families in Iwate (as elsewhere) and is the case of Kazuo discussed in the previous chapter, who married into his wife's family and became head of the pharmacy business, although it is not unusual for the son-in-law today to keep his own family name and for the wife to take his family name, even while he may function as a *mukoyōshi* in his wife's family in terms of his role and position.

For our purposes here, the key point is that household/family and business enterprise are often so closely intertwined that separating them is not particularly meaningful nor analytically useful. However, as is evident in the examples of the three women I have discussed to this point in the book, there are many variations in how the expression of familial and business structures occur. In the case of Akiko, her role in the family has similarities to the typical successor in terms of her running a family business, but the business was started through her own activities and not inherited from her father, and she does not carry responsibilities as head of her lineage. Keiko, on the other hand, while having a fairly non-traditional "family" business beyond the pharmacy that is structured as a limited corporation, to some extent fits into the traditional pattern of an adult child taking over the headship of the business but varies somewhat from the norm in that her brother has taken on responsibilities of household head. Mariko's case is yet another variation on the *ie* theme. As one of three daughters, there is, of course, no eldest male to follow the normative pattern of primogeniture. In the case of a family with daughters and no sons, it would be normal for her eldest sister, Maeri, to take on that role. However, Maeri had a career as a manager in an advertising firm in Tokyo which she continued through retirement at about the age of 60, following which she took a job in advertising in another part of Iwate, which allows her to visit their natal household on a regular basis, but also limits her ability to be involved with her sister's business (note that I do not write "family business" here, because the family actually views the shop as Mariko's business). Mariko is actually the youngest of the three daughters, which means that in terms of ideology she is not expected to take on the role of household head, nor necessarily the role of farm/business head. The reason for her to have taken on these roles is related to her personal interests as well as a desire to care for her parents, now mother, as they grow older. Had she not been interested in learning cheese-making, it is unlikely that she would have been pressured to return home given her position within the birth order and, in fact, neither of the other two sisters experienced any pressure from parents to return to Kanegasaki prior to Mariko's decision to move back to their natal home.

Nonetheless, having returned to Kanegasaki and entered into the family dairy business, even if not continuing the farm, creates an image of Mariko as the successor from the perspective of people outside the family, and in many ways also from her sisters. In one of our conversations, I asked her about her role in the family and its relationship to the work she pursued developing the business of her family farm into a cheese and gelato shop and it became clear that she prefers not to see herself as the successor:

> If there were a sense of defining myself as *atotsugi* [successor 後継ぎ] in my mind, I don't think I could do it. I still believe that my older sister is my family's successor. However, it's true that some people think I'm the successor. My family is the main lineage [*honke* 本家] so we have more burden [responsibility]

> than branch families. My father's role was taking care of the farm; and mine was taking care of the shop. So, when he was alive, our responsibilities were separate and I didn't feel like the successor. However, he passed away, so people think I'm the successor now. I still wish my older sister would return home and manage family issues like taking care of the family grave, funerary rituals, and so on as the successor of the *honke.* In reality, it's difficult to both run a business and take care of family issues at the same time. For instance, in terms of family rituals I'm expected to carry out as successor of the *honke,* I need to think carefully about who we should invite or not. I wish somebody else would do this for me [laughs].

Like Keiko, Mariko's life as an entrepreneur has been shaped by the context of family, although the ways in which this has occurred has been different. Mariko has no concerns about raising a family, but, as shown in the interview excerpt above, she has had to deal with the expectations that come with being the successor following her father's death, although recently her sister Maeri's return has mitigated some of those responsibilities. On a daily basis, however, Mariko is viewed as successor and must take on some elements of that responsibility, given that her sister is employed and does not live nearby, even if she is within about 45 minutes driving distance. Part of Mariko's identity as successor is also closely tied to the manner in which she started her business, which was possible as a result of the emotional and financial support of her father.

> My father helped in starting the business. He set me up with twenty million yen (roughly U.S. $190,000) that I could use to develop the business. He paid for the building and machinery necessary to operate and paid for my trip to The Netherlands to learn cheese making. This was a loan, which I paid back to him at the rate of about 100,000 yen per month. Because my father had both money and agricultural land, I didn't feel a great deal of financial risk in starting the business. Borrowing money [from a bank] would have been much more difficult, given the high interest rates.

A Hybrid Life, A Hybrid Business

Over the course of several conversations and through my own limited activities helping in the shop—mostly folding napkins or placing flavor decals on lids for take-out gelato—one of the themes that has arisen through my analysis of these interactions is the depolarization and hybridization that characterize both Mariko's business and family identities. Structurally, her experience follows historically normative patterns of succession in relation to both household and business/farm despite her somewhat atypical position in the birth order. However, in many ways she also simply functions as an entrepreneur working to maintain a small business that is located in a rather remote place.

She leads the life of a busy businesswoman. On hot summer days customers visit from mid-morning until early evening. At times, cars are parked in the small lot in front of the shop as well as in the hayfield directly across the street and Mariko's work often involves much more than selling cheese and gelato. One afternoon, in particular, was notable. Mariko had sent me out to get bread for the cheese sandwiches she includes on the menu and tomatoes so that she could make tomato sorbet (the tomatoes from her own garden were not yet ripe enough), one of the regular summer flavors she produces. As I was deciding on the best tomatoes, I received a call on my cell phone from Mariko that was quite difficult to understand. She spoke quickly and seemingly somewhat incoherently. Amidst the blur of Japanese, words like police and accident were readily audible, so I quickly headed back to the shop. When I arrived, I found a rather odd scene—half-way through the front glass doors of the shop was a car surrounded by a great deal of shattered glass. By the time I arrived, Mariko had calmed down quite a bit and explained what happened. "My back was to the front of the shop when I heard the loud revving of an engine. I turned around and screamed as a car came right through the glass doors! Thankfully, there was no one sitting at the table in front of the doors and there was only one customer in the shop at the time. No one was hurt." It turned out that the driver had mistakenly put the car in drive instead of reverse, panicked, and drove right into the shop.

Mariko closed the business for several days while carpenters repaired the damage, the cost of which, including loss of revenue while out of action, was covered by the driver's insurance. During this period of time, Mariko had to manage repairs to the shop and make sure that her employees' pay was taken care of through insurance, and, of course, she worked to clean the damaged part of the store. The period of closure also allowed Mariko time to get ahead on her cheese and gelato making, which, although she would have much preferred not having a car drive into her shop, was something of a blessing in disguise. In other words, the accident placed Mariko in the position of having to manage a variety of unexpected problems associated with the business, which are different from her professed desire to make cheese and gelato, but which are also not unusual activities for owners of small businesses as they attempt to respond to unexpected events or crises.[9]

I asked if Mariko was angry about what happened and she said that rather than angry, she was glad that no one was hurt and also felt bad for the women who caused the accident, particularly since when her husband arrived he berated her in front of all those around the store. This is important, because in many ways for Mariko, her business is focused less on making cheese and gelato than it is on interacting with her customers, about whom she cares a great deal. Many of her customers are regulars and the location of the shop—in the middle of corn and hay fields—means that those who visit must make a conscious effort to do so (people don't usually just happen upon the shop, given its location) and also that many people from the surrounding area are customers. Some of her customers are the same people whose ancestors and grandparents settled the area and built dairy farms after the war in various parts of Kanegasaki.

In many ways, the accident emphasized the values that Mariko brings to her business, and as Mariko and I discussed the accident in the seating area of her shop one day, the front window now covered by plywood as it awaited repair, I asked her about the purpose of her business:

> The purpose of running the business is to enjoy working and earn money for maintaining life. I appreciate my customers who come to eat the gelato. And I'm happy to see customers having gelato with happy faces. Also, some customers come to my shop to chat with me, eat gelato, and enjoy the natural beauty of the area around the shop. I enjoy seeing they are having fun with my gelato.

We can see in this passage from my conversation with Mariko that she has blended a combination of elements into her conceptualization of the business: international food, local customers, and rustic scenery. She also is engaged in creating a context in which people can experience leisure activities in a form that, as Mariko's father once told me, were not available when she was young. At that time, he explained, "the only opportunity for leisure and fun happened during the shrine festivals a couple of times a year." In fact, it was the opportunity to pursue leisure activities, in addition to education and work, that often drew people of Mariko's generation to the cities after graduating from high school, and continue to do so to this day.[10]

Kanegasaki Creamery provides an excellent example of both the hybridization and depolarization of the cosmopolitan and rustic that is occurring in parts of Japan like Kanegasaki and Ōshū. The shop itself is constructed as a cosmopolitan space, architecturally modelled after a house one might find in Europe rather than Japan, with the inside a brightly lit space, lacking anything that one would specifically associate with Japan in terms of décor. In fact, the shop is decorated with objects that either Mariko purchased during her time in the Netherlands or that others have brought to her as souvenirs from travels around the world. There are pieces of Delft Porcelain, a large bottle of champagne, and even a couple of cheesehead hats from Wisconsin that are worn by fans of the Green Bay Packers American football team. The floor of the shop is covered with terra cotta tile and there is red brick trim throughout the restaurant that contrasts with the modern light oak tables, chairs, and counters at which customers sit while eating gelato or a sandwich.

Mariko has also attempted to develop a bed and breakfast component to her business using the apartment above the store. Like the restaurant, the apartment has a cosmopolitan feeling, with hard-wood floors, and Delft Blue porcelain tiles imported from Holland on the wall of the bathroom. Guests sleep on beds rather than futon and tatami mats, and the only element that would suggest the apartment is located in Japan is the entry area where one puts one's shoes and dons slippers upon entering the apartment. As Mariko explained to me, it was her intent when designing the interior and exterior of the building to create a space that would have the feel of something not only beyond the Japanese countryside, but beyond Japan itself from both aesthetic and cultural perspectives. In other words, it was Mariko's intent to create a space that was not specifically Japanese, but that transcended geographically specific cultural themes.

Elements of the cosmopolitan are evident throughout the building. The sign that she hangs on the main shop entrance to show whether she is open or closed is written in English, not Japanese, although potential customers rarely pay much attention to the shop hours, which is something that Mariko describes as one of the more decidedly rural (she used the word *inaka*) or non-cosmopolitan aspects of her location. Like with Keiko's experience at the pharmacy, if people see that Mariko is inside, they will usually come in regardless of the visibly displayed hours of operation or the sign that states very clearly "CLOSED."[11] This is a behavior that Mariko has noted differs markedly from what she experienced working in large department stores in Tokyo, where store hours are clearly understood and people normally do not attempt to purchase items outside of those hours.[12] Although Mariko rarely complains, it is fairly obvious that at times she finds the off-hours demand something of an intrusion either into her work time (preparing for the next day) or the rare opportunities she has for leisure and rest.

GLOBALIZED RUSTICITY

Kanegasaki Creamery is interesting in that it forms not only a locus of innovative entrepreneurialism situated in an unlikely place—a rustic locale seemingly remote from mainstream Japanese society—for a gelato and cheese shop, but also because that entrepreneurial activity is intentionally situated within the global flow of cultural themes, images, and ideas. Both the design aesthetic Mariko employs and the products she produces are incongruent with what one might expect for a shop located amidst rice and hay fields deep in the Japanese countryside. And the creation of this locus was not an accident; it was a planned and designed product of Mariko's entrepreneurial goals in creating the shop, as well as her experiences living in the cosmopolitan spaces of Tokyo and Europe. Although Mariko clearly has aimed at something with a cosmopolitan feel, the fact of where she chose to do this cannot be ignored. Part of her locating the shop was related to proximity to dairy products, but also an articulated business decision that she believed being situated among dairy farms would actually make the business more attractive to customers. She was counseled against this by local business people when she was developing a business plan, because they thought few people would venture that far away from the more densely populated areas of the region. Mariko was correct in her analysis and she has added "farm" elements to the business, including keeping goats and at one time a horse in a penned area near the shop that is easily accessible by customers and that attract young families who bring the children to see the animals. In this sense, Mariko's shop represents a hybridization of cosmopolitan and rustic themes—a kind of globalized rusticity expressed in the cosmopolitan form of the shop, its products, and its décor, and the local and rustic in the form of the source of materials for its products and the taste of traditional farm life that a visit to Kanegasaki Creamery brings.

Researchers have typically viewed hybridization as a process through which cultural forms become abstracted from existing practices, recombining to form novel practices, cultural themes, and expressions of identity. Hybridity exists in the context of tension with what in some places represents its opposite—the reproduction and maintenance of tradition. Viggo Vestel explores this issue of the tension between hybridity and reproduction of tradition in a multicultural youth center in Oslo, drawing on Friedman's important point that the concept of hybridity is problematic from an analytical perspective unless we can empirically identify ways in which individuals subjectively associate and identify themselves with some combination of multiple sign complexes connected to distinct cultural traditions.[13] Vestel uses a semiotic approach to argue that the experience of subjective transformations in identity that incorporate multiple tradition complexes are negotiated over time and often involve ambiguities and ambivalences related to the direction in which individuals choose to orient their identities. Positionality in relation to the context of hybridization, particularly in an environment that includes immigrant populations, involves a process of self-transformation within the context of a social milieu that may at once challenge traditional practices and ideas, encourage individuals to preserve tradition, and offer alternatives to those practices and ideas.[14] Vestel's work raises an important point in the context of hybridization within an immigrant context that tension between the traditional and new forms a limiter on the process of hybridization in individuals as they subjectively attempt to negotiate often competing cultural themes and practices, and Vestel notes that practices of exclusion can counteract the hybridization process in an immigrant community.[15]

Here I want to argue that the entrepreneurial identity adds yet another layer to the complexity of hybrid contexts in that it not only identifies with, but actively employs multiple sign complexes in the creation of one's business. The tension between the hybrid and the traditional is actively employed in a hierarchy of part/whole relationships that follows the flow of harmonic tension and resolution extant among the different sign complexes that result in some form of unity of character.[16] This process is similar to what happens in the context of a musical performance in which there is a continuous interplay of tension and relaxation that is closely related to processes of "expectancy build-up, violation or fulfillment of expectancies" as well as to emotions related to anticipation of resolution after a breach of expectancy.[17] In a rather interesting definition of music, Kathleen Coessens and Douglas Walter Scott argue that music can be understood as "the possibility of carving out of an infinite number of possible experiences that allow stable interactions."[18] This would be equally applicable to a definition of culture, and it certainly is a useful way to think about the process of hybridity, in which individuals subjectively select from experiences and ideas those that generate some sense of stability.

Mariko's shop is itself a set of semiotic tensions that resolve into a coherent whole in the form of a node of signification that intersects with the broader web of signification in which it is embedded. The symbolic themes of the shop play on cosmopolitan tropes related to notions of global/European both in the décor and in the food. At the same time, the location of the shop is amidst symbolic themes of rusticity and tradition—the milieu of agricultural Japan. These frames exist in tension with each other but not tension in the sense of conflict or disorder. Rather, they inhabit a web that exists in a state of tensegrity, a portmanteau of the words tension integrity, meaning a condition in which tensional forces that pull on a structure generate stability.[19] The context of hybridity and hybridization that exists in relation to Mariko's shop is in this state of tensegrity—the tensions among the different cultural tropes actually create a stable framework that is internally coherent and cohesive.

Mariko herself is something of a hybrid in terms of her own identity, which displays the intersection of symbolic structures also evident in her shop. I have known Mariko for roughly 30 years, during which time I have seen significant changes in her speech patterns, particularly since she returned from Tokyo to Iwate. Over the past ten years, she has come to increasingly make use of the local dialect in Kanegasaki as opposed to the standard Japanese she used when I first met her, which could no doubt be analyzed in terms of William Labov's work related to social identity and dialect usage, although that is a project for a different scholar.[20] Mariko has travelled to several countries outside of Japan, including the U.S., Mexico, Turkey, and Holland and has interests in world politics—and world soccer—that developed earlier in life when she lived in Tokyo. When I first met Mariko, she tended to dress in stylish clothing fairly typical of women living in Tokyo at the time; today she rarely dresses in the stylish clothes that once were part of her daily routine. Whether at the store or taking some time off, Mariko is usually dressed in work clothes—pants, rubber boots, a white apron and a white hat, although not the type of hat farm women in the area typically wear while working. The hat is of the style one would find at a gelato shop in Tokyo. These hybrid and globalized traits I describe related to Mariko are actually quite common among residents of the immediate area, and one of Mariko's employees—and second-in-command—has also travelled widely and has relatives living in the U.S.

As I conclude this chapter, I want to emphasize that there is a close relationship between Mariko's entrepreneurial activities and identity and the hybrid symbolic complex that informs her outlook on the world and has shaped the ways in which she has gone about creating her business. Mariko's business is situated in what Homi Bhabha refers to as the third space of hybridity, which represents a space in which individuals construct hybrid identities and roles within society and that arises when cultural systems intertwine.[21] This third space can be understood as a dynamic process of agency in which actors articulate, negotiate, contest, and innovate themes, practices, and ideas associated with the cultural and symbolic systems that are in immediate contact.[22] Through the process of hybridization, third spaces emerge as diverse, rather than homogenous, contexts that innovatively mix past and present, traditional and modern, rustic and cosmopolitan. In making this point, I do not want to argue that Mariko or others who frequent her shop necessarily conceptualize themselves as hybrid—in fact, I would suspect that Mariko sees herself as entirely Japanese.[23] However, Mariko's approach to innovation as an entrepreneur is clearly one that engages and employs hybrid themes and concepts that cannot be neatly situated in cultural, geographical, or social frames unambiguously identifiable as cosmopolitan globality or rustic reflections of "traditional" Japanese cultural themes. Kanegasaki Creamery is the product of an intersection among social constructs related to entrepreneurialism and processes of hybridization, as well as Mariko's personal interests, which have converged to generate a third space of cosmopolitan rurality within the corn and hay fields conceptualized as *inaka* at the western end of Kanegasaki that has become a locus for the expression of both ideational and cultural tropes related to the rustic and cosmopolitan, local and global.

Figure 9. Kanegasaki Creamery.

Notes

1. cf. Mariko Tamanoi, *Memory Maps: The State and Manchuria in Postwar Japan* (Honolulu: University of Hawaii Press, 2009).
2. Hokkaido is a more typically thought of as dairy country in Japan, although one can find dairy farms in most of the northern areas. See Hansen or a detailed discussion of the dairy industry in Hokkaido. Raymond Adelard Jussaume, *Japanese Part-Time Farming: Evolution and Impacts* (Iowa State University Press, 1991); Paul Hansen, "Hokkaido's Frontiers: Blurred Embodiments, Shared Affects and the Evolution of Dairy Farming's Animal-Human-Machine," *Critique of Anthropology* 34, no. 1 (2014/03/01 2014), accessed 2018/08/13, http://dx.doi.org/10.1177/0308275X13510186.
3. Akiko Yoshida, *Unmarried Women in Japan: The Drift into Singlehood* (New York: Routledge, 2016).
4. Anne S. Aronsson, *Career Women in Contemporary Japan: Pursuing Identities, Fashioning Lives* (London: Routledge, 2014), 101.
5. Matthews M. Hamabata, *Crested Kimono: Power and Love in the Japanese Business Family* (Ithaca: Cornell University Press, 1991), 31.
6. Brown.
7. Robert J. Smith, *Ancestor Worship in Contemporary Japan* (Stanford: Stanford University Press, 1974).
8. Fumie Kumagai and Donna J. Keyser, *Unmasking Japan Today: The Impact of Traditional Values on Modern Japanese Society* (Westport, CT: Praeger, 1996), 93-94; Mitsuhiro Yoshida, "Contesting Powers: A Cultural Analysis of Water Distribution, Personhood, Gender and Ritual in a Japanese Hot Spring Town" (University of Pittsburgh, 1998).
9. Brahim Herbane, "Small Business Research: Time for a Crisis-Based View," *International Small Business Journal* 28, no. 1 (2010), http://dx.doi.org/10.1177/0266242609350804.
10. Sepp Linhartt and Sabine Frühstück, *The Culture of Japan as Seen through Its Leisure* (State University of New York Press, 1998), 10.
11. It might be argued that this is due to the fact that she chose to use English on the sign, but many people in the area, and most people under the age of 60, read at least some English and would be aware of the meanings of the words open and closed in the context of a store—both are commonly

used in place of their Japanese equivalents at numerous shops throughout the region.

12. I suspect that Mariko's juxtaposition of urban and rural in this case may be somewhat misplaced. Small shops in the Tokyo area, many parts of which have a close neighborhood feeling, may also encounter this type of "always open" feeling among at least local residents who are regular customers.
13. Jonathan Friedman, "The Hybridisation of Roots and the Abhorrence of the Bush," in *Spaces of Culture: City, Nation, World*, ed. Mike Featherstone and Scott Lash (London: Sage, 1999), 249–50.
14. Viggo Vestel, "Limits of Hybridity Versus Limits of Tradition? A Semiotics of Cultural Reproduction, Creativity, and Ambivalence among Multicultural Youth in Rudenga, East Side Oslo," *Ethos* 37, no. 4 (2009): 484, http://dx.doi.org/doi:10.1111/j.1548-1352.2009.01069.x.
15. Ibid., 485.
16. Caroline Palmer, "Music Performance," *Annual Review of Psychology* 48, no. 1 (1997): 119, http://dx.doi.org/10.1146/annurev.psych.48.1.115.
17. Moritz Lehne et al., "The Influence of Different Structural Features on Felt Musical Tension in Two Piano Pieces by Mozart and Mendelssohn," *Music Perception: An Interdisciplinary Journal* 31, no. 2 (2013): 171, http://dx.doi.org/10.1525/mp.2013.31.2.171.
18. Kathleen Coessens and Douglas Walter Scott, "Multiple Tensions in Music's Semiotic Eigenbehavior," *Constructivist Foundations* 12, no. 3 (2017): 360, http://ezproxy.lib.utexas.edu/login?url=http://search.ebscohost.com/login.aspx?direct=true&db=a9h&AN=124217184&site=ehost-live.
19. cf. Karol Winkelmann, Filip Kłos, and Mateusz Rąpca, "Experimental Study and Numerical Optimization of Tensegrity Domes—A Case Study," *AIP Conference Proceedings* 1922, no. 1 (2017), http://dx.doi.org/10.1063/1.5019127.
20. William Labov, *Sociolinguistic Patterns* (Philadelphia: University of Pennsylvania Press, 1972).
21. Homi K. Bhabha, *The Location of Culture* (London: Routledge, 1994).
22. Alice Lam, "Boundary-Crossing Careers and the 'Third Space of Hybridity': Career Actors as Knowledge Brokers between Creative Arts and Academia," *Environment and Planning A: Economy and Space* 50, no. 8 (2018), http://dx.doi.org/10.1177/0308518x17746406.

23. Maria Amoamo, "Tourism and Hybridity: Re-Visiting Bhabha's Third Space," *Annals of Tourism Research* 38, no. 4 (2011/10/01/ 2011): 1270, http://dx.doi.org/https://doi.org/10.1016/j.annals.2011.04.002.

CHAPTER 6

THE SAMURAI PIZZA CHEF

Sharing tea with a fascinating stranger is one of life's true delights.
–Iroh, Episode 2.08 "The Chase", Avatar: The Last Air Bender

At the opposite side of town from Kanegasaki Creamery, along the Kitakami River that separates Kanegasaki from neighboring Esashi to the East, there is a village divided into several neighborhoods, two of which are known as Jōnai and Suwa-kōji, which I will collectively refer to as Shiraito. Quite unlike the area in which Mariko's gelato shop is located, Shiraito is densely packed with large houses, many of which are several hundred years old and are occupied by descendants of the group of samurai who were once connected to the lord of the castle that occupied the center of Shiraito until the later part of the nineteenth century, when it burned to the ground. Shraito rests adjacent to the merchant district of town, just to the west, where one finds the main road that runs through Kanegasaki–the old National Route 4–which is the second longest highway in Japan at 854.9km and was established during the Edo period (1603–1868) as the Ōshū Kaidō (奥州街道), one of the five routes built to link Edo (present-day Tokyo) with outlying domains as a means of maintaining centralized political control over the country.

The downtown part of Kanegasaki is interesting in the fact that one can clearly see the old divisions between merchant and samurai classes in the geographical structure of the space. The samurai descendants live in the Shiraito area along the Kitakami River, while the merchant descendants live just to the west largely on the other side of Route 4. Class distinctions remain evident in the area and are visible in shrine festivals in which the representatives from Shiraito walk at the head of the processional, wearing traditional clothing associated with the samurai class from the Edo Period. In general, class distinctions in Kanegasaki are not evident in terms of economic status of households as they once were. There are wealthy, middle-class, and disadvantaged households in all classes—merchant, farmer, and samurai—although only one household among samurai descendants has struggled from an economic perspective (I discuss this briefly in what follows). The two other households that I have encountered in the downtown area that were in dire economic situations were both in Shiraito, but neither of these was among the descendants of the samurai class. Regardless of economic status, people in the area tend to recognize some level of social status differentiation that reflects the caste system that operated during the Edo Period, although this is not particularly meaningful in terms of distribution of political power. Members of the city council come from all areas of town and all social classes, and the mayor during my longest stays in Kanegasaki was a prominent descendant of the merchant class. My reason for noting the class structure is that it continues to contribute to the self-construction of and ascription of identity to people living in the area. On several occasions, I have encountered descendants of the merchant class disparaging those of the samurai class by describing them as haughty and arrogant. As one woman from a merchant family put it: "I don't think the samurai families are any different, but those people have pride from the past and particularly the older people sometimes seem like they see themselves as high status" [*erai* 偉い]. Old identities die hard. I will return to a discussion of class later in the chapter.

While the samurai past of the area may dominate its image, and is important in the example I discuss in this chapter, Shiraito is actually somewhat diverse in terms of ancestry, as many of the residents are not descendants of samurai. As noted, the castle that occupied part of Shiraito and rested at the border between the Date and Nambu feudal domains burned more than a century ago. The land it once occupied was sold and is now home to buildings constructed by "newcomers" or households that have occupied their land for close to 150 years. There are other areas of the neighborhood on which more recent housing construction has occurred, including one lot that had been owned by a samurai descendant named Nakano Hiroshi. Although the eldest son and successor, he lost his property after his father passed away. He did not speak to me directly about the history of this; however, neighbors indicated that his father had remarried after the death of his mother and when he died, the second wife absconded with the family fortune, including the property. There was a lawsuit and Nakano was awarded a small corner of the property, on which he was able to build the two-room shack in which he lived in relative poverty, while behind the shack had been built five modern, two-level houses in the early 1990s that are now occupied by families that moved into the neighborhood at that time. After losing his family property, according to neighbors, Nakano experienced years of alcoholism and was admitted to a mental hospital on at least on occasion—one neighbor indicated that he had been found passed-out on the street near his house. When I met him, he had been sober for several years and attributed his sobriety to joining the group of Jehovah's Witnesses who used one of the old samurai houses in the neighborhood as its meeting space (and who regularly dropped by my house when I lived there in hopes of getting me to join). That house is no longer used by the Jehovah's Witness group, having been converted into a restaurant and souvenir shop run by the government as part of the historical preservation efforts which began in the neighborhood in the late 1990s and that are central to the example discussed in this chapter.

My first visit to Shiraito was in the summer of 1994 when I was looking for possible locations to conduct my dissertation fieldwork. At the time, the community was active with children visible on a daily basis playing in the public park at the center of the village and also due to the kindergarten that occupied the area right next to the Jehovah's Witness meeting house. Older residents were often outside early in the mornings playing a game known as gateball or weeding their gardens. There were a few empty houses at the time that were ancestral homes of the samurai descendants who lived in the neighborhood, who had often built a modern house next to or in front of the old samurai house. In many cases, the old houses were simply used as storage, while the families lived in the new and much more convenient (and much less cold and drafty in the winter) modern buildings. When my wife and I moved to the area in 1995, we settled in a four-room apartment in the center of the neighborhood on the land that had once been occupied by the local castle, where we lived for about 1.5 years.

Much has changed since we returned to the US, perhaps most notably being the increasing number of empty houses that are evident throughout the neighborhood. On a walk through Shiraito in 2016, I made a rough estimate that 40% of the houses in the neighborhood were vacant, which was confirmed by one of the residents with whom I met as I walked through the area. Our immediate neighbor's house from 1995-96 was empty, and remains so as of 2019, the husband having passed away and the wife having moved to a nursing home. And many other houses have closed curtains throughout the day and night and no evidence of occupation visible from the outside. In front of one house near our apartment a parked, gray automobile has been in the same spot for at least the past five years, as far as I can tell, and is even visible on Google Maps.

Japan and Historical Preservation

While there has been significant loss of population in the neighborhood as older residents have died or moved to nursing homes, there has also been a major effort on the part of the town government and local residents to convert the neighborhood into a tourist attraction and to that end the area became a registered traditional architectures preservation district (*dentōteki kenzōgun hogochiku* 伝統的建造群保護地) in 2001. Conversion of the Jehovah's Witness meeting hall into a restaurant and gift shop, which involved restoration of the building to a state reminiscent of its early Meiji Era (1868–1912) condition, was one component of a much larger project to renovate several buildings and gardens so that they look more like the village did in the early-to-mid nineteenth century.

Although the Japanese government has supported historical preservation—particularly in the form of ancient artifacts—since at least the 1870s, the postwar era witnessed several laws aimed at establishing broad parameters for protecting cultural artifacts. In 1950, Law 214 was issued by the Supreme Commander for the Allied Powers (SCAP, a title that referred not only to American General Douglas MacArthur, but also to the offices and staff associated with the Occupation) that followed guidelines set up in 1929 and extended the list of cultural artifacts beyond imperial sites to a variety of archeological sites under the concept of "cultural space."[1] The law allowed regular citizens to participate with municipalities in preservation efforts, as well as in archaeological digs, which has no doubt contributed to the large number of amateur archaeologists working on historical sites in Japan, and this contributed to a growth in civic involvement in historical preservation in many parts of the country. From 1966 to 1975, historical preservation efforts where shaped by the Ancient Capitals Preservation Law, which was enacted for the purpose of preserving historical landscapes. This was followed by an amendment to that law that focused on traditional buildings and the creation of conservation districts, which shaped the creation of the preservation district in Kanegasaki. Much of this legislation was a response to the fact that rapid urbanization in the postwar era during the 1960s led to the destruction of historical spaces and buildings, which were frequently razed and replaced with modern buildings. As Barbara Galli notes, the historical preservation process in Japan has evolved in relation to internal politics that have often shifted between interests in becoming more Western and resistance to becoming too Western in approach, leading to a situation in which Japanese historical preservation tends itself to have a somewhat hybridized conceptual basis that does not function in isolation from Western ideas about preservation.[2]

Much like what Hiroyuki Hashimoto discusses in relation to Japanese folk-performing arts, understanding the nature of historical preservation in Shiraito should be understood as being closely tied to the tourism industry. Hashimoto views this process in relation to folk-performing arts as one of objectification, in which the arts observed by tourists are not "authentic cultural phenomena" but instead emerge through the process of tourism as part of a distinctively tourist-oriented culture.[3] In the context of Kanegasaki, this is an overtly articulated element of historical preservation efforts; several local residents and government officials have indicated that in addition to preserving the character of the village and documenting its historical significance, the hope is that preservation efforts will attract tourists to the town and, thus, also benefit the town economically. My goal in the remainder of this chapter is not to enter into a discussion of historical preservation efforts in the Japanese countryside, although it is worth noting that there has been some interesting work done related to the legislative and social contexts influencing historical preservation in Japan in recent years.[4] Instead, I want to explore the manner in which historical preservation activities in Shiraito became intertwined with the entrepreneurial interests of one of its resident families that is among the samurai descendants in the village.

RESTORING SHIRAITO

Work on turning the Shiraito village into a historical district dates back to 1991, when a general study of the area was conducted by local residents, which was followed by a 1993 geographical survey of the formal gardens found on many of the properties in the village. Both of these studies were completed with the assistance of historical and archaeological researchers from universities located in Tōhoku. Over the past twenty years, efforts aimed at historical preservation of Shiraito have led to the restoration of several houses, including the former Jehovah's Witness hall mentioned earlier, which was originally owned by the forest magistrate, a member of the samurai class who served the lord of the castle. The building is notable due to its grand four-legged gate at the entrance to the property, which includes a beautiful garden in which one can find *enoki* trees (榎 *Celtis sinensis*) and large maple trees that turn a vivid red color in autumn.

As noted, historians and archaeologists from regional universities (particularly Tōhoku University) have been involved in several stages of the restoration work and helped to guide the process of surveying the area and interpreting a significant number of objects owned by residents or excavated in archaeological digs. In the process of developing the area, the city has built a visitor center that greets occasional busloads of tourists (including some of my students from Waseda University) most of whom are from surrounding areas of Iwate and neighboring prefectures and conducts tours of the historically interesting sites led by residents of the village. Interestingly, this not only attracts tourists, but provides work and volunteer opportunities for local residents, particularly those who are retired (see figure 10). Additionally, the city converted the kindergarten at the south end of the village into a museum that details Shiraito's history and has a fascinating collection of artifacts such as paintings and tools from its earlier days.

At the center of the village, and only accessible either by footpath or a very rough gravel road, one finds an old house with a large thatched roof. The building lacked indoor plumbing when I first encountered it; instead it had an outhouse in front of the horse stalls adjacent to the house. When I lived in the village in the mid-1990s, a single man lived in the house, which was run-down and must have been difficult to occupy in the winters given the lack of indoor plumbing and modern insulation. Upon his rather sudden death at the age of 55, the town purchased the building from the samurai descendant that owned the property for the purpose of converting the house and its surrounding buildings into a centerpiece of the historical district. The building was fully renovated, including an expensive reconstruction of the thatched roof, and is now a tourist attraction open most days of the year, where one can learn about living-styles and construction techniques from the late Edo period. Visitors can walk through the kitchen with its traditional fire pit, and two five-tatami mat rooms, over which one can observe the soot-covered rafters darkened from decades of burning wood for heat and cooking.

About 350 meters from the old house one finds a visitor center along the main road that runs through Shiraito and leads from Kanegasaki to the neighboring town of Esashi (which is today part of the City of Ōshū). The building has a parking area in front large enough to accommodate a bus and is designed to look like a traditional house from Shiraito on the outside, but inside it has an office and meeting space, which is used by residents of the village as a community meeting hall. The building displays the large, dark timbers holding up the roof and sliding doors that one would find in the type of house after which it is modeled, but beyond that it is a completely modern building.

The visitor center is administratively situated within the administrative framework of a system in Kanegaski known as Life Long Learning Centers (*shōgai kyōiku sentā* 生涯教育センター) that represent a localized version of the *kōminkan* （公民館）or community centers that are found in most municipalities throughout Japan. Kanegasaki's Life Long Learning Centers are focused on adult education and typically involve not only opportunities for classroom-based education through lectures and classes but also may involve volunteer activities or community sporting events such as field days in which different districts of town compete in various games.[5] In many parts of Japan, these centers form important locations for members of the community to not only meet for learning purposes but also to engage political leaders in discussions about healthcare and other services available to residents.[6] And in Kanegasaki they are integrated into the overall political ideology of *machizukuri* (町づく

り), which has played an important role in rural or revitalization efforts in Japan for several decades.[7] Normally, the center is staffed by a government employee who is a woman and who wears the uniform typical of female town employees. And staff members from other government facilities, such as the public library, also spend time at the center. Several shelves are immediately visible inside the building that display books related to historical preservation, including a book that lists and describes all of the historical preservation districts in Japan, including Shiraito.

Shiraito, Class, and the Cosmopolitan

Shiraito is an interesting mix of old and new. A walk around the village leads one through narrow pathways and roads that connect houses that range from over 200 years old to less than ten years old. There are several religious sites, including a Soto Zen Buddhist temple, at which one can find the family graves for most of the residents of samurai descent and a large Shinto shrine at the opposite end of the village from the temple as well as a few smaller religious structures that are neither overtly Buddhist nor Shinto. The class structure of the village is evident in the religious rituals of the village, particularly in relation to a small shrine located on the southeastern end called *ofudō-sama* or *fudō-myōō* (不動明王) by locals which, although associated with Buddhism, occupies a building that has ornamental and architectural features normally associated with a Shinto shrine. It is an interesting building in terms both of its construction and its importance to the community, as became evident one day as I was walking around the village and observed two community leaders who were cleaning the area around the shrine and offered to open it up so that I could see what was inside. After struggling with the somewhat rusty bolt that held the doors closed and finally getting it open after using penetrating oil, they unceremoniously opened the doors to reveal a box with two very old wooden monkeys sitting on it that were described as two of the see-no-evil, speak-no-evil trio, but it was unknown why all three were not there. Other objects included a statue of the deity of the shrine (*Ofudō-sama*) with a bright orange image of fire in the background, and a pair of statues placed on each side that protect the deity. There was also an old sword and a spent mortar shell that had been placed there to commemorate a resident who had died in the army during the Russo-Japanese War (1904–1905). This particular shrine is largely used only by the residents who are of samurai descent, although anyone can pray to the deities of the shrine, and it is the location of an annual ritual held in April that is only open to the samurai families who reside in the southern end of the village. There are separate rituals for the samurai families in the northern part of the village.

I raise this to underscore the point that patterns of social organization dating back more than two centuries continue to be important elements of the overall social structure of Shiraito and, as noted earlier in the chapter, there remains a visible class distinction between those families that are samurai and those that are not in terms of perceptions of status as well as in access to religious rituals. Many of the men among the samurai families also have important political roles in the town and there is a perception, at least, that these families tend to be the most highly educated in the area. Indeed, several of the samurai households have teachers among their members, but I have encountered teachers who live in and are descended from all social classes; therefore, I am not convinced that this actually represents an important component of social status other than being a representation of the perceptions related to class among some residents. In short, by virtue of their samurai descent, members of these families have social and symbolic capital that distinguishes them from other residents both in the village of Shiraito and from residents of other parts of town such as the merchant district to the west. There is a sense in which that symbolic capital—one's accessible reputation, honor, or prestige that determine one's status within a social space[8]—is constructed in terms of ancestry, which itself is associated with Japanese ideas related to Japanese historical tradition. The identities of the samurai families living in Shiraito are socially constructed in terms of tradition in the sense that they retain elements of class and status hierarchies associated with the caste system that operated during the Edo Period, and in some ways this is also exhibited in the process of historical preservation that is focused on the samurai village, while not extending to the adjacent merchant district, which also has some architecturally and historically interesting buildings that remain from earlier times.

At the same time, current residents of Shiraito live in a modern capitalist society in which the historical divisions between merchant and samurai classes may still be subtly evident in some social contexts but have limited influence on one's role in society. In contemporary Japan, merchants, teachers, doctors, and so on can come from any socioeconomic background and the country has been portrayed as being largely middle-class during the postwar era.[9] The roots of a broadly middle-class consumer-oriented society has origins in the first half of the twentieth century and in the postwar era, as William W. Kelly points out, there has emerged a process of typification in which Japanese scholars and others often have represented the society as virtually entirely middle class.[10] By typification, Kelly follows Renato Rosaldo's concept of the term as involving cultural and social constructs that provide frameworks within which action is limited and shaped and becomes interpretable and intelligible.[11] Although it has undergone changes and fissures over the past twenty years, there remains a sense in which the construct of Japan as a broadly middle-class society continues to influence the ways in which contemporary people interpret their social and economic surroundings.

This process of typficiation, of course, is complex and the expression of lifeways continues to be interpreted and contested by people as they react to changing social environments. For example, writing in the mid-1980s, Kelly noted that in many parts of the Japanese countryside community continuity had been eroded by increasing autonomy of the workplace and emphasis on privacy within households, which in agricultural areas was accompanied by the decline of full-time farming. In response to this, the area known as Shōnai that Kelly studied, made efforts to "define and reconstruct local community identity in this encounter with mass culture [via] a novel and subtle juxtaposition of *nōson* (farming village) as both *furusato* (the old homeplace) and *inaka* (the backward boonies)."[12] This juxtaposition involved a set of delicately balanced themes as the perceived backwardness of *inaka* became the recipient of the modern in the form of rural development programs, high-speed rail lines, and high-tech healthcare centers.

Kelly's observation remains cogent in the early twenty-first-century context of Shiraito in which local government officials and citizens balance nostalgic renderings of the area's samurai past with modern structures related to the political economies of historical preservation and tourism that have emerged in many parts of the Japanese countryside since the time that Kelly was writing in the 1980s. This juxtaposition is found not only in the nuances of historical preservation in Shiraito but also in the lives of those locals who have lent the town their properties, their village, and in some ways their identities as descendants of the samurai class who exist almost as survivals of a very different Japan accessed through nostalgia tourism. The residents of Shiraito are not only engaged in the historical preservation effort related to their village but also more broadly to attempts to find ways to maintain the economic and cultural viability of Kanegasaki as a whole, of which the historical preservation work has been an important component.

Beyond this, the restoration project through which Shiraito is being reconfigured as a tourist destination has ideological motivations that are tied to nationalism. In his excellent study of restoration of domestic architecture in rural Japan, Adolf W. Ehrentraut rightly situates historical preservation efforts in the context of the construction of national identity. Heritage conservation, mass tourism, and national identity intertwined in the sites he studied to become valued as expressions of qualities represented as unique not only to particular villages but also to the nation as a whole and, thus, are used in ideological constructs that differentiate the Japanese nation from others.[13] Ehrentraut also notes that in the context of historical preservation sites in Japan, "the realities of class relations become submerged under a national culture and the social solidarity it affirms."[14] This is certainly an apt description of part of what is going on in Shiraito; however, while class relations are at one level submerged under the umbrella of national identity in Shiraito, the preservation efforts also to some extent reinforce class distinctions within the town, because they underscore the fact that the samurai village is different from the rest of Kanegasaki, making it worthy of investment of time and money to preserve. This is a rather complex social structure, because on the one hand Shiraito belongs to Kanegasaki as a town, but on the other hand it is differentiated from the other districts of the town. In this sense, the heritage preservation process in Shiraito intersects with local and national class and economic interests as it becomes a node for the construction of local and national identities through domestic tourism and ideology dissemination both in the context of the museum and in the restoration of the architecture itself.

This process of ideological construction and dissemination finds an interesting locus in the expression of innovation and entrepreneurialism through the creation of hybridized forms that express concepts of cosmopolitanism. By hybrid here, I am not referring to the notion of hybridity, creolization, or syncretism that has often been used to point out the problems with bounded notions of culture and identity that have been used in the past in describing immigration contexts.[15] Shiraito is not an immigrant community, even if it is a tourist destination that attracts people and ideas from other parts of Japan and to some extent other parts of the world; nor is it a place where people live situated between two different cultures that somehow constitute distinct entities that have a high level of internal consistency and coherence. Instead, Shiraito itself represents an institutionalized (governmental) entrepreneurial effort that intentionally aims at blending the village's samurai past with the contemporary context of globalizing Kanegasaki and Japan. This temporal hybridization is intended to create a cosmopolitan space that integrates old and new and situates identities such that people can move and drift through a variety of cultural frames without feeling disoriented either in terms of personal identity or cultural affiliation.

In this type of context, the local-cosmopolitan distinction that has characterized considerable writing on rural and urban spaces since at least the 1950s—when Robert K. Merton differentiated the local and cosmopolitan as representing an orientation towards one's own community (local) as opposed to an orientation toward the world outside one's own community (cosmopolitan), which are conceptualized as distinctive and opposed attitudes and interests whereby the local is characterized by parochialism and the cosmopolitan by ecumenicism—does not work well from analytical or descriptive perspectives.[16] The cosmopolitan-local construct, understood largely as existing as binary and oppositional social orientations, continued to be a common trope of social science literature well in to the 1980s.[17] Research over the past twenty-five years, however, has shown that the local and the cosmopolitan in the contemporary world do not exist in binary opposition but are often complementary components of the places and identities in which they are constructed and expressed. Local perceptions are not only structured in relation to "traditional" beliefs and ideas but are also created in relation to national, hemispheric, and global patterns of trade and initiatives, such as historical and environmental preservation and conservation and tourism.[18]

Craig Calhoun notes that following the rapid emergence of globalization trends in the 1990s, the notion of cosmopolitanism has come to have a variety of meanings that have made it less coherent as a theoretical construct, and that for some theorists of cosmopolitanism the ideal has come to be framed as a counter to perceived negative constructs such as religion or nationalism, replacing these seemingly divisive ideas with "a moral vision in which all humanity is equally valued."[19] I certainly think that this has been an element in the emergence of cosmopolitan tropes in Japanese culture for some time, but in Shiraito cosmopolitanism it is more a feature of the politico-economic landscape that is tied-in with the creation of what is hoped will be the emergence of an entrepreneurial ecosystem that will potentially stabilize an area facing likely demographic and economic distress in the near future. I will return to this issue in the last chapter of the book as it has relevance not only in Shiraito but also for all of the cases I have described. In the remainder of this chapter, I want to focus on the specific case of a man I will refer to as Haruki —samurai pizza chef.

The Samurai Pizza Chef

Pizza has become fairly popular in Japan over the past ten years or so. In the summers, I normally spend a month at Waseda University in Tokyo teaching classes to students from abroad. Next to campus there is a restaurant called Takata Bokusha that has been in business since 1905. It started as a "milk hall" which was a type of café that focused on serving milk that became popular in the Meiji Era. The restaurant has gone through various iterations and today it is an upscale pizza shop that specializes in serving Neapolitan-style pizza baked in a wood-burning oven. In some ways, the restaurant encapsulates the emergence of cosmopolitan Tokyo over the years as new forms of food from abroad, such as milk and pizza, have formed an empirical locus for the expression of global things to Tokyo residents, and particularly to the Waseda community.

Like other products and ideas that enter Japan and become reconceived, pizza in Japan can be a bit interesting; there are some unusual flavors, including mayonnaise pizza, which is among the strangest, and likely unhealthiest, I have encountered. This process of appropriation and reinvention from abroad, of course, is not limited to major cities like Tokyo. Indeed, around Kanegasaki, there are several pizza restaurants, including an Italian place in a hotel in neighboring Ōshū that uses cheese from Kanegasaki Creamery. In the center of Shiraito, right next to the public park where old folks play gateball every morning, there is perhaps the most unlikely pizza parlor I have encountered in my travels around the world. The shop, known as Ecru, lacks obvious features that would suggest it is a restaurant from the outside, as is evident in figure 11.

Ecru is situated at the corner of two roads in Shiraito, behind a large formal garden and a hedge that is a little less than two meters in height, making it somewhat difficult to see from the road, although there is a sign along one of the streets that points to the parking area for the restaurant. Indeed, if one did not know it was there, it would be easy to pass by thinking that the restaurant is simply another of the many old samurai houses in the village. Ecru has been set up in a form of domestic architecture known as a *buke-yashiki* 武家屋敷, which is a type of residence associated with the samurai class and is identifiable by a large sloping roof of heavy thatch, which in the case of many such houses,[20] including the building in which Ecru is located, has been replaced with a metal roof making maintenance much easier. The rooves for these houses are supported by large hewn timbers that rest on timber stumps anchored to a stone foundation. Rooms are open and sparse, mostly covered with *tatami* mats and the exterior walls of the building are constructed with a form of stucco known as *wara jyuraku* (藁聚楽), which is made from a combination of sand, clay, diatomaceous earth, and rice straw and is commonly used in older houses in the Kanegasaki area (as in other parts of Japan).

The building in which Ecru is located actually is the ancestral house owned by the family of the proprietor of the restaurant. The family built a separate dwelling in the 1980s adjacent to the old samurai house in part because the older building is drafty in the winter and also because it lacked modern amenities. For years, the family used the old house for storage. Haruki's father worked as a manager for Honda in the city of Sendai and had retired about three years prior to my first visit to the restaurant. Haruki has two siblings, an older sister and a younger brother, thus he represents the eldest son (*chōnan* 長男) and would be the default successor to any family business, although because his father worked as a salaryman for Honda there was actually no family-centered enterprise that Haruki was expected to head—he explained that he grew up without expectations placed on him as a successor and his parents encouraged him to follow his own path in developing his life and career. This is important, because Haruki's decision to start a business in Shiraito was not, at least overtly, influenced by pressure from his parents to assume leadership of a family business and co-reside with them as head of household, although I think it is likely, being a frequently expressed feeling among adults with whom I have spoken in the area, that he had at least some internal pressures to assume the role of household head and provider of care for his parents due to his position as eldest son.[21]

Haruki was 38-years-old, married, and had two children—a boy and a girl—when I first met him. After he graduated from high school, he chose not to attend college (which is unusual for children of samurai descent in the village), instead deciding to move to Hokkaido. He explained, "although I like the environment of the countryside, surrounded by nature, I wanted to live in an urban area, so I moved to Sapporo" which is about 600km north of Kanegasaki. When Haruki departed for Sapporo, he had no plans to return to Kanegasaki and did not think he would ever take on the role as successor to his family's estate and household. In Sapporo, he started working in the food industry, eventually becoming a cook at a large restaurant chain that had outlets not only in Hokkaido, but also in the Tokyo area. However, according to Haruki the company overreached in terms of expansion and went bankrupt around 2010. Haruki lost his job and started the process of looking for a new job in the restaurant industry, but he decided that, given that he wanted to own a restaurant eventually, his situation provided an opportunity to "realize his dream." He moved back to Kanegasaki with his wife and children and began the process of developing the restaurant idea; however, his wife actually opposed not only the move to Kanegasaki, but also his desire to open his restaurant there. She stayed in Kanegasaki for three years, after which, Haruki explained, she took the children and moved back to Sapporo.

I think it worth noting that I have never met Haruki's wife and I have no knowledge of her side of the story of why she and their children returned to Sapporo. According to Haruki, his wife had a career as a nurse and also her hometown is located just outside of Sapporo and it may be that both of these aspects of her life contributed to the decision, along with her own lack of a desire to live in Kanegasaki. It would be difficult to interpret the motivations of Haruki's wife without data related to her perceptions, but it is worth noting that conflict related to location of residence between women and men is a common narrative I have encountered in talking with people living in Iwate, particularly when the man in a couple is the eldest son and, thus, is expected to live with his parents as they grow old. Thoughts on the nature of this type of conflict were described to me clearly by one woman, whom I will call Chioko (25 years old), and who was staying with her parents in Kanegasaki as she contemplated divorcing her husband (the situation was similar to Akiko's returning home to think about her marriage and life). Chioko explained that she had met her husband through the process of match-making (*omiai* お見合い) in Tokyo and they had been married for about two years:

> The first year was great and he was easy to get along with. But after a while, he decided to return to his natal home in northern Iwate because he is the eldest son. He came home one day and said, "I'm the eldest son, so I will return." I was very angry about this because he had not told me anything about it prior to our marriage. He never indicated that he wanted to return. I was working at a good job in Tokyo as an announcer for a radio station and had to give that up when we got married, because he told me that he didn't want me to work after we were married. I prefer Tokyo and don't want to move back to Iwate. When I talked about this with my parents, they told me that I was being selfish and that I should just be patient [*gaman* 我慢].

As we talked in a corner of a French restaurant on the outskirts of Ōshū, a friend of Chioko's entered and decided to join us for lunch. After Chioko updated her friend on the content of our conversation, Shizuka added her own thoughts:

> Japanese men have not changed much. They are the same as they were in the Edo Period. Particularly the eldest son sees himself as high status [*erai* 偉い] and the head of the household who can order around the other members of the household.

Both women indicated that they do not like this characteristic that they associate with Japanese men and find this aspect of married life dissatisfying. Chioko's situation was difficult and although she was considering divorce at the time, she also indicated hesitance due to her perception of stigma as being attached to divorce. Much of the thinking of both Chioko and Shizuka is encapsulated in Shizuka's comment about men behaving as they did in feudal times, which was another way of juxtaposing frameworks of typification associated with these women's images of backwardness/tradition/rusticity as being opposed to modernity/cosmopolitan and as we can see in the comments of these women, there are gendered and generational elements in the ways these frameworks are interpreted. Both women explained that they believe there is a large gap between the ways in which older and younger people think in areas like Ōshū—in fact, Chioko held her arms widely apart as she explained this to add emphasis:

> The older generations still think in old-ways, particularly in relation to first sons. And men continue to think in old ways.

Interestingly, in addition to perceptions about age-related differences in the construction of values, for both women there seems to be a gendered construction of modernity and tradition in which women are associated with the modern and men (at least eldest sons) with the traditional.[22] They believe that firstborn sons tend to follow more traditional patterns of thought while women are less traditional in their thinking. Ideas about the gendered and age-related aspects of ideological and attitudinal differences among men and women, young and old, are closely related to notions of tradition as being set in opposition to modernity. Chioko, in fact, made it a point to avoid the traditional term for wife or bride, *yome* 嫁, because, she explained, it connotes traditional ideas about the social content of kinship relationships and also distribution of power within the household that privileges males and elders. For both of these women, the gendered and generational aspects of power are intertwined and within a traditional household tend to reinforce each other—parents support the power and position of their son and the son supports the position of status of his parents—and this relationship is not perceived as being conducive to a modern marriage that focuses on the conjugal pair. In fact, Chioko stated that she did not want to live with her husband in the context of his natal household because, "he puts more emphasis on the needs and wants of his parents than he does on mine. And he makes decisions unilaterally or with discussion with his parents, but I am not a part of those decision-making processes."

In other words, in relation to her marriage, Chioko describes herself as being marginalized from the household in which she is expected to reside, in large part because her gender and position within the kinship structure exclude her from decision-making related to her own life and residential situation as long as she remains married. For Chioko, these feelings of marginalization are tied to their return to Iwate and to perceptions about a traditional pattern of patrilocal residence that typifies kinship patterns among many households in the area. Note that she describes the first year of their marriage, the year they spent in Tokyo as a conjugal pair, in positive terms. It is only upon his decision to return and co-reside with his parents—to follow traditional and from Chioko's perspective feudal patrilineal and patrilocal patterns of household formation, kinship organization, and power structures—that things went south (or north, actually).

I do not have sufficient data to generalize Chioko's case to the experiences of other women, but Akiko's description of the difficulties she faced with her first husband echo those of Chioko—her husband made (rather poor) decisions that were addressed between he and his father and kept secret from Akiko—and I have had similar conversations with other women living in the area. It is reasonable to hypothesize that at some level Haruki's wife also may have been resisting not simply the move to (rustic) Kanegasaki and his starting a restaurant business but also the expectations of co-residence with his parents that are associated with the primogenitural patterns of kinship in Japan that continue to characterize patterns of behavior in many households in the area. Admittedly, I am speculating here, because I have never met Haruki's wife, but Haruki described his wife's decision to return as being at least partly tied to her distaste for rustic life in Kanegasaki and her discomfort with being away from her own family, which may also have been tied to discomfort with being close to his family.

Interestingly Haruki is a rather mild-mannered individual. He is soft spoken and has a delicate laugh, gentle smile, and a calm demeanor. He does not, at least on the surface, exude a sense of feudal masculinity that Chioko and Shizuka associate with Japanese men, and particularly men from the "traditional" families like Haruki's, although, as noted, Haruki's parents did not impose expectations on him to adhere to traditional patterns of primogeniture. However, it was also clear that, as he described his move back to Kanegasaki, he made the decision and his wife and children followed. I do not know the extent to which there were consultations between husband and wife before they moved, but Haruki did indicate that there were arguments about the move, and the emotional aspects of his relationship to his conjugal family became evident one day when I asked him how often he is able to see his children. Haruki and I began to discuss his relationship with his children:

> I see my family three times a year and I miss them very much. I want to live together in the near future. We don't plan to divorce and I also have a business relationship with my father-in-law, who provides fish for my restaurant. I hope I can open another restaurant in Sapporo in the future so I can be with my family.

As Haruki talked about his children, he stopped and tears began to form at the corners of his eyes. We sipped our coffee in silence as he composed himself and as I contemplated the emotional pain that he experiences due to his children being so far away. Haruki's comments on his family situation do not sound like those of someone who expects divorce, but, again, I have no idea what his wife thinks about his plans or what her ideas might be about divorce. And, of course, his relationship to his wife also has business implications, because Haruki purchases fish from his in-laws, who operate a fishing business and this is a relationship that he wants to continue.[23]

HARUKI'S BUSINESS

It is not clear when Haruki's natal family came into the services of the lord who resided in Shiraito a few centuries ago, but family histories suggest that they moved to the area around 1644 and the family took control of a plot of land 750 *tsubo* (坪) which totals about 2500m^2 in size. The restaurant building dates to the late Edo Period (early nineteenth century) and follows a floor plan typical of houses in the area, with a wood-floored platform area on the left side of the building next to the entrance and an expanse of *tatami* (畳) mat rooms to the right. There have been several renovations to the building over the years, including two significant ones in the Meiji era (1869–1912) and two in the Showa era (1926–1989), the most significant being the reconstruction of the thatched roof into a gabled metal roof. Inside, the feeling of the building is one of open spaciousness with a 15-*tatami* room (about 25m^2) that today is used as the main dining area with five low tables at which between 4 and 6 people can sit on the floor. To the left of the entrance is a small lantern room that has a high table and chairs at which one can sit either alone or with one other person for a quick bite or cup of coffee. The main dining area is bounded by sliding doors opening onto the formal garden that separates the building from the road, and this provides a lovely view to enjoy while dining. It also functions to cool the room on hot and humid summer days, when fans bring in cooler air from outside —the restaurant does not have air conditioning.

Ecru derives its name from a French term, which the website indicates is translated into Japanese as meaning natural or "as it is in nature" (*shizen no mama* 自然のまま) and although not necessarily organic in approach, to the extent possible Haruki makes use of locally sourced ingredients, including onions and other vegetables from his family garden. He is quite explicit in his representation of the concept of the restaurant as fusion cuisine; the goal was to create food that would be appealing to both younger and older patrons and he describes the restaurant as a combination of Western (European) and Japanese cuisines to create a hybrid concept restaurant.[24] The business is very much a family affair. Haruki's mother often waits tables and his father tends the gardens and does maintenance to the building and the kitchen when needed. Haruki also employs a few part-time employees, including two women in their early twenties who wait tables and a male assistant to help with the cooking.

Ecru's menu is eclectic and to some extent changes on depending on what Haruki decides he wants to cook and the ingredients that he has available. For example, in the summer one can find asparagus flavored ice cream that he makes himself and for which he uses locally sourced asparagus, while in the winter one might find *ganzuki* (がんづき), which is a sweet steamed bread or cake with sesame seeds on top that is often made in the area during the colder months. The restaurant also serves typical Japanese lunch foods such as *onigiri* (おにぎり rice cakes) that are accompanied with miso soup and *takuan* (たくあん pickled daikon). The menu has been designed to integrate the restaurant into the surrounding historical district as a way of providing tourists (and locals) with opportunities to eat unusual traditional Japanese foods local to the region. *Ganzuki* is one example of this and another is a stew known as *suiton* (すいとん)—a winter food with a clear broth, chicken, carrots, gobo, and dumpling skins (that are not filled)—that despite its seasonal association Haruki often has on the menu throughout the year. The purpose of having these foods available throughout the year is to offer tourists an opportunity to taste something of traditional local cuisine when they visit Shiraito. Locals have told me that *suiton,* for example, is viewed as being unique to the area, although I have encountered people from other parts of Japan who are aware of the dish, and historically was a poverty food eaten in times of poor crop yields. Thus, it has a connotation for some locals, at least, linking it to the rural and agricultural past. It also has an association in the minds of some people with the immediate post-war period, in which food was in short supply.

Haruki is creative and often develops dishes that blend elements of Japanese and Western cooking, a good example of which are the pasta dishes he makes that may come with a tomato sauce or may have another sauce using Japanese ingredients and crushed seaweed on top (this is not particularly innovative, since most Japanese spaghetti restaurants fuse Western and Japanese culinary approaches). I have seen dishes on the menu that have shrimp on spaghetti with a tomato sauce, avocado ice cream, tomato sorbet, chocolate cake, and some deserts that blend Western and Japanese flavors such as vanilla ice cream with red bean paste on top. One particularly interesting desert is whisked green tea with red beans and mochi floating on top. Ecru has a wide range of cold and hot drinks, including mango juice and various hot teas and coffees.

In some ways, the most interesting dish on the menu—and the food that was the talk of the town for quite a while after Ecru opened—is pizza. Ecru's pizza is baked on a stone slab and served on a flat wooden cheese board. The pizzas are small, usually with only four slices, and customers typically order several different versions in a way similar to ordering tapas or snacks in a Japanese *izakaya* (居酒屋 drinking establishments) in which one selects small portions of various foods until everyone at the table has eaten their fill. The style of pizza at Ecru is Neapolitan and one of the flavors he always has on the menu is Margherita. Additionally, toppings such as bacon and sweet corn, fried egg and spinach, and four cheese are mainstays of the restaurant's menu. One can also order a pizza flavored with fish row (pollack) and mayonnaise, which represents a fairly good example of the fusing of Japanese and Western tastes (although mayonnaise is so ubiquitous in Japan that I am not sure Japanese really think of it as non-Japanese food and, in fact, I have encountered people who argue Japanese mayonnaise is better than the American variety).

Among the more interesting characteristics of Ecru's menu is that it blends some very traditional dishes that are associated with the region, like *ganzuki* and *suiton,* with clearly foreign dishes like pizza, creating a milieu that exists in part as a result of the emergence of post-industrial globalized social, political, and economic structures that have opened Kanegasaki to the flow of international goods and ideas—in this case in the tangible form of food. Indeed, when I first lived in Kanegasaki in the mid-1990s, there was limited Internet access and it was quite difficult to purchase ingredients for making Western foods—tomato sauce was a challenge, and peanut butter was impossible without taking a trip to Tokyo. There were a few restaurants that specialized in Western cuisine, including one that focused on Russian food and was widely known for its cheesecake in the nearby city of Kitakami, but access to non-Japanese ingredients was limited. I remember distinctly the excitement among some residents in the area when a bakery opened that sold "bagels" in 1997 in Kitakami. My wife and I were living in Ōshū at the time and decided to take the forty-minute drive to purchase some bagels only to be disappointed that they were actually just bread rolls shaped like bagels.

By contrast, although I still have not found good bagels near Kanegasaki, today I can purchase excellent French-style bakery goods right along the Route 4 bypass that skirts around the center of town. Less than five kilometers from Ecru, there is a quaint tan building with wood siding on the front and an awning over the main window and entry. The bakery, which is across the street from an Isuzu farm equipment store and just down the road from a shopping mall with a chain pharmacy and a supermarket, is open early in the morning until mid-afternoon and sells a variety of baked goods such as croissants, cinnamon rolls, and Danish pastries. One can also find products common in other bakeries in Japan, such as curry bread and pigs in a blanket. Takashi, the owner of the bakery who is in his early forties, produces very high-quality pastries, which are light and flakey and often delicately covered with powdered sugar for the more Western products among his offerings.

Takashi was single, 42 years-old, and lived with his parents when we met. After high school he worked at an automobile manufacturing company, but he disliked his work—he said he was bored—so he quit and started working at a bakery in Sendai, where he stayed for 13 years. In 2012, he returned to Kanegasaki and began plans to open his shop, which he did in 2013. He had been interested in cooking since he was a child, so the opportunity to start a bakery represented a chance to do something he truly enjoyed. Takashi stated that when he was in high school, he had given up on the dream of cooking for a living and followed a more conventional path of work, but, as he put it, "a twist of fate" led him to follow his interests and start the bakery, where he now employs three women who help with both serving customers and baking.

Like Haruki, Takashi is pursuing his dream of owning his own business in the food industry, or perhaps more precisely they are both following their desire to cook and to develop innovative businesses in their home towns and to bring a touch of the cosmopolitan to Kanegasaki. Indeed, both shops represent a locus of cosmopolitanism, much like Mariko's gelato shop, within the context of a region associated with rusticity and agriculture, which in some ways is visually evident in the interesting juxtaposition of Takashi's bakery and the farm implement store across the street. Both men also took advantage of parental support and local social networks to help them in establishing their businesses. For example, on one of the days when it was a little slow at Ecru, I had the opportunity to ask Haruki why he decided to open his restaurant in Kanegasaki as opposed to somewhere else, like Sapporo.

Haruki: Restaurants are risky. So, I decided to open it in my hometown and on my family property. This eliminated the need to rent space. And because my family home is located in the historical district, we received funds from the government to restore the building. We thought that having a restaurant in the middle of the historical district would attract tourists without having to advertise. This has worked out well. I employ three part-time workers and the finances for the restaurant are in good shape.

JT: How did you obtain the financial backing necessary to start a business?

Haruki: My parents received the money to renovate the building from the national and municipal governments. And they provided help from their retirement savings to pay for equipment such as the refrigerator and various cooking supplies. That was really the only thing we spent our own money on—there was very little financial risk in starting the restaurant. Without the help of my parents, including the labor they provide now, I couldn't have started or continued the restaurant.

JT: What is your objective for the business?

Haruki: My business is for making a living. I sustain my life doing what I like to do. I don't work for becoming rich or expanding my business. My objective of having this restaurant is making my customers happy through what I want to do; what I'm good at doing. In addition, I want to contribute to the development of tourism in this town. I like cooking, so I liked my previous job as well. However, the reason I opened my own restaurant rather than being employed by someone, like in my previous job, was that I wanted to develop and manage the restaurant on the basis of my original idea and style.

FOLLOWING ONE'S STYLE

Throughout the conversations I have had with entrepreneurs in Kanegasaki, I have been struck by how frequently I hear comments that emphasized desires: 1) to contribute to the local community and 2) to create something that reflected the personal tastes, ideas, and styles of the entrepreneurs. As I have discussed elsewhere, among many of my interlocutors in Kanegasaki and Ōshū, entrepreneurialism is closely tied to the search for existential meaning that is represented through the nature of one's occupation and an interest in running a business for the purpose of helping others. Existential meaning is generated not necessarily through entrepreneurial activity *per se*, although certainly the process of designing and building the business generates meaning for these individuals. Rather, for these entrepreneurs existential meaning is primarily associated with the creation and maintenance of social relationships that come through the daily operations of the business and the creation and extension of personal networks that contribute to the creation of meaning in life. Personal fulfillment arises in the process of satisfying the needs of others along with one's own needs, but this process involves a delicate balancing of the tensions that exist between family and work.[25] Haruki, for example, along with building a business that interests and excites him, has fulfilled his role as eldest son and successor, even if the demands from his parents related to that role were limited. And the other entrepreneurs I have discussed to this point all encounter the need to balance expectations related to family with personal desires related to running a business, although Akiko seems to have minimal tensions along these lines because both her husband and father have supported her in creating the business and she has not indicated that she experiences demands placed upon her as successor either from within her family or from others.

For Haruki, perhaps more than the other entrepreneurs with whom I have spoken in Kangeasaki and Ōshū, the pursuit of his entrepreneurial dreams to start a restaurant brought with it significant risk but not in the form of financial risk. Indeed, none of the entrepreneurs with whom I have spoken indicated that there was any significant financial risk involved with starting or maintaining their businesses, although Keiko has experienced financial risk associated with the expansion of her pharmacy into other areas of the healthcare industry and Akiko has struggled to maintain her store in Ōshū due to the demographic problems in the center of town. But emotional and personal risk are experiences encountered by these entrepreneurs and Haruki provides a particularly clear example of how this type of risk has been connected with his activities as a restauranteur.

As Haruki described his life and his activities as an entrepreneur, it was clear that he lives at the center of a complex set of relations that involve conflicting demands related to his conjugal family, his natal family, and his interests as an entrepreneur/restauranteur. This is a path that he has chosen, but it is also a path that is connected to his position as eldest son and the default value he holds within the traditional Japanese kinship structure that automatically defines his identity as successor of the family unless an alternate option exists. Mariko has similar responsibilities related to family due to perceptions of her as successor to the family dairy farm (although being the youngest, she does not hold the default value of successor—she is an alternative). However, because Mariko is not married and has no children, her situation is different from Haruki's; for Mariko is no tension or conflict between different ways of life that Haruki experiences resulting from his complex family interests and expectations and his desire to follow a career path to his liking.

Haruki has struggled emotionally to balance competing demands related to work and family, in part as a consequence of his being the eldest son and successor in his natal family but also because he chose to develop a career path that had the potential to alienate him from his wife and, as a result, physically distance him from his children. Part of the reason he chose to do this was practical—he had access to a relatively low-risk situation financially that would allow him to start a business that interested him, and that low-risk situation would not have existed were he to have started a similar restaurant in Hokkaido. In other words, Haruki put himself into a position where he had to choose between his conjugal family, his natal family, and his interests as an entrepreneur, and in the end his natal family and entrepreneurial interests won out. He might have been able to start a similar business with help from in-laws in Sapporo, but the well of social capital available to Haruki necessary to start a business in Shiraito was considerably deeper as evident in his networked connections through consanguineal kin in Kanegasaki than it would have been through the affinal kin network he had available through his wife's family, although he has maintained a linkage to that network by purchasing fish products through his father-in-law. Of course, access to economic capital also played a major role in the decision to locate the business in Kanegasaki, given his receipt of financial help in renovating the farmhouse from the government. And in Haruki's efforts to build a business, social and economic forms of capital are intertwined both in relation to his family's involvement in the business and also because the interconnectedness of government officials and his family and neighbors (many of them are the same people) is tightly woven. In fact, Haruki's ability to make use of the government as a source of economic support was integrated with his pre-existing social networks in Shiraito as one of the samurai families who owned and occupied an important estate that could contribute to the overall project of heritage preservation in the village. And Haruki exploited that situation.

Local Policies, Heritage Preservation, and Entrepreneurial Ecosystems

Nonetheless, the economic context in which Haruki and the other entrepreneurs I have discussed is difficult to ignore. While there are a variety of projects like the heritage preservation efforts in Shiraito that have complex and varied goals, most of them fit in one way or another into a broader effort on the part of local governmental leaders to create an entrepreneurial ecosystem that will contribute to maintaining or improving the overall economy of the region and, most importantly, build a social and employment infrastructure that has the potential to at least maintain and hopefully attract potential residents. There are many government-sponsored efforts designed to accomplish these ends in one way or another, including a recently created program that provides government subsidies to purchase land and build a new house in Kanegasaki.

While I would not argue that the creation of an entrepreneurial ecosystem is necessarily an overtly articulated goal of programs like the heritage preservation effort in Shiraito or other attempts to create new businesses in Ōshū to revitalize the downtown business district from which Akiko benefited, there exists a context of interconnected entrepreneurial actors and institutions that are engaged in entrepreneurial processes related to projects as small as Ecru and as large as the International Linear Collider discussed in chapter 2.[26] These projects and the rhetorical structures associated with them have their roots in a long-standing political framework of *machizukuri*[27] discussed earlier in the chapter, which in the past tended to center around nostalgic aims of native-place building that have been a part of local and national Japanese politics since the 1970s.[28] The current iteration of the *machizukuri* ideological trope in Kanegasaki and its neighboring towns involves engagement with the main domains typically associated with entrepreneurial ecosystems—social, economic, technological, financial, infrastructural, and policy—that are interacting in the context of southern Iwate.[29] However, one key domain usually associated with an entrepreneurial ecosystem that is not operating in a supporting way is the demographic characteristics of the region. And a significant feature of the web of activities associated with creating an entrepreneurial ecosystem in the region are directly tied to efforts to combat the loss of population and its associated economic problems.

Nonetheless, despite efforts to generate what we can view as an entrepreneurial ecosystem by local government leaders, all of the entrepreneurs located in southern Iwate with whom I have spoken recognize that the economic future of the region is potentially bleak as a result of the demographic transition that is currently unfolding. In fact, many of the entrepreneurs with whom I have spoken, like those discussed here, situate their entrepreneurship within local policies and rhetorical structures that integrate business innovation with the social and political themes expressed by community leaders that encourage tying one's life and work to the needs of the community. Entrepreneurs like Haruki, Mariko, Keiko, and Akiko are cognizant of local governmental attempts to develop programs that support community development and generate contexts that are economically beneficial to the community and are also useful in building a sense of local identity; hence, they actively situate their own business activities within the larger context of the needs of the community.

Indeed, Shiraito should be understood not simply as an attempt at historical preservation, but also as the symbolic expression—in both the policies and the creation of a physical and social space of both tradition and modernity—of an ambition among local leaders to make Kanegasaki a destination for domestic tourism that also can provide employment and entertainment opportunities for local residents. In Kanegasaki, the context of heritage conservation is one that involves an interplay between the town's (and Japan's) historicity and modernity that communicates a sense of Kanegasaki as at once traditional and modern.[30] In this sense, Shiraito represents a node of cultural emergence in which the countryside, rather than existing as a homogeneous space, becomes articulated and constructed in a process of co-constitution and entanglement of various themes associated with both the modern and the traditional, generating a locus of hybridity—and an emerging entrepreneurial ecosystem—that at times overtly and other times covertly synchronizes the rustic with the cosmopolitan.[31]

Rosabelle Boswell argues in her study of heritage preservation projects in southern Africa that such projects can involve an "ongoing conquest of space" in which hybridity and identity are expressed in a context of multiple historical narratives and mixed identities and through which the concept of cultural heritage functions as a means to reconstitute a sense of bounded cultural identities.[32] I think something similar is going on in Shiraito, but rather than an attempt to generate bounded identities, the goal is to create a social environment that is non-bounded or less bounded than the "traditional" social environment associated with the region's agricultural and rustic past. The heritage component of Shiraito is important, but it is continually being situated in the context of the modern and international through linkages to the outside world in the form of the museum and the attempt to bring in tourists—and Ecru symbolically embodies localized globality in its capacity to express the hybridization of historicity and modernity, rusticity and the cosmopolitan, in the same physical and conceptual space. In this sense, what is occurring in Shiraito is the constitution and expression of cosmopolitan rurality, or a hybrid space in which ideational and physical elements of the rustic and cosmopolitan become merged or linked together and expressed in novel forms, in the case here typically through the activities of entrepreneurial innovation.

I will return to this point in chapter 8. Now, I want to revisit and explore in somewhat greater depth the demographic dimension of the emergent entrepreneurial ecosystem I have been discussing throughout this book by considering a domain of social and economic activity that has been at the leading edge in experiencing problems associated with population decline. To accomplish this, I will turn to a discussion of Buddhist temples and the difficulties some temples located in neo-rural areas are experiencing as a result of declining memberships associated both with the local demographic issues and a perceived lack of interest among younger generations in the types of activities in which Buddhist temples typically engage.

Figure 10. Tourists in Shiraito await the beginning of their guided tour through the historical district.

Figure 11. The entrance to Ecru.

NOTES

1. Barbara Galli, "In the Service of National Culture: Japanese Preservation and Its Political Context, 1871–1994," *Future Anterior: Journal of Historic Preservation, History, Theory, and Criticism* 10, no. 1 (2013): 27, http://dx.doi.org/10.5749/futuante.10.1.0023.
2. Ibid., 36.
3. Hiroyuki Hashimoto, "Between Preservation and Tourism: Folk Performing Arts in Contemporary Japan," *Asian Folklore Studies* 62, no. 2 (2003): 230, http://www.jstor.org.ezproxy.lib.utexas.edu/stable/30030287.
4. Peter David Siegenthaler, "Looking to the Past, Looking to the Future: The Localization of Japanese Historic Preservation, 1950–1975" (University of Texas at Austin, 2004).
5. Austin Uzama and Pierre Walter, "Incorporating Ecotourism into Social Education (Shakai Kyouiku 社会教育) and Lifelong Learning (Shougai Gakushuu 生涯学習) in Japan," *Journal of Adult and Continuing Education* 24, no. 1 (2018/05/01 2018), accessed 2019/02/11, http://dx.doi.org/10.1177/1477971417753975.
6. Traphagan, *Taming Oblivion : Aging Bodies and the Fear of Senility in Japan.*
7. Tadashi Ushino, "Comprehensive District Plan by Inhabitants and "Kande" System," *Journal of the Rural Planning Association* 1, no. 3 (1982), http://dx.doi.org/10.2750/arp.1.3_19;裕一 福川 and 真理子 西郷, "民間非営利組織(町づくり会社)による再開発；その必要性と成立条件 [Redevelopment by Private Non-Profit Organizations (Town Development Companies); Its Necessity and Conditions for Establishment,]" 日本建築学会計画系論文集 *[Architectural Institute of Japan Planning Papers]* 60, no. 467 (1995), http://dx.doi.org/10.3130/aija.60.153_1.
8. Pierre Bourdieu, *The Field of Cultural Production* (New York: Columbia University Press, 1993); Diana L. Miller, "Symbolic Capital and Gender: Evidence from Two Cultural Fields," *Cultural Sociology* 8, no. 4 (2014/12/01 2014), accessed 2019/02/11, http://dx.doi.org/10.1177/1749975514539800.
9. Vogel.
10. Andrew Gordon, "Consumption, Leisure and the Middle Class in Transwar Japan," *Social Science Japan Journal* 10, no. 1 (2007), http://www.jstor.org.ezproxy.lib.utexas.edu/stable/30209680; William W. Kelly,

"Rationalization and Nostalgia: Cultural Dynamics of New Middle-Class Japan," *American Ethnologist* 13, no. 4 (1986).

11. Renato Rosaldo, *Ilongot Headhunting, 1883-1974: A Study in Society and History* (Stanford: Stanford University Press, 1983), 153.
12. Kelly, 611.
13. Adolf W. Ehrentraut, "Visual Definition of Heritage: The Restoration of Domestic Rural Architecture in Japan," *Visual Anthropolgy* 2, no. 2 (1989): 157.
14. Ibid., 158.
15. Antoine Pécoud, "Cosmopolitanism and Business among German-Turks in Berlin," *Journal of the Society for the Anthropology of Europe* 2, no. 1 (2002), http://dx.doi.org/doi:10.1525/jsae.2002.2.1.2.
16. Robert K. Merton, *Social Theory and Social Structure* (Glencoe, IL: Free Press, 1957); Robert K. Merton, *Social Theory and Social Structure* (New York: Free Press, 1968), 447.
17. cf. Larry R. Petersen and K. Peter Takayama, "Local-Cosmopolitan Theory and Religiosity among Catholic Nuns and Brothers," *Journal for the Scientific Study of Religion* 22, no. 4 (1983), http://dx.doi.org/10.2307/1385769; Edward C. Lehman, "The Local/Cosmopolitan Dichotomy and Acceptance of Women Clergy: A Replication and Extension of Roof," *Journal for the Scientific Study of Religion* 25, no. 4 (1986), http://dx.doi.org/10.2307/1385911; Andrew J. Grimes and Phillip K. Berger, "Cosmopolitan-Local: Evaluation of the Construct," *Administrative Science Quarterly* 15, no. 4 (1970), http://dx.doi.org/10.2307/2391332; Victor E. Flango and Robert B. Brumbaugh, "The Dimensionality of the Cosmopolitan-Local Construct," *Administrative Science Quarterly* 19, no. 2 (1974), http://dx.doi.org/10.2307/2393889.
18. Hannah Elizabeth Parathian, "Understanding Cosmopolitan Communities in Protected Areas a Case Study from the Colombian Amazon," *Conservation & Society* 17, no. 1 (2019): 33, https://www-jstor-org.ezproxy.lib.utexas.edu/stable/26554468.
19. Craig Calhoun, "The Elusive Cosmopolitan Ideal," *Berkeley Journal of Sociology* 47 (2003): 6, http://www.jstor.org.ezproxy.lib.utexas.edu/stable/41035579.
20. 宮沢智士, "民家における書院的座敷の成立時期の一例 : 長野県南佐久郡八千穂村の場合, [An Example of the Arrangement of a Shoin-style Room in a Private House: Yachiho Village, Minamisaku-gun, Nagano" 日本建築学会論文報告集 [Transactions of the Archtectural Institute of Japan] 95 (1964), http://dx.doi.org/10.3130/aijsaxx.95.0_27; B. Shelton,

Learning from the Japanese City: Looking East in Urban Design (New York: Routledge, 2012).

21. John W. Traphagan, "The Liminal Family: Return Migration and Intergenerational Conflict in Japan," *Journal of Anthropological Research* 56, no. 3 (2000), http://www.jstor.org.ezproxy.lib.utexas.edu/stable/3631089.
22. John W. Traphagan, "The Oddness of Things: Morality Games and Interpretations of Social Change among Elders in Rural Japan," *The Asia Pacific Journal of Anthropology* 10, no. 4 (2009).
23. Over the years I have known him, I have thought quite a lot about this relationship and wondered the extent to which it is actually important to his business. There are plenty of sources of fresh fish much closer to Kanegasaki than Sapporo so it is possible, at least, that the business relationship is more important for Haruki as a means of maintaining ties to his wife and children than it is for his business. However, I have no clear evidence that this is the case—he has never indicated this to me directly.
24. The website states, "...和食と洋食を融合させた和洋食道エクリュ..."
25. Traphagan, "Entrepreneurs in Rural Japan: Gender, Blockage, and the Pursuit of Existential Meaning."
26. Freitas and Kitson, 268.
27. In official government documents, this is written as #####, but locally the kanji character is often used in place of the hiragana for *machi*. http://www.mlit.go.jp/totikensangyo/totikensangyo_tk2_000067.html
28. Eyal Ben-Ari, "Contested Identities and Models of Action in Japanese Discourses of Place-Making," *Anthropological Quarterly* 68, no. 4 (1995): 213, http://dx.doi.org/10.2307/3317283; Jennifer Robertson, "A Dialectic of Native and Newcomer: The Kodaira Citizens' Festival in Suburban Tokyo," *Anthropological Quarterly* 60, no. 3 (1987).
29. Ivan Bull and Frederick Winter, "Community Differences in Business Births and Business Growths," *Journal of Business Venturing* 6, no. 1 (1991/01/01/ 1991), http://dx.doi.org/https://doi.org/10.1016/0883-9026(91)90004-W; Michael Fritsch and Yvonne Schindele, "The Contribution of New Businesses to Regional Employment—an Empirical Analysis," *Economic Geography* 87, no. 2 (2011).
30. Francesca R. Sborgi Lawson, "Music in Ritual and Ritual in Music: A Virtual Viewer's Perceptions About Liminality, Functionality, and Mediatization in the Opening Ceremony of the 2008 Beijing Olympic Games," *Asian Music* 42, no. 2 (2011).

31. Michael Woods, "The Local Politics of the Global Countryside: Boosterism, Aspirational Ruralism and the Contested Reconstitution of Queenstown, New Zealand," *GeoJournal* 76, no. 4 (2011/08/01 2011): 495, http://dx.doi.org/10.1007/s10708-009-9268-7.
32. Rosabelle Boswell, "Heritage Tourism and Identity in the Mauritian Villages of Chamarel and Le Morne," *Journal of Southern African Studies* 31, no. 2 (2005): 295, http://dx.doi.org/10.1080/03057070500109466.

Chapter 7

Abandoned Graves, Empty Temples, Religious Entrepreneurialism

A flower falls, even though we love it; and a weed grows, even though we do not love it.

—Dōgen Zenji (1200–1353)

In the western end of Kanegaski, near the border with Ōshū, there is a Soto Zen temple nestled into the hills amidst dark evergreens skirted by carpets of florescent moss glowing in the rods of sunlight that dissect the black forest shade of spring and summer. The temple, which I will call Yamadera, was founded in 1356 and is difficult to find without a map. After a drive of several kilometers from the center of town, one encounters a road the width of a single car that goes ahead while the main road veers to the left. The nameless lane runs through rice paddies to the left and farm houses abutted by verdant mountain forest to the right. Careful navigation of the narrow road leads to a 90-degree bend bordered by a dented and scratched guard rail that terminates in a parking area a few meters from the temple. Everything about the area feels ancient and damp, including the trees with a stand of cedars some of which are close to 600 years old. The two exceptions are a modern, bright yellow house near the temple building where the head priest and his wife live, and, interestingly, the temple building itself which is only about 10 years old. Although relatively new, the temple building fits in well with the surroundings, while the house seems oddly incongruent with the setting.

Yasu and Eri run the temple together, Yasu being the only son in his family, which to some extent predestined him to eventually take over the headship of the temple from his father. Yasu is a tall, slender man who looks the part of the temple priest. His head is always shaved and he has a very calm and quiet demeanor; although this can be deceiving, because he has a quick wit and enjoys a good laugh. Eri and Yasu are highly educated and enjoyed travel when they were young, although the demands of the temple have made it impossible for the couple to travel overseas—and rarely in Japan—for the past twenty-five years. Yasu holds a degree in sociology from one of Japan's top universities, and Eri graduated from a major university in Tokyo, spending a year abroad in Canada. I originally met Eri at an English dinner, a gathering that was held monthly at the international center in Ōshū and that Eri attended regularly in the 1990s to keep her already strong English skills active. Today, she rarely attends these types of gatherings, because she is too busy helping Yasu with the demands of the temple and also caring for her aging parents who are in declining health.

The new temple building replaced a much older building (at least 300 years old) that was collapsing under its own weight, having endured not only centuries of dampness and winter weather but also occasional earthquakes. The old buildings of the temple, a few of which remain standing, had long been in poor condition, with numerous rotting timbers and a rather disconcerting tilt of the main pillars to the left as one faced the buildings, which was the result of a large earthquake that occurred several years ago. When I first visited the temple, there was a long disused priest's residence adjacent to the main hall, in which rested two small refrigerators that had actually fallen through a partially collapsed floor. The dank, earthy smell of mold and mildew was overpowering, and the long cracks in plaster walls and open areas of roofing left me wanting to depart the building as quickly as possible. In the main hall, there were various statues and other objects typical of a Buddhist temple, including a strangely deformed elephant statue that, Eri explained, was the result of the fact that the ancient priest who made it had never actually seen an elephant. In a corner of a side room from the main hall, there rested an old *mikoshi* (神輿) or palanquin used to carry a Shinto deity around the neighborhood during shrine festivals. Eri had no idea when the festival took place or when it had ended, but the *mikoshi* was covered with a tarp and Eri did not believe it had been used in decades.

The old temple structures are a stark contrast to the modern building that was constructed about 10 years ago to replace the collapsing main temple hall (*hondō* 本堂). The new building is typical of the temple architecture in the area, but is a modern building with central heating and an alarm system due to the fact that some geographically isolated temples in Japan have experienced problems with thieves stealing statuary and other objects that are then sold overseas. Eri described the new building as expensive, costing the equivalent of roughly 1.7 million American dollars, half of which was covered by donations (*kifu* 寄付) from related temples in Iwate and other parts of Japan and the remaining half contributed by households in the Yamadera parish (*danka* 檀家), which includes the neighborhood surrounding the temple and also has households from other parts of Kanegasaki and Ōshū. The costs were so high that planners (members of the parish and the head priest) were forced to cut corners in the construction. There are no complex wood carvings in the building, unlike the old temple, and the large wooden pillars that support the roof are made of imported cypress from Canada, which I was informed is much cheaper than using Japanese trees.

Yasu explained to me that the costs were quite difficult to cope with because there are many members of his parish who are elderly individuals living alone on a fixed, and often minimal, income. They lacked the financial ability to contribute significantly to the construction efforts and as a result the costs were not divided evenly among all households in the parish, but instead were divided in part on the basis of a household's level of financial ability to contribute. Eri described some of the challenges they faced in completing the project:

> The process of getting the building of the new main hall to happen was very difficult. There are three districts in the parish for Yamadera, one in Ōshū and the other two in Kanegasaki. The one in Ōshū was largely in favor of rebuilding the main hall, but the households in the other two districts ranged from neutral to opposed. The cost was significant, with the average cost per household at 5.5 million yen [roughly 50,000 USD in 2019]. Most of the households in the parish set up a monthly payment plan to make it more manageable, although some did pay in a lump sum.
>
> There have been so many problems! There has been a lot of complaining from members of the temple parish, particularly those who live near the temple. They think because they paid they can say anything! And then there were all of the issues related to the construction. The new town sewer and water systems were being installed in the area at the time we built the main hall, and that meant that many households experienced a double punch—they had to cough up money for both connecting their houses to the sewer and water lines and for the construction of the temple hall. Fortunately, only a few households refused to pay for the temple building, and those families have been somewhat stigmatized by other members of the parish—people view them as strange or unpleasant families. We created a committee to manage the construction and costs and they met once a month to make absolutely sure everything stayed within the budget—people here really can't afford more than what this cost. Yasu, ever the sociologist, wanted to do a survey of the households to see what each was willing to pay when we decided to replace the main hall. This was strongly opposed by members of the parish, who seemed to think that having circled a particular amount, they would be held to that amount or might be embarrassed by having chosen to

pay too little or unhappy about having chosen to pay too much. I have a copy of the survey, but Yasu never was able to distribute it.

Clear from Eri's comments is the fact that gaining consensus on replacing the old temple building was difficult and the process did not always move forward smoothly. They were able to obtain some help from the town's historical preservation commission, although due to the fact that the temple is a religious establishment the commission could not contribute to the actual construction of the new building. Instead, they were able to support the project by repaving the road to the temple and repairing footpaths that lead from the village to the temple compound. As we discussed the costs, I asked Eri if there was any national organization of Soto Zen temples that might offer help and she replied somewhat cynically, "it exists, but it won't give money—they only collect money—we have to pay to the national organization for special events like the celebration of Dōgen's birthday, but they won't help with reconstructing the temple."

Incongruities

There is a strange incongruity in the expensive effort to construct a new temple building to replace the crumbling structure of Yamadera's main hall while populations in the area are declining rapidly. This incongruity is not lost on Yasu and Eri. Although in conversation Yasu has tended to be somewhat circumspect about the difficulties they faced in building the new main hall, Eri's description of the process raises an interesting question of why they would go to so much effort in a context where the population is already declining and will continue to do so for the foreseeable future. In fact, temples and shrines throughout the region (and throughout Japan) are facing major problems related to the loss of population and the associated decline in parish membership. In addition to projects like replacing the main hall at Yamadera, the daily operation of most temples and shrines in Japan is based on contributions provided by parish members. Much of the work of a Buddhist priest in Japan centers on ritual care of the dead.[1] Although there is no set amount and contributions are voluntary, for a typical funeral Yasu is given between 200,00 and 300,000 yen (1,800 to 2,800 USD), by the family of the deceased. Because Yasu's temple is run like a company, and Yasu is in fact an employee, the money is put into company funds and used to pay for things like maintenance of the temple and Yasu's salary. The obvious problem is that if the number of households in a parish declines, then the income to the temple also will decline, making it difficult to maintain buildings and the cemetery and, ultimately, making it difficult to employ a head priest and provide living space for his or her family. This problem is not limited to Iwate but is occurring throughout Japan and there are predictions that as many as 40% of Buddhist temples will close over the next twenty years, which translates to roughly 30,800 of the 77,000 temples throughout the country .

Yasu and Eri are, of course, aware of this problem and it was part of the reason that they felt it necessary to replace the old building. As Yasu explained it, "in the future I think the relationship with temples will become more on an individual basis, rather than a family basis. There will be less of a sense of families belonging as there are fewer children and fewer families. But the rituals for the dead will continue to need to be done, so there need to be institutions where people can take care of that." This, however, does not really explain why they would go to such trouble and expense to replace the building in a context that is losing its parish membership. The answer, which came from Eri, is in fact directly tied to the population problem.

> There were several reasons, but one of the main ones was the fact that Yasu and I don't have children. Therefore, we do not have a successor to eventually take over the temple. There are some other options that we have explored, including adopting an adult couple into Yasu's family to take over the responsibilities of the temple, but nothing has come of that to date. The problem of having no successor is serious and the new building was intended in part to address that. If we want to bring in a disciple [*deshi* 弟

> 子] for Yasu from a Zen monastery, he is unlikely to want to come with the temple in such bad shape. Also, there is a clear need for replacing the temple and we didn't think it would make sense to dump this on Yasu's successor. So, part of what we were thinking is that if we rebuild the temple before finding a successor, it might help with attracting someone to replace Yasu.

The reconstruction of Yamadera represents an excellent example of the ways in which Japan's population decline is beginning to significantly affect long-established institutions such as Buddhist temples and Shinto shrines. The current and projected loss of population means that temples like Yamadera face significant obstacles to their operations in the present and their long-term viability is open to question. Yasu has indicated that he believes Yamadera will eventually be forced to combine with another Soto Zen temple in the area in order to maintain a sufficient parish membership to continue operations, and I think it is reasonable to conclude that the new temple building may represent a strategy for managing possible amalgamation in the future in that the new construction might allow Yamadera to have more control over the nature of any alliance they are forced to make, although Yasu has never indicated this directly to me. Such an alliance could come in the form of adopting a second or third son from a related Soto Zen temple who would take on the role as successor, which also has financial implications for Eri and Yasu in that adopting an adult successor can generate tax benefits and the successor would be treated as family in terms of inheriting the responsibilities of managing the temple and its headship and taking over Yasu and Eri's personal estate, which would include caring for their ancestral spirits when they die. This is one of the reasons that formally adopting a successor has advantages over simply finding someone to take over the temple, although that option also is on the table.

Both Eri and Yasu would like to eventually move away from Yamadera and live in a city in their retired years, although neither is convinced that such a future lies ahead. Eri, in particular, longs for urban life and has stated on several occasions that she dislikes living in the mountains, remote from friends and family, as well as from the lifestyle associated with urban areas. A common theme she brings up when talking about their life is her hatred of snakes, of which there are many around her house and the temple and which seem to symbolically encapsulate her dislike of living in the mountains. Yasu, on the other hand, seems to be largely resigned to the inevitability that they will spend the rest of their lives at the temple, even if he retires from the work of head priest.

TEMPLES AND GRAVES

A few kilometers north of Yamadera there is another Buddhist temple which I will call Antai-ji that is, like Yamadera, located amidst a clump of trees on a hillside, but Antai-ji is also surrounded by wide expanses of rice paddies, a few small housing developments, and the occasional apartment building. The entrance to the temple is along one of the main roads in Kanegasaki, which leads to the town's industrial park including the Toyota factory as well as a sports complex that includes a small baseball stadium, tennis courts, and indoor facilities for swimming, training, and racket ball. It is also fairly close to the public golf course that attracts golfers from throughout the region and is a regular haunt of local politicians. The temple looks like other temples in the region with its tiled roof, large central gate under which one climbs uneven stone steps to reach the area with a large temple bell, and formal garden. In this sense, Antai-ji is quite different from Yamadera, where there is no formal garden, no artificial pond with carp swimming in it, and few family members to help with the maintenance of the grounds—at Antai-ji, it is not unusual to find the head priest's mother weeding or carefully tending the flowers in the garden.

The head priest of Antai-ji, whom I will call Ichiro, is a bespectacled man in his mid-fifties, of slight height and build, but whom I have often seen around the grounds with a pitchfork in hand tending the grounds and taking care of the large cemetery that climbs the side of the hill next to the temple buildings. Antai-ji is different from Yamadera in the fact that, rather than experiencing a shrinkage in the size of its parish, there are today roughly 500 families which represents a modest increase over the past few years. The relative proximity of Antai-ji to the central part of Kanegasaki as well as the industrial park has contributed to the comparative stability of the temple. Ichiro explained to me at one point that the Toyota factory, in particular, has brought in some people to the area for work who have moved into the newer houses built between the factory and the limited-access highway a few kilometers to the east. Some of these families have chosen to permanently relocate to Kanegasaki and become members of Antai-ji.

It should be pointed out here that temple membership is typically a matter of either family tradition or convenience in Japan rather than having much of anything to do with faith or commitment to a particular religious tradition.[2] One is a Soto Zen Buddhist, for example, not so much because one believes in anything specifically related to the philosophical tradition of Zen, but because one's ancestors are buried at a Soto Zen temple.[3] If a family moves to Kanegasaki from another part of Japan and expects to remain, they may choose to join a local temple and move the family grave to that temple's cemetery, although this is not necessary. As long as someone is caring for the ancestral grave site—regardless of where it is located—it is not usually necessary to change temples or to move the family grave nearby. But if there are no relatives left in one's natal town and one has permanently relocated, it may make sense to move one's ancestral grave to a local temple and this would represent a potentially significant reason why one might join a temple like Antai-ji after having moved to Kanegasaki.

Even while Antai-ji has experienced a moderate increase in the size of its parish, population issues are a significant concern for Ichiro, who intimated that although there have been a few families who recently joined, the newer families have little interest in temple activities or have no immediate relatives who have died, thus they do not participate in rituals associated with the temple. Indeed, in Japan if no one has died in one's immediate family, there is little reason to become involved in temple rituals—the temple is not normally a locus of community worship or even community activities as one might imagine the role of a church or synagogue in a community in the United States.[4] The main reason to visit one's temple is to care for deceased relatives. If one has no close relatives who are deceased, or if someone else in the family is providing care, it is not necessary to be involved with the activities of a Buddhist temple, even if one has chosen to become a member of the parish (which has implications for the care of one's own ancestral spirit in the future).

Despite its population stability today, Ichiro anticipates that the parish will begin to experience a decline in membership in the near future, because there are quite a few families in the parish that lack children and that consist of elder couples or individuals. Not only does this present a problem in terms of issues like financing temple operations, it also has implications for the work of the temple priest, because adult children are expected to care for the ancestral spirits of their families, which is done through a combination of ritual memorialization and maintenance of the family grave-site.[5] As we wandered around his temple cemetery one day, Ichiro explained the problems that arise with depopulation in relation to maintenance of grave sites and ancestral care:

> There are several families in which there are no children and for which there is no one to care for the grave. These graves become like discarded trash [ゴミ *gomi*] in that there is no one to care for them and they are just scattered around without anyone cleaning the area or making offerings. This is a growing problem. It's not that people have moved away; it's just that there isn't anyone left [alive] to care for the graves. I wind up having to do it, although in some temples people pay for long-term care of the grave provided by the priest. I don't do that here.

It has long been the case that concern for and care of one's ancestors is perhaps the most important element of religious practice in Japan.[6] Many people believe that it is necessary and morally right for the living to show their concern and love of those who have died through the performance of rituals and offerings, in part, at the family grave site.[7] Ancestral spirits that are ignored are normally understood as becoming *muenbotoke* (無縁仏) or unattached spirits. These spirits have been historically viewed as dangerous to the living, although neither Yasu nor Ichiro have ever indicated that they view them as presenting dangers, and I suspect most younger Japanese do not view them in this way. Both Yasu and Ichiro see wandering spirits as being sad and lonely (*sabishii* 寂しい) because no one is caring for them.

The problem in places like Kanegasaki is that there are a growing number of abandoned graves dotting cemeteries in much the same way that the abandoned houses are evident throughout the landscape of the countryside, and both houses and graves often are left without living people to provide care and maintenance. The problem of *muenbotoke* today is exacerbated by the aging and declining population. As the average age of the local population increases, many find it physically difficult to attend to the needs of maintaining family grave sites, although doing so is certainly a priority, and this may become impossible if one is living in a nursing home and lacks relatives nearby to attend to grave-site needs or to bring one to the family grave.

Reinventing Buddhism Through Religious Entrepreneurialism

Necessity is the mother of innovation and several head priests in Kanegasaki and Ōshū have explored ways to ensure that their temples are able to continue operation. Often, this is done by attempting to make Buddhism more immediately relevant to younger people and to reduce the widespread image of the religion as being only associated with care of the dead. On a rainy June morning a friend of mine drove me from her house in the center of Ōshū to a temple deep in the mountain range that separates the central plains of southern Iwate from the eastern coastal areas. As we headed up a twisting road, passing tiny farming hamlets with old houses covered by metal roofs painted a faded red, brown, or blue, my friend told me that I was in for a bit of a surprise. When we arrived at Ichijō-ji, I realized that I had been to the temple in the past for a festival known as *hadaka-matsuri* (裸祭) in which throngs of naked men engage in mock battles through a cold winter night in the attempt to gain control over a collection of wooden amulets. The temple is quite famous throughout Iwate both for the festival and for its architectural beauty.

As we extracted ourselves from my friend's BMW, we were greeted by Fusako, a woman in her mid-fifties with shining black hair cut in a bob. Fusako is slender and somewhat taller than average for a woman in Japan at about 1.7 meters in height. She was wearing a black *samue* (作務衣), the cotton casual clothing consisting of loose pants and a loose-fitting top that closes like a robe. This clothing is typically worn for sitting meditation or working around the temple by Buddhist monks (and also laypersons) in Japan. Fusako wears thick glasses in wire frames that tend to magnify her eyes somewhat. She has a strong and loud voice, a robust laugh, and is very talkative; and contrary to stereotypes of Japanese as indirect, she is both blunt and direct in conversation with a dry sense of humor.

We walked together along the path to her house, which is adjacent to the main temple buildings, most of which are about 150 years old. The wood on the outside of the buildings is weathered and gray and the walls consist of wood and a tan plaster; the entire compound is surrounded by a yellow-tan wall decorated with tiles along the top, and through the gate at the bottom of the hill on which the temple is located one finds a large parking lot with a shop that sells souvenirs and has a toilet for the occasional tourists who visit the temple.

Fusako was the surprise, although I was not as surprised as my friend had expected because I had seen her several years earlier at a meeting in Kanegasaki where she gave a talk on Buddhism to local residents at a community center. As head priest of Ichijō-ji, Fusako has made significant efforts to bring Buddhist ideas and philosophy beyond the confines of her temple by giving lectures throughout the region. She is quite well known for her interesting and rather humorous lectures, as well as the fact that she is unusual being a woman functioning as head priest of a well-known and historically important temple. Her lectures also provided needed income for her family and the temple because, despite the high visibility of the temple, her parish is quite small even compared with much less well-known temples like Yamadera.

Fusako is aware of the fact that being a woman is unusual, and when we talked about the fact that men are typically Buddhist priests, her comments were quite clear:

> **Fusako**: That's a prejudice, isn't it? [She used the term *henken* 偏見 , which means prejudice, bias or a limited perspective]. It's prejudice against women. There is nothing in Buddhism that prohibits women from being priests. Women can do this [when she said this, she moved her hands over her clothing].
>
> **JT**: Your head isn't shaved...
>
> **Fusako**: I shave it just like the men do—when I need to for ritual purposes. Maybe it's a little unusual [*mezurashii* 珍しい] for a woman to be doing this job, but there are other women who are Buddhist priests. However, from the perspective of other Japanese it is very unusual [*sugoku mezurashii* すごく珍しい].
>
> **JT**: Why did you decide to become a priest?
>
> **Fusako**: I like Buddhism. You are kind in the face of other humans —there is a sense of being kind to others. That is very important and I like that. Buddhism is peaceful. It gives you peace of *kokoro* [心 heart/mind/center]. There are so many problems in Japan today, like bullying, and I think it's because Japan has lost the values associated with Buddhism. I also like the fact that Buddhism focuses on living in the moment, although that can be difficult to accomplish. I find thinking about the future disagreeable. I don't want to think about the future, about saving for the future, or that

> sort of thing. It is the wrong approach for a temple and for life. If the temple comes to an end, it comes to an end.

As we sat on tatami sipping green tea in her living room, I asked about how Ichijō-ji is coping with population decline and how that affects her temple.

> There are only 15 families in the parish for this temple. It's always been this way. There have been about 1200 years of history. It's always been small. These are the people who were in the parish from the past. The parish has not increased, but it has not decreased particularly either. If the temple has problems, my family pays for them. If the roof needs to be fixed, we don't get significant contributions from the parish. We might get 10,000 yen (USD 90) from each family, so 150,000 yen altogether, but that isn't enough to take care of the temple by any means. So, we pay for whatever needs to be done. It is difficult [*taihen* 大変]. We don't get any help from the government because of separation of religion and state, unlike the monastery up the road which gets about half the money they need because the main hall is designated as a historical building.[8] Right now, the altar in the main hall needs repairs and we will need to take care of that soon.

As we talked, Fusako scolded me somewhat jokingly after one of my questions was too vague. She said, "fix your question" as she got up to bring more water for tea. When she returned from the kitchen, she started to explain more about how they finance the operations of the temple. They have about 3,000 people who participate in a public organization that runs the annual festival (the naked man festival) and that group contributes money to support maintenance of the temple for cultural reasons. Each member of the organization pays about 300 yen as a membership fee, which helps with costs associated with the temple (there are additional costs related to the festival that are obtained from other sources). The temple also has income from the amulets (*omamori* お守り) that the temple sells to tourists and those on pilgrimage who visit, and they collect about one million yen (USD 9,000) annually from rituals and other activities that she and her son perform (excluding her lectures). Altogether, from all sources, the temple income is between 2 and 3 million yen per year, although it can be lower during difficult economic times. After the costs associated with the festival, they typically have 1.5 to 2.0 million yen to cover all costs associated with the temple for the following year.

The family receives income from work outside of the temple, such as Fusako's lectures and her husband works in a grocery store as a manager, which brings a steady income to support their family. Fusako's son, who attended graduate school in the United Kingdom and works for the local international center, in part due to his strong English skills, also brings income and will eventually take over as head priest of the temple. The family has struggled somewhat with finances because one of Fusako's parents is bedridden and that has caused the accumulation of significant medical expenses. Her husband's income covered all of the expenses related to raising their three children, including attendance at college, which has allowed her to use much of her own income to take care of the temple.

At one point in our conversation, I mentioned that we had met many years earlier at one of her talks and that it's a small world, to which she replied, "then we can't do anything bad!" [*de warui koto dekinai desu"* で悪いことできないです], over which we had a good laugh and then she turned to a more serious tone when I asked about the future of her temple.

> I have no idea, really. The temple has been here for 1200 years. There are good times and bad times. We are in a bad time right now, but it may change. When the samurai were around it was a very good time. It is what it is. In Buddhism, you simply take things the way they are; you don't really look to the future, but focus on the present. If the economy gets better, more people will come. Maybe they build an apartment building nearby and a lot of people join the parish. We don't know what will happen. It would be too bad if the temple went away, but in Japan there have been many other more important temples that have gone away. Don't

> churches in the US go away sometimes? There are a lot of temples in the area, so if it goes away, it goes away. Maybe it would be combined with another temple. Those things do happen.
>
> I suppose we could make the temple a big one with a big parish if we wanted, but I have no desire to do so. I'm not a hard worker! It's ok the way it is... [*watashi hataraki mono jya nai kara, tekitō de ii*... 私働き者じゃないから...適当でいい]. I don't actually like it when bus-loads of people show up—it's a lot of work. There are a few days when a lot of people come, but it's not often. It would be very difficult if it were often.

Like the organizational structure of Yamadera, Ichijō-ji does not belong to Fusako's family nor does it belong to the parish, but operates like a company—in essence, she said, the temple belongs to the Tendai sect of Buddhism. And regardless of Fusako's desire to live in the present, it is difficult to avoid thinking about the future. The current average age of parish members is around 70 and there are very few adult children and no elementary school children in the parish. And as for her own successor, Fusako noted that it can be quite difficult to find a spouse for a head priest, because priests are public figures and there is little privacy.

> You can't do whatever you want. I don't care what others think about me, so I go ahead and do what I want and operate the way I think is best. That's part of how I came into giving lectures on Buddhism, which is unusual for priests. But following my path could be difficult for a successor when it comes to finding a spouse. Not everyone likes the way I approach being a priest.

Fusako is one example of a religious entrepreneur operating within the context of Buddhism.[9] She is clearly quite different from other priests in the area, not only because she is a woman but also because she has approached her work as a priest in a more comprehensive way than most of her colleagues. Other priests, at least in southern Iwate, rarely give talks on Buddhist philosophy, or on how to live life, but Fusako has actually made a living out of leveraging her identity as an unusual priest

—a priest who is a woman and who has strong philosophical ideas—into a career as a public speaker. When I have attended her lectures, comments on her sense of humor, her entertaining style, and the interesting content of her talks—as well as her being a woman—have been common among the groups that gather to hear her. She is something of a minor celebrity in the area and many people look forward to hearing her talks; I have attended several of her lectures and the room is always packed.

Fusako's entrepreneurial activity is in part related to income—she needs income to maintain the temple and to a lesser extent for her family and the lectures help with that. But it is also related to her desire to express a particular view of Buddhism as a philosophy rather than simply as a set of rituals designed to care for ancestors. This is evident in her explanation of why she chose to take on the role of head priest. She has a brother, but, as she described it, he had little interest in becoming a priest; given her own attraction to Buddhism from a philosophical and lifestyle perspective, there were good reasons to take on the work of the temple. And she certainly has made her temple more visible in the area, which attracts not only tourists but also other priests to see the buildings and also talk about the situation that most temples in the area face. One day while Fusako and I were walking around the grounds together and chatting, a priest and his parishioners (all of whom were over 60) from another temple in neighboring Miyagi Prefecture visited to see the main temple building and the ancient Buddha statue it houses.

Fusako toured the group around the grounds and the temple, describing its history and explaining the functions of different parts of the complex of buildings. As she was talking about the main hall, one of the men in the group of visitors asked about the size of the parish. When Fusako told him, everyone was amazed at how small it is. Then he started to talk about their own temple, at which they are having significant problems because of the decrease in parish size to only 40 families at the time, following which the visiting priest agreed that they are all facing a serious problem related to the population decline. Fusako joked to me that the topic must have come up because of my research, but the fact was that it actually arose spontaneously—I was simply standing to the side following her around, but not talking, and Fusako had not actually mentioned my interests when she introduced me to the group. She simply described me as a visitor from America. Clearly, the future of temples like Ichijō-ji in relation to demographic decline is something people think about. And priests like Fusako, who have found innovative ways to attract interest to either their temple buildings or to Buddhism itself, are of interest to some who are concerned about the fate of Buddhism.

It is this last point, the attempt to innovate Buddhism, that is perhaps most interesting when one looks at religious entrepreneurialism in neo-rural parts of Japan like southern Iwate (and the country more generally). Buddhism has long had a somewhat stale image and at times even a negative perception among many. Juzo Itami's wonderful 1984 film *The Funeral* (お葬式 *Osōshiki*), explores feelings of loss and grief as members of a family interact during the process of preparation for the funeral of the family patriarch. The film was quite successful in Japan, winning five Japanese Academy awards, including Best Film. One scene in the film is interesting in its portrayal of Buddhist priests. The head priest of the family's temple shows up to discuss preparations driven by a chauffeur in a Rolls Royce, conveying an image that is not unusual in Japan that priests are often wealthy as a result of the fact that they obtain income via preying on vulnerable relatives of the deceased. I have never met a priest who drives a Rolls Royce. Yasu, for example, drives an old Toyota Prius, but this negative image of both priests and Buddhism is not uncommon in Japan and has raised concerns about the future of the religion. My interest here is not to focus on these negative images of Buddhism or Buddhist priests, but simply to note that, as Stephen G. Covell argues, "negative images of priests abound, based on views of contemporary Buddhism as corrupt or on certain ideas...about what constitutes a real priest."[10] And even when images are not necessarily negative, survey research has shown that Japanese are generally not particularly enamored of anything defined as "religion" due to concerns that religious institutions will attempt to manipulate people into giving money or that new religions, in particular, are prone to odd or dangerous behaviors, an idea that was underscored by the Aum attack on the Tokyo subway system in 1995.[11]

The image problems associated with Buddhism are widely understood by Buddhist leadership in most sects and, as John K. Nelson shows in his study of experimental approaches to Buddhism in Japan, a common concern is that priests focus on funerary rituals but lack awareness of and fail to respond to social problems. Nelson argues that among the problems facing contemporary Buddhism in Japan are public perceptions that temples serve only as places for funeral rituals, priests are aloof and motivated by money, and most denominations have failed in determining good ways to get people into temples.[12]

A few temples throughout the country have attempted to develop novel approaches to engage the public more directly in temple activities and through that to become more familiar, even if only tangentially, with Buddhist practice and philosophical ideas. For example, in 2013 Hirotake Asano, who is the head priest at Shingyo-ji Temple outside of Tokyo, opened Tera Café within the temple compound. "Tera" is a word for temple in Japanese and Tera Café is a coffee shop located at the temple that was created with the aim of bringing people into the proximity of the temple—particularly young adults. This goal should not be viewed as evangelism; there was no intention of drawing in people to necessarily engage in the religious, philosophical, or ritual activities of the institution. The goal is instead to make Buddhism seem less distant and the business also functions as a source of income in the face of declining contributions.[13] Other temples, including one in Kanegasaki, have opened day-care centers that serve the purpose not only of providing child care but also of producing much needed income. Among the more interesting innovations has been a rent-a-monk service available through Amazon through which one can obtain religious expertise and leadership for funerals and other death-related rituals. And some temples have employed modern technology to encourage ancestor memorialization and engage younger people—one temple in the center of Tokyo has developed video services in which people can view photos of the deceased and can even participate in rituals remotely. In addition to their use of electronic technology, the temple employs modern advertising techniques, including large posters in subway stations and on trains around Tokyo. As for the Tera Café, it is rated at four stars on Yelp Japan and reports on the café have indicated that business is good, as women in their 20s–40s visit the restaurant to socialize and enjoy coffee along with eating foods like *shabu-shabu* pork and ginger-flavored chicken.

THE CHAPATSU PRIEST

As noted above, one of the major problems Buddhist temples face is that they are associated with death rituals and, thus, are not particularly appealing places for younger people. Temples can function as a center of community, but the normal pattern in which they do this is as the locus for taking care of the dead. People will gather monthly to help with maintenance of the temple, such as weeding the gardens, but beyond that and funerary rituals there is little that ties one to a temple. For younger people, there often is little reason to visit a temple other than to memorialize ancestors, and if no one in one's immediate family has died, there may be very few opportunities to visit a temple other than as a tourist.[14] In many respects, temple activities revolve around older members of the community and, in fact, some temples have capitalized on this fact by creating or emphasizing ritual and statuary structures that attract older people who visit to pray to avoid a prolonged process of dying. Susan Orpett Long discusses in her research on death and dying in Japan the fact that that some older people hope for a sudden death in which they would be healthy right up to the moment of passing, and these temples are locations in which they hope to invoke assistance from Buddhism-related divine beings in attaining this goal.[15]

The pattern of Buddhist temples developing innovative ideas in order to generate income is nothing new in Japan. During the Tokugawa Period some Buddhist temples managed to attain financial stability by emphasizing the healing powers associated with the temple when activities related to funerary rituals were insufficient sources of income.[16] Nonetheless, the demographic environment of contemporary society, notably in the countryside, has exacerbated problems associated with finances, as noted above. At one temple, a few kilometers north of Kanegasaki, I encountered one of the more novel approaches to securing increased stability for a Buddhist temple that I have observed.

Kosho-ji is a temple of the Jōdo Shinshū (浄土真宗) sect of Buddhism set among rice paddies in the municipality of Kitakami. On a pleasant summer afternoon, Kenyu (the son of the current head priest), a married couple from his parish, fellow anthropologist Satsuki Kawano, and I talked about his ideas related to running a temple and the future of Buddhism. Kenyu arrived in the same type of loose-fitting work clothing worn by Fusako, although his outfit was a light gray color rather than black. And Kenyu pointed out his own appearance shortly after we started to talk, asking if we were surprised. In fact, both anthropologists were, because he had a full head of flowing hair dyed orange, which is fairly common among Japanese, but rather unusual for a priest. Kenyu seemed proud of the fact that he did not look the part of the typical temple priest.[17]

According to Kenyu, he is the 22nd generation in his family line to function as head of the temple, although when we spoke his father was still officially the head priest, and the temple itself dates back between 300 and 400 years.[18] We sat on the floor of the main hall of the temple, which is a modern building at the center of which is placed a large statue of the Buddha (*honzon* 本尊 or principle object of worship at a temple) that is entirely covered with gold leaf. When I saw the statue, I recalled Yasu's concerns about theft at their temple and asked if they had any concerns about theft, given the highly valuable objects in the room. Kenyu responded,

> We don't lock the door so that anyone can come to pray. If the Buddha statue (*gohonzon* ご本尊) were stolen, then the head priest (住職) is to be blamed. It's not a big deal even if something is stolen unless it's the *gohonzon*. Perhaps, such incidents are a modern phenomenon. We trust the people in our community. But, thieves may come from outside the area.
>
> We collect the donated money periodically from the donation box [in front of the main hall], but we intentionally leave some money inside assuming that really desperate people may need that money to survive. Anyone who steals a temple's money must be in very bad condition. It is annoying if robbery happens often, but we hope those desperate people would be saved (by the money) and there is no need to lose life.

After this comment, the female parishioner voiced a frequently heard refrain in the area, emphasizing the lack of young people: "The priest's challenge is reaching out to youth. People who come to the events are familiar, regular [old] people. That is the community's common problem —not having young people." Kenyu followed this comment with his analysis of the problems that the temple faces:

> Modern society is structured heavily around economic activities. No one can deny that fact and we can't abandon the system. Going to a good college, getting a good job, earning a good salary may be regarded as the best way to pursue happiness. While doing these things in order to be happy, one may feel as though one is missing important things as a human being. Temples can fill that sort of emotional gap and are needed; temples are the only place for people to come talk about such things.
>
> Adults have been lazy or irresponsible not to go to the temples together (with their children) during the economic boom era after the Second World War. After the 3-11 Earthquake, the number of young people who have started to ponder the meaning of life rather than monetary aspects of living is increasing. Life mentioned here is not about the biological process or physical entities [he does not

> define what it is, but seems to imply some type of metaphysical abstraction in relation to the human mind or soul]. The number of social activists who are not controlled by politicians is increasing, which is a positive thing and the number of people who prioritize personal values such as the future of children is increasing.

Kenyu has, himself, tried to be engaged socially, particularly following the disaster in March of 2011. He made Buddhist prayer beads from pine trees that had been swept away by the tsunami so that the tsunami and earthquake would not be forgotten; the beads were sold, and the proceeds from which were donated to support tsunami victims. He also provided bathing services at his temple to help tsunami survivors. Kenyu is interested in developing a more engaged form of Buddhism and in the course of the discussion I asked him if he had explored starting a kindergarten or day-care center like some other temples in the area.

> No. I think it is important to nurture young children in a religious setting. It's difficult to do this not only due to cost, but also because the number of children is decreasing in the area. Therefore, instead of running a school, I want to make my temple a gathering place for children—including my own 6th grade son. We hold events several times a year for children at the temple.

Events for children are among several activities that Kenyu has tried to develop to connect with members of the community in ways that are not specifically tied to Buddhist funerary rituals. For example, in addition to typical ceremonies such as funerals and memorial services, he holds *oshōgyō* (お聖教) or sacred teaching (sutra) study for lay people, barbeque parties, and he has organized group travel to the sect's main temple in Kyoto. Kenyu seems to wear his innovative approach in his brightly colored hair style which, given his initial referencing for his guests, seems to function as something of a symbolic (and clearly embodied) representation of his ideas as being different from his perceptions of traditional Buddhism. When asked about how people respond to his hair, he talked about his hair and then quickly shifted to the nature of Buddhism in Japan:

> It's hard to tell what people really think in mind. My father has black normal length, side-parted hair, and people get used to seeing that, so much so that nobody says anything about my hair color, and sometimes they say they like it.
>
> There are two types of Buddhism in Japan. One type is that through ascetic training the priests or monks get their virtue level up and contribute their cumulative virtues on behalf of the people who cannot do so by themselves. My temple is not that type. Even if one does ascetic training, he would not be able to catch up [he was not clear about what catching up means]; he would not be elevated to the dignified position. This place is for practice and to listen to the words of Buddha. Therefore, I am a listener, not a teacher. I am the listener who happens to be standing at the head of all listeners.
>
> My temple exists with a hope that the teaching of *nanmandabutsu* [spoken in local dialect, this refers to the *nembutsu* 念仏 or ritual recitation of the name Amida (Amitabha), a celestial buddha that is the principal buddha in Pure Land Buddhism, be continued and spread. My role is to connect with the people and to the next generation. I myself am a listener of the teachings. I sit on the flat same level of others, not on an elevated place. I see myself as happening to be sitting in the front row while managing the temple, thus, I am a lay priest (*zaikesō* 在家僧), not a monk and that's why I don't get my head shaved and dye my hair.

Religious Entrepreneurialism, Symbolic Meaning, and Convention

At the end of our conversation, Kenyu wanted to make sure that we understood one important point. "The most joyous moment in my life now," he said emphatically, "is to be told that my temple has a family atmosphere." Indeed, temples in Japan are not usually associated with a family atmosphere; rather they are centers of ritual performance that are of fundamental importance to the family, but that are focused on taking care of the dead and are not generally engaged on a regular basis beyond participation in mortuary ritual. Kenyu has wanted to change that image of his temple, and of Buddhism, by creating an atmosphere that brings families—and particularly children—to the temple for barbeque gatherings and other events that serve the function of generating a sense of community centered on temple life.

Kenyu's religious entrepreneurialism is, of course, situated in a context of symbol-use involving representational elements that are interpreted by members of the temple parish and are intertwined with other symbolic structures associated with conventional ideas about Buddhism shared by members of the community. In some ways, at the center of that symbolic complex is Kenyu's hair, which operates as what Peirce refers to as a sign-vehicle or an object or condition that constrains the ability to signify or express meaning and, therefore, generates a framework from which others engage in interpretive practice. In this case, Kenyu's hair (both its fullness and color) forms a sign-vehicle that operates as a focal point for interpreting conventional ideas related to the function of the Buddhist temple in the community and to the behavior and appearance of a Buddhist priest.[19]

The meaning associated with a sign and conveyed through a sign-vehicle can be understood as a cultural unit or semantic marker that is linked to other sign-vehicles and indexes the conventions that people use to interpret and draw meaning from signs.[20] Kenyu's hair at once indexes convention and also conveys meaning related to his unwillingness to abide by convention. He consciously has chosen not to follow the conventions of shaving his head, instead having a full head of hair and actually goes somewhat beyond this by dyeing his hair in a color that has typically been associated with youth and at one time with unconventional behavior (although it is now common for people of many ages, particularly women, to dye their hair brown or burnt orange). In this sense, his hair conveys meaning associated with his desire to contest conventional symbolic structures and practices associated with both the priesthood and the function of Buddhism. In short, Kenyu's hair represents a desire on his part to deconstruct and challenge the dominant discourse of Buddhism and contest the religious meanings associated with the temple in contemporary Japanese society.[21]

This is similar to what we see in the case of Fusako who has engaged in an attempt to, at least at some level, contest and reinvent the nature of Buddhism as it functions and is perceived in southern Iwate. Her identity as a woman itself challenges the dominant discourse about who and what a Buddhist priest is, and she actually strategically employs her gender as a way of generating interest in her particular take on Buddhism, which in turn helps her temple financially and also increases its visibility, which draws in tourists. Fusako's gender functions as a sign-vehicle in a way similar to Kenyu's hair—it indexes the conventional discourse of Buddhism by contesting that discourse. Agency is located in the disjuncture between conventional notions of Buddhism and of the personhood and expected identity of priests and a reconceptualization of those conventional notions by Fusako and Kenyu.[22] We see in both cases a contrast between the dominant discourse and a reconstituted social reality of Buddhism evident in the embodied existential character of their bodies as representations of a reconfigured Buddhism within the context of reconfigured rurality.[23]

Kenyu and Fusako are both good examples of religious entrepreneurs operating in the context of Buddhism. Both priests are interested in addressing the changing—some would argue declining—role of temple Buddhism in response to processes of secularization.[24] The two priests I discuss here represent examples similar to the socially active Buddhist priests that Nelson describes, whose entrepreneurial activities have focused on experimental approaches to Buddhism in response to the collapsing parish system. Nelson argues that a small group of priests have become "primary protagonists" who are not particularly interested in directives from denominational headquarters, nor are they necessarily shaped or inspired by basic teachings associated with philosophical Buddhism. Instead, they are motivated by an interest in changing the role of temples and their priests in society by generating a meaningful connection between priests and their communities beyond their function as leaders of funerary ritual.[25]

Nelson calls these approaches "experimental Buddhism" and defines this as practices that are "selective, pragmatic, and concerned primarily with achieving a satisfactory result that somehow improves human life or advances the agenda of an individual or group in ways thought to be beneficial."[26] This form of experimental or entrepreneurial Buddhism represents an expression of localism that forms a practice of contesting conventional tropes of Buddhist temple work and engagement in the community. In this sense, entrepreneurial Buddhism, at least for these two priests, can be understood as a form of progressive localism that engages in the production of alternative religious narratives through which individual and community interests are prioritized over those of distant religious authorities and institutions.[27] Nelson shows in some detail the variety of innovations Buddhist priests have developed to change conventional images and also financial situations of temples, and these innovations include activities ranging from fashion shows to reinterpretations of rituals, traditions, and religious objects such as altars.[28] Here, I want to emphasize that the religiously related entrepreneurial activities I have observed in Iwate are embedded in the context of depopulation and are tied into both overt and tacit discourses aimed at generating an entrepreneurial ecosystem that might mitigate the effects of depopulation. In the case of religious entrepreneurialism and Buddhism, the capacity to create innovative structures and themes is often viewed as imperative for the survival of often ancient institutions that are in peril.

Even the more traditional efforts of Yasu and Eri can be understood as fitting within this overall context of innovation in the face of depopulation, despite the fact that the basic approach is conventional rather than innovative. Their approach has been to focus on creating an enduring physical space in which parish members can continue to engage in conventional Buddhist practices related to caring for the dead. But this has broader consequences in that they hope the creation of a new building might provide a means for attracting a successor. In other words, at one level the new temple building is an attempt at marketing, the success of which will determine the long-term viability of the temple as a cite of ancestor memorialization for its parish and, potentially, for other temples/parishes with which it may cooperate or amalgamate in the future. Religious entrepreneurs such as these in neo-rural Japan are walking a line between convention and the necessities generated by contemporary population movements and a highly secularized society in which religious activity is often not seen as being particularly important or meaningful among younger people in particular.

NOTES

1. Traphagan, *The Practice of Concern: Ritual, Well-Being, and Aging in Rural Japan.*
2. Ibid.
3. Blaine P. Connor and John W. Traphagan, "Negotiating the Afterlife: Emplacement as Ongoing Concern in Contemporary Japan," *Asian Anthropology* 13, no. 1 (2014).
4. Traphagan, *The Practice of Concern: Ritual, Well-Being, and Aging in Rural Japan.*
5. John W. Traphagan, "Empty Houses, Abandoned Graves: Negative Population Growth and New Ideas in Neo-Rural Japan," *The Brown Journal of World Affairs* 24, no. 2 (2018).
6. Herman Ooms, "The Religion of the Household: A Case Study of Ancestor Worship in Japan," *Contemporary Religions in Japan* (1967); Traphagan, "Empty Houses, Abandoned Graves: Negative Population Growth and New Ideas in Neo-Rural Japan."
7. John W Traphagan, "Older Women as Caregivers and Ancestral Protection in Rural Japan (1)," *Ethnology* 42, no. 2 (2003).
8. Fusako used the term *bunkazai* 文化財, which refers to cultural assets or cultural properties and falls within the Law for the Protection of Cultural Properties 文化財保護法. The monastery to which she refers is protected due to its architecture, which, it is claimed, has the largest thatched roof in Japan over the main hall.
9. The reader is directed to the work of John Nelson (2013) on experimental Buddhism in Japan that provides several excellent examples of entrepreneurial behaviors related to religious institutions.
10. Stephen G. Covell, *Japanese Temple Buddhism: Worldliness in a Religion of Renunciation* (University of Hawaii Press, 2005), 108.
11. Akira Kawabata and Takanori Tamura, "Online-Religion in Japan: Websites and Religious Counseling from a Comparative Cross-Cultural Perspective," *Journal of Computer-Mediated Communication* 12, no. 3 (2007): 1002, accessed 2/22/2019, http://dx.doi.org/10.1111/j.1083-6101.2007.00360.x.
12. John K. Nelson, *Experimental Buddhism: Innovation and Activism in Contemporary Japan* (Honolulu: University of Hawai'i Press, 2013), 67-68.

13. Yiyuan Wang, "Buddhist Cafe Gives Tokyo Caffeinated Enlightenment," *The Japan Times* 2016.
14. Traphagan, *The Practice of Concern: Ritual, Well-Being, and Aging in Rural Japan.*
15. Fleur Woss, "*Pokkuri* Temples and Aging," in *Religion and Society in Modern Japan*, ed. Mark R. Mullins, Shimazono Susumu, and Paul L. Swanson (Berkeley: Asian Humanities Press, 1993); Susan Orpett Long, "Becoming a Cucumber: Culture, Nature, and the Good Death in Japan and the United States," *Journal of Japanese Studies* 29, no. 1 (2003), http://www.jstor.org.ezproxy.lib.utexas.edu/stable/25064363.
16. Kawashima Tinka Delakorda, "The Healing Jizo: Soto Zen Koganji Temple Adapting to Varying Social Conditions," 臺灣東亞文明研究學刊 13, no. 1 (2016), http://dx.doi.org/10.6163/tjeas.2016.13(1)77.
17. As something of an aside, Kenyu has something of an interesting back story in which he was headed down a very different path from becoming a priest. During the car ride from Kanegasaki with the parishioner couple who had joined us for the conversation with Kenyu, we learned quite a bit about his experience in college and the fact that it was a significant sore spot among members of the temple parish. Kenyu attended college in Kyoto at Ōtani University, a private Buddhist university associated with the Ōtani School of Jōdo Shinshū that was founded in 1665 as a seminary for Shin Buddhism, although today it teaches fields such as education and sociology along with its primary focus on Buddhism studies. In fact, Kenyu had been sent to the university via the efforts of the temple parish, as each family donated money to pay for his expenses with the expectation that he would become the future head priest of the temple. However, after about two years, he decided that he preferred music to study and quit university to join the boy band in which he performed for several years. His father had counseled him not to quit school, but as Kenyu put it, "I did not follow what my father told me. I don't think I really understood what I was being taught in school at that time, although now I think I understand much better."Kenyu's decision to leave college did not sit well with members of the parish, who were quite angry at the head priest and his son, in part because they had paid the bills involved with Kenyu's education. When he turned thirty, Kenyu found himself at a crossroads in life, "I wasn't sure how to live and swung between monetary concerns and non-monetary values. I re-evaluated the priorities of life such as time and money relationships and decided that I wanted to return to the temple." Members of the parish

were quite suspicious of his motivations and of whether or not he could be relied upon to actually take on the responsibilities of being head priest and, according to the couple, continued to be somewhat concerned even several years after his return.

18. I have no way to confirm or dispute this statement about his lineage, but if we think of there typically being 7 generations every 200 years, then this seems inflated, although shorter life spans could perhaps account for this. Among some families in Japan, particularly nobility, kinship records are very detailed and precise. However, Kenyu did not show us these records.
19. S. Long and J. Manley, *Social Dreaming: Philosophy, Research, Theory and Practice* (London: Routledge, 2019).
20. Umberto Eco, *A Theory of Semiotics* (Bloomington: Indiana University Press, 1976), 72.
21. Gerd Baumann, *Contesting Culture: Discourses of Identity in Multi-Ethnic London* (Cambridge: Cambridge University Press, 1996), 178.
22. Taha Kazi, "Religious Television and Contesting Piety in Karachi, Pakistan," *American Anthropologist* 120, no. 3 (2018/09/01 2018): 532, accessed 2019/03/05, http://dx.doi.org/10.1111/aman.13061.
23. Thomas J. Csordas, "Words from the Holy People: A Case Study in Cultural Phenomenology," in *Embodiment and Experience: The Existential Ground of Culture and Self*, ed. Thomas J. Csordas (Cambridge: Cambridge University Press, 1994), 269.
24. Ian Reader, "Secularisation, Rip? Nonsense! The 'Rush Hour Away from the Gods' and the Decline of Religion in Contemporary Japan," *Journal of Religion in Japan* 1, no. 1 (2012); John K Nelson, "Japanese Secularities and the Decline of Temple Buddhism," *Journal of Religion in Japan* 1, no. 1 (2012).
25. Nelson, 20.
26. Ibid., 21.
27. David Featherstone et al., "Progressive Localism and the Construction of Political Alternatives," *Transactions of the Institute of British Geographers* 37, no. 2 (2012): 179, http://dx.doi.org/10.1111/j.1475-5661.2011.00493.x; ibid.; Nelson, 142.
28. Nelson.

Chapter 8

Cosmopolitan Rurality and Entrepreneurialism

> My personal decorating style is cozy, romantic and a little rustic, with a sense of whimsy.
>
> —Kimberly Schlapman

There is something wonderfully ironic in the way the term *rustic* is so often used in the modern American vernacular. Rustic refers to feelings or images of the simple, unsophisticated, and perhaps rural while it is used at the same time to index a sophistication of style among cosmopolitans in relation to interests such as food or decorating. The rustic at once defines the cosmopolitan by its alterity while being appropriated by the cosmopolitan constructed within an imaginary rustic authenticity that invokes aesthetic sensibilities employed to distinguish elites from others and provide social status among bourgeois circles.[1] In other words, as an ideational category rusticity is polysemous and, when used from the perspective of the cosmopolitan him or her, has the capacity to simultaneously index images of simplicity and sophistication, rural and urban. Of course, the rustic also continues to reference spatiality as a place associated with the pastoral/agricultural that is remote from urban spaces and expresses practices and value structures associated with conventional tropes of rurality. The structures of alterity through which the rustic and the cosmopolitan co-construct each other are, in other words, spatial, social, and ideational, and rusticity has found its way into the cosmopolitan, at least in American decorating circles, from a conceptual standpoint. Schlapman's comment underscores the fact that the gap between the rustic and cosmopolitan is not unambiguously articulated in American society, and I think this is true in Japan, as well.

Indeed, the cosmopolitan in Japan also, as I have argued throughout this book, has found its way into the rustic imaginary as those living in areas deemed rural engage in processes of reconceptualizing their own social and physical space. Much of this reconfiguration in the past has been associated with the diffusion of industrial structures into rustic areas and characterized as rural industrialization and the new rusticity. Rural industrialization tends to focus more on the economic and physical reconstruction of rural spaces, while the new rusticity tends to deal with modalities of socialization that are constructed in relation to the penetration of economic and social activities typically associated with metropolitan areas and the integration of those activities with neighboring urban areas and more extensive networks of economic and social activity that extend ultimately to the global.[2] When we take these processes together, we can think of this process in terms of the conceptualization and creation of a cosmopolitan rurality, or the restructuring of rural and conceptually rustic spaces and lifeways to incorporate and engage elements of the cosmopolitan.

The Cosmopolitan and Neo-Rural Japan

Bronislaw Szerszynski and John Urry offer a useful way of thinking about the nature of the cosmopolitan as involving a set of predispositions and practices which I somewhat modify here as including: (1) extensive *mobility* both corporeally and virtually, (2) the ability to *consume* different things and environments, (3) *curiosity* about other places and cultures,

(4) an *openness* to taking risks related to the encounter with "others", and (5) the *semiotic* ability to consume and interpret complex images and symbols from cultures different from one's own.[3] One of the key points of this definition is that it places the cosmopolitan in the heads of individuals, rather than in the features of the land, although obviously elements such as a built landscape are the products or expressions of what is going on in the heads of individuals. Cosmopolitanism and rusticity are both embodied and can be understood as expressions of habitus, or the collection of embodied habits and dispositions found among a particular group of people that limit how they perceive and react to their social and physical environments and that is acquired through processes of socialization.[4] This means that both cosmopolitanism and rusticity are constantly changing—there is no objective cosmopolitanism nor rusticity—and in contexts like the one I have described here, we can see the creative generation of a hybrid structure that combines elements typically associated with both concepts and that is being constructed, at one level, through the innovations and actions of local entrepreneurs.

Habitus, of course, in essence is another way to think about culture, one that situates culture in the bodies of individuals. And like culture, it is always on the move—it changes as individuals continually interpret and reinvent their surroundings. In my own research related to both concepts, I have come to think of this process as being very much like the way jazz musicians read what is known as a lead sheet. For those less versed in musical vernacular, a lead sheet is a way of writing music that only involves presenting the melody and the chords that should be played at different points while one is performing the piece. These chords are called changes, because they change as one moves through the melodic structure of the tune. When a jazz musician reads a lead sheet, she usually first plays the tune largely straight—without much improvisation—and then during solos begins to improvise, which involves taking the changes and the melody and innovating these into new forms through the embodied action of playing the instrument. The basic melodic and harmonic structure of the tune will remain largely the same and often can be heard during the solos, although a good jazz musician may veer very far away from that structure in the process of creating and expressing innovative and original ideas. However, if the musician deviates too far from the basic form of the tune, either in terms of the melody or the changes, it may become difficult for the listener to interpret—it loses its internal logic and, thus, does not really make sense in relation to the form and structure of the tune being performed. Part of what makes a great jazz musician, like Thelonious Monk or Charlie Parker, is the ability to deviate significantly from the melody or changes while staying enough within the parameters outlined in the lead sheet so that the song continues to make sense. The structure evident in the lead sheet may be stretched considerably, but the good jazz musician is able to work the changes and melody in such a way that eventually she finds his way back to the original structure. Part of what makes jazz interesting is to see how the musician expresses her musical ideas and innovates *within the context of each tune.*

Culture works in largely the same way. The discourses and tropes that we associate with or that are employed in a particular cultural context are permeable and are constantly being interpreted and innovated upon by the individuals within a context. If one pushes the edges of those interpretive structures too far, they stop making sense and people have difficulties interpreting and understanding behaviors. In other words, innovative expressions of ideas and behaviors that are too far outside the structure of the changes or melody—the value structures and practices—associated with a given cultural context create difficulties in interpreting their meanings.

When we look at the performers I have discussed in this book—from gelato shop owner, to politicians trying to build the International Linear Collider, to samurai pizza chef—we see actors operating within the context of a social ecosystem in which innovation is being encouraged and applauded, both by political leaders and by people who patronize these establishments or engage in trying to work for the attraction of institutional structures like the ILC. This, I would argue, is what constitutes an entrepreneurial ecosystem. It is a social, political, and economic context in which multiple players engage in improvisation by innovating the confines of the cultural lead sheet in which they happen to live and operate on a daily basis. In other words, an entrepreneurial ecosystem is not necessarily one that simply fosters entrepreneurship; rather it is a cultural context in which people feel comfortable improvising off of the underlying social themes operating in that environment. One way that this improvisation can be expressed is through the creation of new businesses that engage and exploit opportunities evident in the larger social and economic contexts in which they are situated and that allow for particular types of entrepreneurial activities to succeed.

Businesses like Kanegasaki Creamery and Ecru operate and are successful because people in the area are already linked into cosmopolitan flows that they have encountered through schooling, travel, and the media while retaining an interest and connection to the rustic that has typically characterized life in the region. They, themselves, are social and cultural hybrids that bring together the rustic and the cosmopolitan and these innovative businesses are hybrid contexts that bring together objects and associated meanings like gelato and goats that capture and resonate with those people. I doubt that at the moment in southern Iwate a TexMex restaurant with extremely spicy food would be particularly successful, because it is too much of a stretch in the lead sheet that shapes how people think about food in the area. However, in ten or fifteen years it might work just fine as more people in the region have changed their concepts of the limits of good food through travel or simply cooking different recipes that they find on the Internet. Predicting the future is difficult and not part of my interests here; rather, my point is that the limits of interpretation of the cultural lead sheet change over time, just as the lead sheet itself changes as a result of innovation and improvisation. Indeed, the key point that I want to emphasis here is that culture itself is an entrepreneurial ecosystem, because it is an environment in which innovation and creativity are constantly emerging and being strategically used and exploited by individuals and groups. Even in cultural contexts that attempt to restrain innovation such as religious orders that suppress ideas or beliefs that diverge even minimally from doctrine or schools that have strict requirements about how uniforms are worn, people in various ways contest practices of subordination with practices of innovation. In southern Iwate, I have often seen male school students mildly contesting school-uniform codes by wearing pants that are several sizes too big and are synched together with a belt. Basically, the uniforms meet code, but they still manage to look sloppy.

In short, the data and examples I have discussed throughout this book emphasize that from the perspective of thinking about entrepreneurialism the question is less one of how do we create entrepreneurial ecosystems than it is one of how do we identify the right types of innovation and creativity to take advantage of particular social, political, economic, and geographical contexts. Humans are inherently creative and innovative beings and, in fact, I would argue that creativity is the most important adaptive trait or tool humans developed through the process of evolution. An entrepreneurial ecosystem is one that creates frameworks in which that adaptive trait is able to flourish among residents and within the confines of the cultural lead sheet operating in a given social context.

IT'S ALL ABOUT PEOPLE

In the examples from northern Japan that I have discussed throughout this book, every aspect of entrepreneurialism must be contextualized within the processes of demographic change and depopulation that are operating in the region. There is a broad awareness among residents of Iwate and its surrounding prefectures that the situation of population loss is serious in most places and dire in some and reaction to that loss requires innovative ideas and approaches in order to adjust business, governmental, religious, and other institutions to a rapidly changing demographic environment. Nonetheless, the effects of population loss are quite different depending upon the type of business or institution one considers. For people working in health-related businesses like pharmacies or eldercare, the current political and economic environment is quite good and supportive of creating new ideas. This is in part a result of the existence of the long-term care insurance program and also the movement of the average age of the population upward, which is a trend that will continue for the near-term. Ecru is another example of a business that is working well, but the environment is different. Ecru works well because it is situated in an environment where historical preservation is being encouraged, while people also want access to new and interesting foods like pizza, which the owner of Ecru produces at a high level of quality. And a similar point can be made about Kanegasaki Creamery, which takes advantage of the dairy production in the town, while providing cosmopolitan products in the form of cheese and gelato, tapping the larger context of rustic farm country in which the store is located.

Unlike these small businesses that may only tangentially be thought of by their owners as contributing to the creation of an entrepreneurial ecosystem in that they provide a contribution to the community, the much larger project of the ILC is an overt attempt by local leaders to generate an entrepreneurial ecosystem that has the potential to retain and attract people. In other words, it is aimed at reconstituting the local social and economic climate as a cosmopolitan space that can draw in scientists and technicians from around the world, which will, in turn, change the overall nature of the local cultural context. Although this type of aim is not part of the ideas presented by the small-business owners with whom I have spoken, their capacity to create interesting businesses is in part a product of a political climate that encourages innovation and a public that is interested in accessing and experiencing innovative foods, clothing, and other items or approaches to eldercare and health care.

Most of these activities either overtly or covertly index themes and tropes associated with the cosmopolitan and the rustic at the same time. And this is where we find the emergence of neo-rural Japan, or a cosmopolitan rurality that neither fits neatly into the framework of the urban nor the rural. Instead, areas like the towns I have discussed in Iwate are engaged in a process of reconfiguring or reinventing the social and cultural landscape to express a distinct lifeway or set of lifeways that is fully engaged with cosmopolitan structures—it is integrated with global flows of ideas and goods—while also retaining elements of the rustic patterns of life such as a slower pace or an emphasis on face-to-face interactions and the embeddedness of local businesses within the community. In other words, this is a social and physical space that cannot be understood in terms of binaries such as the cosmopolitan and the rustic, the urban and the rural, the industrial and the agricultural, the modern and the traditional. The people living there engage all of these elements of post-modern society at the same time and are involved, either consciously or tacitly, in a process of innovating a different type of social space that employs themes and ideas from each of the elements simultaneously.

As I bring the book to a close I want to emphasize this point—that at least in contexts like Japan, the notion of rurality is being reconfigured to incorporate or appropriate the cosmopolitan, which is leading to a different kind of space that I have called neo-rural or one in which people living in a social frame that I am calling cosmopolitan rurality. In relation to attempts to generate an entrepreneurial ecosystem, we see the presence of a triangular set of relationships between demographic conditions, entrepreneurial ideologies and policies, and personal interests that are constantly interacting to generate a milieu that exhibits this sense of cosmopolitan rurality.

To live in "rural" Japan, or at least the part of Japan I have discussed throughout this book, is to live in a region that is as easily characterized by its global interconnectedness as it is by its forested mountains and broad expanses of rice fields. It is a social and geographical space in which the binary juxtaposition of rural and urban, rustic and cosmopolitan really do not have a great deal of meaning from an analytical perspective, even while people living in those areas may continue to think and talk about the differences between life in the cities and in the countryside. And, indeed, there are differences, but those differences are not ones of a sharp dichotomy between cosmopolitan and rustic but are found in the processes of hybridization that continually construct the experiences of the rustic and cosmopolitan in neo-rural lifeways.

NOTES

1. Craig J. Thompson and Siok Kuan Tambyah, "Trying to Be Cosmopolitan," *Journal of Consumer Research* 26, no. 3 (1999): 219, http://dx.doi.org/10.1086/209560.
2. Rocío Rosales Ortega, "Urban-Rural Relations in the Central Region of Mexico a Viewpoint from Tlaxcala," *Urbani Izziv* 23 (2012): S16, http://www.jstor.org.ezproxy.lib.utexas.edu/stable/24920837.
3. Bronislaw Szerszynski and John Urry, "Visuality, Mobility and the Cosmopolitan: Inhabiting the World from Afar," *British Journal of Sociology* 57, no. 1 (2006): 114-15, http://dx.doi.org/10.1111/j.1468-4446.2006.00096.x.
4. Bourdieu, *Outline of a Theory of Practice.*

Bibliography

Altaweel, Mark and Andrea Squitieri. "Material Culture Hybridization." In *Revolutionizing a World: From Small States to Universalism in the Pre-Islamic Near East*, 179-98. UCL Press, 2018.

Amoamo, Maria. "Tourism and Hybridity: Re-Visiting Bhabha's Third Space." *Annals of Tourism Research* 38, no. 4 (2011): 1254-73. http://dx.doi.org/https://doi.org/10.1016/j.annals.2011.04.002.

Aronsson, Anne S. *Career Women in Contemporary Japan: Pursuing Identities, Fashioning Lives.* Taylor & Francis, 2014.

Asano, Satoshi. "The Conservation of Historic Environments in Japan." *Built Environment (1978-)* 25, no. 3 (1999): 236-43. http://www.jstor.org.ezproxy.lib.utexas.edu/stable/23287816.

Auerswald, Philip E. *Enabling Entrepreneurial Ecosystems: Insights from Ecology to Inform Effective Entrepreneurship Policy.* Kaufman Foundation, 2015.

Baer, Howard, Vernon D. Barger, and Jenny List. "The Collider That Could Save Physics." Last modified 2016. Accessed 18 January, 2018. https://www.scientificamerican.com/article/the-collider-that-could-save-physics/.

Bailey, Jackson. *Ordinary People, Extraordinary Lives: Political and Economic Change in a Tohoku Village.* Honolulu: University of Hawaii Press, 1991.

Baumann, Gerd. *Contesting Culture: Discourses of Identity in Multi-Ethnic London.* Cambridge University Press, 1996.

Baumol, William J. "Entrepreneurship: Productive, Unproductive, and Destructive." *Journal of Political Economy* 98, no. 5 (1990): 893-921.

Beardsley, Richard K., John W. Hall, and Robert E. Ward. *Village Japan.* Chicago: University of Chicago Press, 1959.

Ben-Ari, Eyal. "Contested Identities and Models of Action in Japanese Discourses of Place-Making." *Anthropological Quarterly* 68, no. 4 (1995): 203-18. http://dx.doi.org/10.2307/3317283.

Bernstein, Gail L. *Haruko's World: A Japanese Farm Woman and Her Community.* Stanford: Stanford University Press, 1983.

Bestor, Theodore C. *Neighborhood Tokyo.* Stanford: Stanford University Press, 1989.

Bhabha, Homi K. *The Location of Culture.* London: Routledge, 1994.

Boret, Sabastian. *Japanese Tree Burial: Ecology, Kinship, and the Culture of Death.* London: Routledge, 2014.

Boswell, Rosabelle. "Heritage Tourism and Identity in the Mauritian Villages of Chamarel and Le Morne." *Journal of Southern African Studies* 31, no. 2 (2005): 283-95. http://dx.doi.org/10.1080/030570705 00109466.

Bourdieu, Pierre. *Outline of a Theory of Practice.* Translated by Richard Nice. Cambridge University Press, 1977.

Bourdieu, Pierre. *The Field of Cultural Production.* New York: Columbia University Press, 1993.

Bradley, Harriet. *Fractured Identities: Changing Patterns of Inequality.* Cambridge: Polity Press, 1996.

Brown, Keith. "The Content of Dozoku Relationships in Japan." *Ethnology* 7, no. 2 (1968): 113-38. http://dx.doi.org/10.2307/3772742.

Brown, L. Keith. *Shinjō: The Chronicle of a Japanese Village.* Pittsburgh: University Center for International Studies, University of Pittsburgh, 1979.

Bull, Ivan and Frederick Winter. "Community Differences in Business Births and Business Growths." *Journal of Business Venturing* 6, no. 1 (1991/01/01/ 1991): 29-43. http://dx.doi.org/https://doi.org/10.1016 /0883-9026(91)90004-W.

Calhoun, Craig. "The Elusive Cosmopolitan Ideal." *Berkeley Journal of Sociology* 47 (2003): 3-26. http://www.jstor.org.ezproxy.lib.utexas.edu/ stable/41035579.

Campbell, John Creighton. *How Policies Change: The Japanese Government and the Aging Society*. Princeton University Press, 2014.

Campbell, John Creighton and Naoki Ikegami. "Long-Term Care Insurance Comes to Japan: A Major Departure for Japan, This New Program Aims to Be a Comprehensive Solution to the Problem of Caring for Frail Older People." *Health Affairs* 19, no. 3 (2000): 26-39.

Carsrud, Alan and Malin Brännback. "Entrepreneurial Motivations: What Do We Still Need to Know?" *Journal of Small Business Management* 49, no. 1 (2011): 9-26.

Cazzolla Gatti, Roberto, Brian Fath, Wim Hordijk, Stuart Kauffman, and Robert Ulanowicz. "Niche Emergence as an Autocatalytic Process in the Evolution of Ecosystems." *Journal of Theoretical Biology* 454 (2018/10/07/ 2018): 110-17. http://dx.doi.org/https://doi.org/10.1016/j.jtbi.2018.05.038.

Clark, Scott. *Japan: A View from the Bath*. University of Hawaii Press, 1994.

Coessens, Kathleen and Douglas Walter Scott. "Multiple Tensions in Music's Semiotic Eigenbehavior." *Constructivist Foundations* 12, no. 3 (2017): 359-68. http://ezproxy.lib.utexas.edu/login?url=http://search.ebscohost.com/login.aspx?direct=true&db=a9h&AN=124217184&site=ehost-live.

Connor, Blaine P and John W Traphagan. "Negotiating the Afterlife: Emplacement as Ongoing Concern in Contemporary Japan." *Asian Anthropology* 13, no. 1 (2014): 3-19.

Covell, Stephen G. *Japanese Temple Buddhism: Worldliness in a Religion of Renunciation*. University of Hawaii Press, 2005.

Cox, Benjamin Davis. "Gods without Faces: Childhood, Religion, and Imagination in Contemporary Japan." University of Texas at Austin, 2018.

Crane, Diana. "Culture and Globalization: Theoretical Models and Emerging Trends." In *Global Culture*, edited by Diana Crane, Nobuko Kawashima, and Ken'ichi Kawasaki, 1-28. New York: Routledge, 2016.

Creighton, Millie. "Consuming Rural Japan: The Marketing of Tradition and Nostalgia in the Japanese Travel Industry." *Ethnology* 36, no. 3 (1997): 269-54.

Csordas, Thomas J. "Words from the Holy People: A Case Study in Cultural Phenomenology." In *Embodiment and Experience: The Existential Ground of Culture and Self*, edited by Thomas J. Csordas, 269-190: Cambridge University Press, 1994.

Denoon, Donald, Mark Hudson, Gavan McCormack, and Tessa Morris-Suzuki, eds. *Multicultural Japan: Palaeolithic to Postmodern*: Cambridge University Press, 2001.

Desjarlais, Robert and C. Jason Throop. "Phenomenological Approaches in Anthropology." *Annual Review of Anthropology* 40 (2011): 87-102. http://www.jstor.org.ezproxy.lib.utexas.edu/stable/41287721.

Dore, Ronald. *City Life in Japan: A Study of a Tokyo Ward*. Berkeley: University of California Press, 1958.

Dore, Ronald. *Shinohata: A Portrait of a Japanese Village*. Berkeley: University of California Press, 1993.

Eco, Umberto. *A Theory of Semiotics*. Bloomington: Indiana University Press, 1976.

Ehrentraut, Adolf W. "Visual Definition of Heritage: The Restoration of Domestic Rural Architecture in Japan." *Visual Anthropology* 2, no. 2 (1989): 135-61.

Embree, John F. *Suye Mura: A Japanese Village*. University of Chicago Press, 1939.

Featherstone, David, Anthony Ince, Danny Mackinnon, Kendra Strauss, and Andrew Cumbers. "Progressive Localism and the Construction of Political Alternatives." *Transactions of the Institute of British Geographers* 37, no. 2 (2012): 177-82. http://dx.doi.org/10.1111/j.1475-5661.2011.00493.x.

Feld, Brad. *Startup Communities: Building and Entrepreneurial Ecosystem in Your City*. New York: Wiley, 2012.

Fielding, Anthony J. and Yoshitaka Ishikawa. "Migration and the Life Course in Contemporary Japan." *Geographical Review of Japan* 76, no. 12 (2003): 882-93. http://dx.doi.org/10.4157/grj.76.12_882.

Flango, Victor E. and Robert B. Brumbaugh. "The Dimensionality of the Cosmopolitan-Local Construct." *Administrative Science Quarterly* 19, no. 2 (1974): 198-210. http://dx.doi.org/10.2307/2393889.

Flannery, Maura C. "The White Coat: A Symbol of Science and Medicine as a Male Pursuit." *Thyroid* 11, no. 10 (2001): 947-51.

Freitas, Carmen and Michael Kitson. "Perceptions of Entrepreneurial Ecosystems in Remote Islands and Core Regions." *Island Studies Journal* 13, no. 1 (2018): 267-84. http://dx.doi.org/10.24043/isj.44.

Friedman, David B. *The Misunderstood Miracle: Industrial Development and Political Change in Japan.* Cornell University Press, 1988.

Friedman, Jonathan. "The Hybridisation of Roots and the Abhorrence of the Bush." In *Spaces of Culture: City, Nation, World*, edited by Mike Featherstone and Scott Lash, 230-56. London: Sage, 1999.

Fritsch, Michael and Yvonne Schindele. "The Contribution of New Businesses to Regional Employment—an Empirical Analysis." *Economic Geography* 87, no. 2 (2011): 153-80.

Fujimura, Shinya. "The Samurai Ethics: A Paradigm for Corporate Behavior." *Kennedy School Review* 11 (2010): 212.

Fujioka, Toru and Connor Cislo. "Rural Japan's Folk Traditions Fading as Residents Age." *The Japan Times* 2017, https://www.japantimes.co.jp/news/2017/02/09/national/rural-japans-folk-traditions-fading-residents-age/#.XLYJZy2ZPOQ.

福川裕一 and 真理子 西郷. "民間非営利組織(町づくり会社)による再開発；その必要性と成立条件 [Redevelopment by Private Non-Profit Organizations (Town Development Companies); Its Necessity and Conditions for Establishment."] 日本建築学会計画系論文集 *[Architectural Institute of Japan Planning Papers]* 60, no. 467 (1995): 153-62. http://dx.doi.org/10.3130/aija.60.153_1.

Galli, Barbara. "In the Service of National Culture: Japanese Preservation and Its Political Context, 1871–1994." *Future Anterior: Journal of Historic Preservation, History, Theory, and Criticism* 10, no. 1 (2013): 23-38. http://dx.doi.org/10.5749/futuante.10.1.0023.

Gill, Tom, Brigitte Steger, and David H. Slater, eds. *Japan Copes with Calamity: Ethnographies of the Earthquake, Tsunami and Nuclear Disasters of March 2011.* Oxford: Peter Lang, 2013.

Goldstein-Gidoni, Ofra. "Being Happy as a Woman: The Promise of Happiness for Middle-Class Housewives in Japan." In *Life Course, Happiness and Well-Being in Japan*, 97-115: Routledge, 2017.

Gordon, Andrew. *A Modern History of Japan: From Tokugawa Times to the Present.* Oxford University Press New York, 2003.

Gordon, Andrew. "Consumption, Leisure and the Middle Class in Transwar Japan." *Social Science Japan Journal* 10, no. 1 (2007): 1-21. http://www.jstor.org.ezproxy.lib.utexas.edu/stable/30209680.

Grimes, Andrew J. and Phillip K. Berger. "Cosmopolitan-Local: Evaluation of the Construct." *Administrative Science Quarterly* 15, no. 4 (1970): 407-16. http://dx.doi.org/10.2307/2391332.

Gulinck, Hubert and Carl Dortmans. "Neo-Rurality: The Benelux as a Workshop for New Ideas About Threatened Rural Areas." *Built Environment (1978-)* 23, no. 1 (1997): 37-46. http://www.jstor.org/stable/23287850.

Hall, John B. "Negative Population Growth: Why We Must, and How We Could, Achieve It." *Population and Environment* 18, no. 1 (1996): 65-71. http://www.jstor.org.ezproxy.lib.utexas.edu/stable/27503504.

Hamabata, Matthews M. *Crested Kimono: Power and Love in the Japanese Business Family.* Cornell University Press, 1991.

Hannon, Paul D. "Why Is the Entrepreneurial University Important?" *Journal of innovation management* 1, no. 2 (2013): 10-17.

Hansen, Paul. "Hokkaido's Frontiers: Blurred Embodiments, Shared Affects and the Evolution of Dairy Farming's Animal-Human-Machine." *Critique of Anthropology* 34, no. 1 (2014/03/01 2014): 48-72. Accessed 2018/08/13. http://dx.doi.org/10.1177/0308275X13510186.

Hashimoto, Akiko. *The Gift of Generations: Japanese and American Perspectives on Aging and the Social Contract.* Cambridge: Cambridge University Press, 1996.

Hashimoto, Hiroyuki. "Between Preservation and Tourism: Folk Performing Arts in Contemporary Japan." *Asian Folklore Studies* 62, no. 2 (2003): 225-36. http://www.jstor.org.ezproxy.lib.utexas.edu/stable/30030287.

Hendry, Joy. *Marriage in Changing Japan: Community & Society.* Routledge, 2010.

Herbane, Brahim. "Small Business Research: Time for a Crisis-Based View." *International Small Business Journal* 28, no. 1 (2010): 43-64. http://dx.doi.org/10.1177/0266242609350804.

Hogan, Jackie. "Constructing the Global in Two Rural Communities in Australia and Japan." *Journal of Sociology* 40, no. 1 (2004/03/01 2004): 21-40. Accessed 2019/01/16. http://dx.doi.org/10.1177/1440783304040451.

Holthus, Barbara and Wolfram Manzenreiter. "Conclusion: Happiness as a Balancing Act between Agency and Social Structure." In *Happiness and the Good Life in Japan*, edited by Wolfram Manzenreiter and Barbara Holthus, 243-55. London: Routledge, 2017.

Hopson, Nathan. *Ennobling Japan's Savage Northeast: Tōhoku as Postwar Thought, 1945 - 2011.* Vol. 407. Harvard East Asian Monographs. Cambridge, Mass.: Harvard University Asia Center, 2017.

Howorth, Carole, Sue Tempest, and Christine Coupland. "Rethinking Entrepreneurship Methodology and Definitions of the Entrepreneur." *Journal of Small Business and Enterprise development* 12, no. 1 (2005): 24-40.

Ichinoseki Linear Collider bulletin, 2017. "Kids Try Their Hand at ILC Posters." Last modified 2017. Accessed 11 January, 2018. http://www.city.ichinoseki.iwate.jp/ilc/en/newsletters/ilc_news_vol20.html#box5.

Ikegami, Naoki. "Public Long-Term Care Insurance in Japan." *Journal of the American Medical Association* 278, no. 16 (1997): 1310-14.

Ikegami, Naoki, Keita Yamauchi, and Yukari Yamada. "The Long Term Care Insurance Law in Japan: Impact on Institutional Care Facilities."

International Journal of Geriatric Psychiatry 18, no. 3 (2003): 217-21. http://dx.doi.org/10.1002/gps.818.

ILC. *Guidelines for Preparation of National Cost Estimates Based on the ILC TDR Value Estimate.* 2013.

ILC 戦略会議. "Announcement of the Results of the ILC Candidate Site Evaluation in Japan." Last modified 2013. Accessed 11 January, 2018. http://ilc-str.jp/topics/2013/08281826/.

Isenberg, Daniel and Vincent Onyemah. "Fostering Scale up Ecosystems for Regional Economic Growth." *Innovations* 11, no. 1/2 (2016): 60-79.

石田正昭. 農村版コミュニティ・ビジネスのすすめ: 地域再活性化とJaの役割 [Advising Rural Communities and Business Recommendations: Regional Revitalization and the Role of Ja]. 東京: 家の光協会 [Home Light Association], 2008.

岩手県政策地域部 [Iwate Prefecture Policy and Region Department].岩手県時計白書 *2018 [Iwate Prefecture Statistical White Paper 2018]*, by 政策地域部, 岩手県, 2018.

岩手日報. "Ilcに関心 64% [ILC Interest 64%]. ." 岩手日報. 24 December, 2017.

岩手日報. "Ilc関連に2.6億円18年度政府予算案 [260 Million Yen Allocated for Ilc-Related Items in National Budget for Fy2018 – an Almost 152 Million Yen Increase from Fy2017]. ." Last modified 2017. Accessed 9 January, 2018. http://www.iwate-np.co.jp/cgi-bin/news.cgi?ilc=20171223_1.

Izuhara, Misa. "Social Inequality under a New Social Contract: Long-Term Care in Japan." *Social Policy & Administration* 37, no. 4 (2003): 395-410.

Jamal, Haroon and Amir Jahan Khan. "The Changing Profile of Regional Inequality." *The Pakistan Development Review* 42, no. 2 (2003): 113-23. http://www.jstor.org.ezproxy.lib.utexas.edu/stable/41260530.

Japan Press Weekly. "Scientists Concerned over Japan's Hosting Ilc Project." Last modified 2013. Accessed. http://www.japan-press.co.jp/modules/news/index.php?id=6377.

Japan Statistics Bureau. "Labor Force Survey." Ministry of Internal Affairs and Communications. Last modified 2018. Accessed 4 January, 2019. http://www.stat.go.jp/english/data/roudou/lngindex.html.

Jayawarna, Dilani, Julia Rouse, and John Kitching. "Entrepreneur Motivations and Life Course." *International Small Business Journal* 31, no. 1 (2013/02/01 2011): 34-56. Accessed 2019/01/30. http://dx.doi.org/10.1177/0266242611401444.

Johnson, Jerry D. and Raymond Rasker. "The Role of Economic and Quality of Life Values in Rural Business Location." *Journal of Rural Studies* 11, no. 4 (1995/10/01/ 1995): 405-16. http://dx.doi.org/https://doi.org/10.1016/0743-0167(95)00029-1.

Jussaume, Raymond Adelard. *Japanese Part-Time Farming: Evolution and Impacts.* Iowa State University Press, 1991.

河北新報. "＜東北市長会＞原発事故対応やILC誘致要望 [Tōhoku Mayors Association Nuclear Accident Response and ILC Invitation Request]." Last modified 2017. Accessed 4 January, 2018. http://www.kahoku.co.jp/tohokunews/201706/20170607_71015.html.

川村保. "販売力強化へ向けて農協販売事業をどう改革するか (特集 農協を立て直す)--(Ja は農業者の所得増大にどう取り組むか) [How to Reform the Agricultural Cooperative Sales Business to Strengthen Sales Power]." 農業と経済 *[Agriculture and Economy]* 82, no. 8 (2016): 15-23.

Kawabata, Akira and Takanori Tamura. "Online-Religion in Japan: Websites and Religious Counseling from a Comparative Cross-Cultural Perspective." *Journal of Computer-Mediated Communication* 12, no. 3 (2007): 999-1019. Accessed 2/22/2019. http://dx.doi.org/10.1111/j.1083-6101.2007.00360.x.

Kazi, Taha. "Religious Television and Contesting Piety in Karachi, Pakistan." *American Anthropologist* 120, no. 3 (2018/09/01 2018): 523-34. Accessed 2019/03/05. http://dx.doi.org/10.1111/aman.13061.

経済産業省. 平成27年度 ものつ#くり基盤技術の振興施策 （概要）東京. : 経済産業省 [*2016 White Paper on Small Enterprises in*

Japan (Summary)]. Tokyo: Ministry of Economy, Trade, and Industry, 2016.]

Kelly, Wiliam W. "Rationalization and Nostalgia: Cultural Dynamics of New Middle-Class Japan." *Amerian Ethnologist* 13, no. 4 (1986): 603-18.

Kelly, William W. "Regional Japan: The Price of Prosperity and the Benefits of Dependency." *Daedalus* 119, no. 3 (1990): 209-27.

Kelly, William W. "Rice Revolutions and Farm Families in Tōhoku: Why Isfarming Culturally Central and Economically Marginal?" In *Wearing Cultural Styles in Japan: Concepts of Tradition and Modernity in Practice*, edited by Christopher S. Thompson and John W. Traphagan, 47-71. Albany: State University of New York Press, 2006.

Kelly, William W. and Merry I. White. "Students, Slackers, Singles, Seniors, and Strangers Transforming a Family-Nation." In *Beyond Japan*, The Dynamics of East Asian Regionalism, ed. Peter J. Katzenstein and Takashi Shiraishi, 63-82: Cornell University Press, 2006.

Kinoshita, Yasuhito. and Christie W. Kiefer. *Refuge of the Honored: Social Organization in a Japanese Retirement Community*. University of California Press, 1993.

Kirkwood, Jodyanne Jane. "One Size Doesn't Fit All: Gender Differences in Motivations for Becoming and Entrepreneur." University of Otago, 2004.

Kjeldgaard, Dannie and Søren Askegaard. "The Glocalization of Youth Culture: The Global Youth Segment as Structures of Common Difference." *Journal of Consumer Research* 33, no. 2 (2006): 231-47.

Klien, Susanne. "Reinventing Ishinomaki, Reinventing Japan? Creative Networks, Alternative Lifestyles and the Search for Quality of Life in Post-Growth Japan." *Japanese Studies* 36, no. 1 (2016/01/02 2016): 39-60. http://dx.doi.org/10.1080/10371397.2016.1148555.

Klien, Susanne. "Entrepreneurial Selves, Governmentality and Lifestyle Migrants in Rural Japan." *Asian Anthropology* 18, no. 2 (2019): 75-90. http://dx.doi.org/10.1080/1683478X.2019.1572946.

Knight, John. "Organic Farming Settlers in Kumano." In *Farmers and Village Life in Twentieth-Century Japan*, edited by Ann Waswo and Nishida Yoshiaki, 267-84. London: RoutledgeCurzon, 2003.

Knight, John and John W. Traphagan, eds. *Demographic Change and the Family in Japan's Aging Society.* Albany: State University of New York Press, 2003.

Kraidy, Marwan M. "The Trails and Tales of Hybridity." In *Hybridity: Pr the Cultural Logic of Globalization*, edited by Marwan M. Kraidy, Or the Cultural Logic of Globalization, 45-71. Philadelphia: Temple University Press, 2005.

工藤雅樹. "考古学から見た古代蝦夷 [Ancient Ezo from an Archaeological Viewpoint." 日本考古学 [*Journal of the Japanese Archaeological Association*] 1, no. 1 (1994): 139-54.

Kühn, Manfred. "Peripheralization: Theoretical Concepts Explaining Socio-Spatial Inequalities." *European Planning Studies* 23, no. 2 (2015): 367-78. http://dx.doi.org/10.1080/09654313.2013.862518.

Kumagai, Fumie. and Donna J. Keyser. *Unmasking Japan Today: The Impact of Traditional Values on Modern Japanese Society.* Praeger, 1996.

Kumagai, Fumie. "Forty Years of Family Change in Japan: A Society Experiencing Population Aging and Declining Fertility." *Journal of Comparative Family Studies* 41, no. 4 (2010): 581-610.

Kumagai, Fumie. *Family Issues on Marriage, Divorce, and Older Adults in Japan: With Special Attention to Regional Variations.* Springer Singapore, 2014.

Kuratko, Donald F, Jeffrey S Hornsby, and Douglas W Naffziger. "An Examination of Owner's Goals in Sustaining Entrepreneurship." *Journal of Small Business Management* 35, no. 1 (1997): 24.

Kuroda, Tashio 日本人口の転換構造 [The Structure of the Japanese Population in Transition]. 古今書院, 1979.

Labov, William. *Sociolinguistic Patterns.* University of Pennsylvania Press, 1972.

Lam, Alice. "Boundary-Crossing Careers and the 'Third Space of Hybridity': Career Actors as Knowledge Brokers between Creative

Arts and Academia." *Environment and Planning A: Economy and Space* 50, no. 8 (2018): 1716-41. http://dx.doi.org/10.1177/0308518x17746406.

Lawson, Francesca R. Sborgi. "Music in Ritual and Ritual in Music: A Virtual Viewer's Perceptions About Liminality, Functionality, and Mediatization in the Opening Ceremony of the 2008 Beijing Olympic Games." *Asian Music* 42, no. 2 (2011): 3-18.

Lebra, Takie S. *Japanese Women: Constraint and Fulfillment.* University of Hawaii Press, 1985.

Lehman, Edward C. "The Local/Cosmopolitan Dichotomy and Acceptance of Women Clergy: A Replication and Extension of Roof." *Journal for the Scientific Study of Religion* 25, no. 4 (1986): 461-82. http://dx.doi.org/10.2307/1385911.

Lehne, Moritz, Martin Rohrmeier, Donald Gollmann, and Stefan Koelsch. "The Influence of Different Structural Features on Felt Musical Tension in Two Piano Pieces by Mozart and Mendelssohn." *Music Perception: An Interdisciplinary Journal* 31, no. 2 (2013): 171. http://dx.doi.org/10.1525/mp.2013.31.2.171.

Lewis, Virginia L and Neil C Churchill. "The Five Stages of Small Business Growth." *Harvard Business Review* 61, no. 3 (1983): 30-49

Ley, David A. "The Effective Gm: Leader or Entrepreneur?" *Cornell Hotel and Restaurant Administration Quarterly* 21, no. 3 (1980): 66-67.

Liaw, Kao-Lee. "Interprefectural Migration and Its Effects on Prefectural Populations in Japan: An Analysis Based on the 1980 Census." *The Canadian Geographer* 36, no. 4 (1992): 320-35.

Linhartt, Sepp and Sabine Frühstück. *The Culture of Japan as Seen through Its Leisure.* State University of New York Press, 1998.

Lit, Phua Kai. "The Japanese Experience with Population Ageing and the Financing of Social Security, Health and Other Social Services for the Elderly: Lessons for Other Nations." *Asian Journal of Social Science* 34, no. 4 (2006): 618-29. http://www.jstor.org.ezproxy.lib.utexas.edu/stable/23654550.

Lock, Margaret M. *East Asian Medicine in Urban Japan: Varieties of Medical Experience.* University of California Press, 1984.

Long, Susan. and Julian Manley. *Social Dreaming: Philosophy, Research, Theory and Practice.* Taylor & Francis, 2019.

Long, Susan Orpett. "Becoming a Cucumber: Culture, Nature, and the Good Death in Japan and the United States." *Journal of Japanese Studies* 29, no. 1 (2003): 33-68. http://www.jstor.org.ezproxy.lib.utexas.edu/stable/25064363.

Maclachlan, Patricia L and Kay Shimizu. "Japanese Farmers in Flux: The Domestic Sources of Agricultural Reform." *Asian Survey* 56, no. 3 (2016): 442-65.

Martin, Rachel. "Buddhism Is Waning in Japan." NPR. Last modified 2015. Accessed 12 December, 2018. https://www.npr.org/2015/11/22/456989131/buddhism-is-waning-in-japan.

Mason, Michele. *Dominant Narratives of Colonial Hokkaido and Imperial Japan: Envisioning the Periphery and the Modern Nation-State.* New York: Springer, 2012.

Matanle, Peter and Anthony Rausch. *Japan's Shrinking Regions in the 21st Century: Contemporary Responses to Depopulation and Socioeconomic Decline.* Amherst, NY: Cambria Press, 2011.

Mathews, Gordon. *What Makes Life Worth Living? How Japanese and Americans Make Sense of Their Worlds.* University of California Press, 1996.

Mathews, Gordon and Carolina Izquierdo. "Anthropology, Happiness and Well-Being." *Pursuits of happiness: Well-being in anthropological perspective (1–19). New York: Berghahn Books* (2009).

McClelland, David C. *Achieving Society.* Vol. 92051: Simon and Schuster, 1967.

Merton, Robert K. *Social Theory and Social Structure.* Glencoe, IL: Free Press, 1957.

Merton, Robert K. *Social Theory and Social Structure.* New York: Free Press, 1968.

Miller, Diana L. "Symbolic Capital and Gender: Evidence from Two Cultural Fields." *Cultural Sociology* 8, no. 4 (2014/12/01 2014): 462-82. Accessed 2019/02/11. http://dx.doi.org/10.1177/1749975514539800.

宮沢智士. "民家における書院的座敷の成立時期の一例：長野県南佐久郡八千穂村の場合. [An Example of the Time of Establishment of a Shoin-style Room in a Private House: A Case Study of Yachiho Village, Minamisaku-gun, Nagano Prefecture]." 日本建築学会論文報告集 [Proceedings of the Architectural Institute of Japan] 95 (1964): 27-32, http://dx.doi.org/10.3130/aijsaxx.95.0_27.

持田昇一. "地域をフィールドとした社会起業新論 [Social Entrepreneurship] "開発工学 *[Development Engineering]* 35, no. 2 (2016): 139-42.

Nakamura, Karen. *Deaf in Japan: Signing and the Politics of Identity.* Ithaca: Cornell University Press, 2006.

Nakamura, Karen. *A Disability of the Soul: An Ethnography of Schizophrenia and Mental Illness in Contemporary Japan.* Cornell University Press, 2013.

Nakamura, Shiori, Masahiro Shigeta, Makoto Iwamoto, Norifumi Tsuno, Rie Nina, Akira Homma, and Yu Kawamuro. "Prevalence and Predominance of Alzheimer Type Dementia in Rural Japan." *Psychogeriatrics* 3, no. 3 (2003): 97-103.

Nelson, John K. "Japanese Secularities and the Decline of Temple Buddhism." *Journal of Religion in Japan* 1, no. 1 (2012): 37-60.

Nelson, John K. *Experimental Buddhism: Innovation and Activism in Contemporary Japan.* University of Hawai'i Press, 2013.

Nogué, Joan. "Neo-Ruralism in the European Context: Origins and Evolution." In *The New Ruralism: An Epistemology of Transformed Space,* edited by Joan Ramon Resina and William Viestenz, 27-39. Madrid: Iberoamericana Vervuert, 2012.

Norbeck, Edward. *Takashima: A Japanese Fishing Community.* Salt Lake City: University of Utah Press, 1954.

Normile, Dennis. "Japan Hopes to Staff up to Host the International Linear Collider." Last modified 2016. Accessed 18 January, 2018. http://www.sciencemag.org/news/2016/01/japan-hopes-staff-host-international-linear-collider.

Ogasawara, Yuko. *Office Ladies and Salaried Men: Power, Gender, and Work in Japanese Companies.* University of California Press, 1998.

Okazaki, Manami and Geoff Johnson. *Kawaii!: Japan's Culture of Cute.* Prestel, 2013.

奥山純子, 中山徹, 斉藤功子, 田中智子, 小伊藤亜希子, and 立松麻衣子. "地方自治体における高齢者福祉施設の配置計画: 生活圏を意識した計画の実態 (都市計画) [Placement Planning of Welfare Facilities for the Elderly in Local Governments: Actual Conditions of Planning for Living Areas (Urban Planning)." 日本建築学会技術報告集 *[The Architectural Institute of Japan Journal of Technology and Design]* 11, no. 22 (2005): 445-50.

奥山純子, 中山徹, 斉藤功子, 田中智子, 小伊藤亜希子, and 立松麻衣子. "介護サービス基盤の圏域設置計画とその整備手法: 地方自治体における高齢者福祉施設の配置計画 その 2 (都市計画) [Planning and Setting of Nursing Care Service Base Area: Placement Planning of Welfare Facilities for the Elderly in Local Governments Part 2 (Urban Planning)]." 日本建築学会技術報告集 *[The Architectural Institute of Japan Journal of Technology and Design]* 12, no. 24 (2006): 381-86.

Ooms, Herman. "The Religion of the Household: A Case Study of Ancestor Worship in Japan." *Contemporary Religions in Japan* (1967): 201-333.

Ortega, Rocío Rosales. "Urban-Rural Relations in the Central Region of Mexico

a Viewpoint from Tlaxcala." *Urbani Izziv* 23 (2012): S11-S21. http://www.jstor.org.ezproxy.lib.utexas.edu/stable/24920837.

太田幸司 and 山本信次. "農山村地域における多様な主体の協働による市町村交通サービスの在り方: 岩手県雫石町 「あねっこバス」 を事例として."" [The State of Rural Transport Services Organized on the Basis of the Collaboration of Various Bodies in Rural Mountain Village Regions: Case Study of Shizukuishi Town in Iwate Prefecture] 林業経済研究 [*Journal of Forest Economics*] 54, no. 3 (2008): 7-18

Palmer, Caroline. "Music Performance." *Annual Review of Psychology* 48, no. 1 (1997): 115-38. http://dx.doi.org/10.1146/annurev.psych.48.1.115.

Parathian, Hannah Elizabeth. "Understanding Cosmopolitan Communities in Protected Areas: A Case Study from the Colombian Amazon." *Conservation & Society* 17, no. 1 (2019): 26-37. https://www-jstor-org.ezproxy.lib.utexas.edu/stable/26554468.

Pavloff, Franck. *Matin Brun*. Devesset, France: Cheyne, 1998.

Pécoud, Antoine. "Cosmopolitanism and Business among German-Turks in Berlin." *Journal of the Society for the Anthropology of Europe* 2, no. 1 (2002): 2-12. http://dx.doi.org/doi:10.1525/jsae.2002.2.1.2.

Petersen, Larry R. and K. Peter Takayama. "Local-Cosmopolitan Theory and Religiosity among Catholic Nuns and Brothers." *Journal for the Scientific Study of Religion* 22, no. 4 (1983): 303-15. http://dx.doi.org/10.2307/1385769.

Plath, David W. *Long Engagements: Maturity in Modern Japan*. Stanford: Stanford University Press, 1980.

Plath, David W. "My-Car-Isma: Motorizing the Showa Self." *Daedalus* (1990): 229-44.

Rausch, Anthony. *Cultural Commodities in Japanese Rural Revitalization: Tsugaru Nuri Lacquerware and Tsugaru Shamisen*. Brill, 2010.

Rausch, Anthony. "Local Identity, Cultural Commodities, and Development in Rural Japan: The Potential as Viewed by Cultural Producers and Local Residents." *International Journal of Japanese Sociology* 14 (2005): 122-37.

Reader, Ian. *Religion in Contemporary Japan*. University of Hawaii Press, 1991.

Reader, Ian. "Secularisation, RIP? Nonsense! The 'Rush Hour Away from the Gods' and the Decline of Religion in Contemporary Japan." *Journal of Religion in Japan* 1, no. 1 (2012): 7-36.

Resina, Joan Ramon. "The Modern Rural." In *The New Ruralism: An Epistemology of Transformed Space*, edited by Joan Ramon Resina and William Viestenz. Madrid: Iberoamericana Vervuert, 2012.

Ritzer, George. "Mcdonaldization." *The Blackwell Encyclopedia of Sociology* (1993): 1-3.

Robertson, Jennifer. "A Dialectic of Native and Newcomer: The Kodaira Citizens' Festival in Suburban Tokyo." *Anthropological Quarterly* 60, no. 3 (1987): 124-36.

Robertson, Jennifer. *Native and Newcomer: Making and Remaking a Japanese City.* University of California Press, 1991.

Rorty, Richard. *Contingency, Irony and Solidarity.* Cambridge: Cambridge University Press, 1989.

Rosaldo, Renato. *Ilongot Headhunting, 1883-1974: A Study in Society and History.* Stanford, CA: Stanford University Press, 1983.

Rosenberger, Nancy. "Rethinking Emerging Adulthood in Japan: Perspectives from Long-Term Single Women." *Child Development Perspectives* 1, no. 2 (2007): 92-95.

Rosenberger, Nancy. 'Making an Ant's Forehead of Difference': Organic Agriculture as an Alternative Lifestyle in Japan." In *Capturing Contemporary Japan*, Differentiation and Uncertainty, ed. Satsuki Kawano, Glenda S. Roberts, and Susan Orpett Long, 105-34: University of Hawai'i Press, 2014.

Salabert, Pere. "A Semi-Peircean Essay on "New Ruralism" by Means of Nature." In *The New Ruralism: An Epistemology of Transformed Space*, edited by Joan Ramon Resina and William Viestenz, 41–54. Madrid: Iberoamericana Vervuert, 2012.

Saleem, Ahmed. "Japan's Alternative Farming Approaches: Farmer-Distributor-Consumer Linkages." *Ambio* 24, no. 6 (1995): 379-80. http://www.jstor.org/stable/4314371.

Salhi, Bisan. "Beyond the Doctor's White Coat: Science, Ritual, and Healing in American Biomedicine." *Understanding and Applying Medical Anthropology* (2016): 204-12.

Schein, Edgar H. *Dec Is Dead, Long Live Dec: The Lasting Legacy of Digital Equipment Corporation.* San Francisco: Berrett-Koehler Publishers, 2004.

Schnell, Scott. *The Rousing Drum: Ritual Practice in a Japanese Community.* Honolulu: University of Hawai'i Press, 1999.

Science Council of Japan. *Report on the International Linear Collider Project.* Tokyo, 2013.

Seales, Chad E. "Corporate Chaplaincy and the American Workplace." *Religion Compass* 6, no. 3 (2012/03/01 2012): 195-203. Accessed 2019/01/09. http://dx.doi.org/10.1111/j.1749-8171.2012.00340.x.

Shelton, B. *Learning from the Japanese City: Looking East in Urban Design.* Taylor & Francis, 2012.

Shigeta, Masahiro. "Epidemiology: Rapid Increase in Alzheimer's Disease Prevalence in Japan." *Psychogeriatrics* 4, no. 4 (2004): 117-19.

Shimizu, Akitoshi. "Ie and Dozoku: Family and Descent in Japan." *Current Anthropology* 28, no. 4 (1987): S85-S90. http://www.jstor.org/stable/2743443.

清水希容子 and 松原宏. "東日本大震災後の東北製造業の回復と産業立地政策 [Tōhoku's Industrial Recovery and Industrial Location Policies after the Great East Japan Earthquake]." *E-Journal GEO* 9, no. 2 (2014): 113-18.

Siegenthaler, Peter David. "Looking to the Past, Looking to the Future: The Localization of Japanese Historic Preservation, 1950 - 1975." University of Texas at Austin, 2004.

Skinner, G. William. "Family Systems and Demographic Processes." In *Anthropological Demography: Toward a New Synthesis*, edited by David I. Kertzer and Tom Fricke, 55-97. Chicago: University of Chicago Press, 1997.

Smith, Robert J. *Ancestor Worship in Contemporary Japan.* Stanford University Press, 1974.

Smith, Robert J. *Kurusu: The Price of Progress in a Japanese Village, 1951-1975.* Stanford: Stanford University Press, 1978.

Souza, Peter de. *The Rural and Peripheral in Regional Development: An Alternative Perspective.* New York: Routledge, 2018.

Sperber, Murray A. "The College Coach as Entrepreneur." *Academe* 73, no. 4 (1987): 30-33.

Staff, Japan Times Editorial. "A Chance to Host Linear Collider." Last modified 2013. Accessed 11 January, 2018. https://www.japantimes.co.jp/opinion/2013/03/05/editorials/a-chance-to-host-linear-collider/#.WleKZSOZNE4.

Stam, Erik. *The Dutch Entrepreneurial Ecosystem.* Utrecht, Netherlands: Birch Research, 2014.

Stam, Erik. "Entrepreneurial Ecosystems and Regional Policy: A Sympathetic Critique." *European Planning Studies* 23, no. 9 (2015/09/02 2015): 1759-69. http://dx.doi.org/10.1080/09654313.2015.1061484.

Stangler, Dane and Jordan Bell-Masterson. "Measuring an Entrepreneurial Ecosystem." *Kauffman Foundation Research Series on City, Metro, and Regional Entrepreneurship* 16 (2015).

Steiner, Artur and Jane Atterton. "Exploring the Contribution of Rural Enterprises to Local Resilience." *Journal of Rural Studies* 40 (2015/08/01/ 2015): 30-45. http://dx.doi.org/https://doi.org/10.1016/j.jrurstud.2015.05.004.

Stewart, Wayne H., Warren E. Watson, Joann C. Carland, and James W. Carland. "A Proclivity for Entrepreneurship: A Comparison of Entrepreneurs, Small Business Owners, and Corporate Managers." *Journal of Business Venturing* 14, no. 2 (1999/03/01/ 1999): 189-214. http://dx.doi.org/https://doi.org/10.1016/S0883-9026(97)00070-0.

Suda, Yuko. "Devolution and Privatization Proceed and Centralized System Maintained: A Twisted Reality Faced by Japanese Nonprofit Organizations." *Nonprofit and Voluntary Sector Quarterly* 35, no. 3 (2006): 430-52.

Sunakawa, Chiho. "Virtual *Ie*: A Three-Generational Houshold Mediated by Webcam Interactions." *Journal of Pragmatics* 69 (2014): 63-81.

Szerszynski, Bronislaw and John Urry. "Visuality, Mobility and the Cosmopolitan: Inhabiting the World from Afar." *British Journal of Sociology* 57, no. 1 (2006): 113-31. http://dx.doi.org/10.1111/j.1468-4446.2006.00096.x.

Takano, Takako. "Exploring the Values of Rural Communities through Place-Based Education in Niigata Prefecture." In *Educating for Sustainability in Japan: Fostering Resilient Communities after the Triple Disaster*, edited by Jane Singer, Tracey Gannon, Fumiko Noguchi, and Toko Mochizuki, 249-63. New York: Routledge, 2017.

Tamanoi, Mariko. *Memory Maps: The State and Manchuria in Postwar Japan.* University of Hawai'i Press, 2009.

Thin, Neil. "Why Anthropology Can Ill Afford to Ignore Well-Being." In *Happiness: Well-Being in Anthropological Perspective*, edited by Gordon Mathews and Carolina Izquidero. New York: Berghahn Books, 2009.

Thompson, Chrisotpher S. and John W. Traphagan, eds. *Wearing Cultural Styles in Japan: Concepts of Tradition and Modernity in Practice.* Albany: State University of New York Press, 2006.

Thompson, Christopher S. "Depopulation in Regional Japan: Population Politics in Tōwa-Chō." In *Demographic Change and the Family in Japan's Aging Society*, edited by John Traphagan and John Knight, 89-106. Albany: State University of New York Press, 2003.

Thompson, Christopher S. "The Ochiai Deer Dance: A Traditional Dance in a Modern World." *The Journal of Popular Culture* 38, no. 1 (2004/08/01 2004): 129-48. Accessed 2019/01/10. http://dx.doi.org/10.1111/j.0022-3840.2004.00103.x.

Thompson, Christopher S. "Preserving the Ochiai Deer Dance: Tradition and Continuity in a Tōhoku Hamlet." In *Wearing Cultural Styles in Japan: Concepts of Tradition and Modernity in Practice*, edited by Christopher S. Thompson and John W. Traphagan, 124-50. Albany: State University of New York Press, 2006.

Thompson, Christopher S. "Population Decline, Municipal Amalgamation, and the Politics of Fok Performance Preservation in Northeast Japan." In *The Demographic Challenge: A Handbook About Japan*, edited by Florian Coulmas, Harald Conrad, Annette Schad-Seifert, and Gabriele Vogt, 361-86. Leiden: Brill, 2008.

Thompson, Craig J. and Siok Kuan Tambyah. "Trying to Be Cosmopolitan." *Journal of Consumer Research* 26, no. 3 (1999): 214-41. http://dx.doi.org/10.1086/209560.

Thompson, Heather Ann. *Whose Detroit? Politics, Labor, and Race, in a Modern American City.* Ithaca: Cornell University Press, 2001.

Tinka Delakorda, Kawashima. "The Healing Jizo: Soto Zen Koganji Temple Adapting to Varying Social Conditions." 臺灣東亞文明研究學刊 13, no. 1 (2016): 77-105. http://dx.doi.org/10.6163/tjeas.2016.13(1)77.

Traphagan, John W. "Reasons for Gateball Participation among Older Japanese." *Journal of Cross-Cultural Gerontology* 13, no. 2 (1998): 159-75.

Traphagan, John W. "Older Women as Caregivers and Ancestral Protection in Rural Japan (1)." *Ethnology* 42, no. 2 (2003): 127-40.

Traphagan, John W. "Culture and Long-Term Care: The Bath as Social Service in Japan." *Care Management Journals* 5, no. 1 (2004): 53-60.

Traphagan, John W. "The Oddness of Things: Morality Games and Interpretations of Social Change among Elders in Rural Japan." *The Asia Pacific Journal of Anthropology* 10, no. 4 (2009): 329-47.

Traphagan, John W and Tomoko Nagasawa. "Group Homes for Elders with Dementia in Japan." *Care Management Journals* 9, no. 2 (2008): 89-96.

Traphagan, John W. "The Liminal Family: Return Migration and Intergenerational Conflict in Japan." *Journal of Anthropological Research* 56, no. 3 (2000): 365-85. http://www.jstor.org.ezproxy.lib.utexas.edu/stable/3631089.

Traphagan, John W. *Taming Oblivion: Aging Bodies and the Fear of Senility in Japan.* Albany: State University of New York Press, 2000.

Traphagan, John W. *The Practice of Concern: Ritual, Well-Being, and Aging in Rural Japan.* Durham, N.C.: Carolina Academic Press, 2004.

Traphagan, John W. "Being a Good Rôjin: Senility, Power, and Self-Actualization in Japan." In *Thinking About Dementia: Culture, Loss, and the Anthropology of Senility*, edited by Annette Leibing and Lawrence Cohen, 269-88. New Brunswick, NJ: Rutgers University Press, 2006.

Traphagan, John W. "Moral Discourse and Old-Age Disability in Japan." In *Disability in Local and Global Worlds*, edited by Benedicte Ingstad and Susan Reynolds Whyte, 259-86. Berkeley: University of California Press, 2007.

Traphagan, John W. "East Asia's Population Problem." *Georgetown Journal of International Affairs* 15, no. 2 (2014): 17-26. http://www.jstor.org.ezproxy.lib.utexas.edu/stable/43773623.

Traphagan, John W. "Entrepreneurs in Rural Japan: Gender, Blockage, and the Pursuit of Existential Meaning." *Asian Anthropology* 16, no. 2 (2017/04/03 2017): 77-94. http://dx.doi.org/10.1080/1683478X.2017.1281534.

Traphagan, John W. "Empty Houses, Abandoned Graves: Negative Population Growth and New Ideas in Neo-Rural Japan." *The Brown Journal of World Affairs* 24, no. 2 (2018): 161-74.

Traphagan, John W. "Empty Houses, Abandoned Graves: Negative Population Growth and New Ideas in Neorural Japan." *Brown Journal of World Affairs* 24, no. 2 (2018): 161-74.

Traphagan, John W. and L. Keith Brown. "Fast Food and Intergenerational Commensality in Japan: New Styles and Old Patterns." *Ethnology* 41, no. 2 (2002): 119-34. http://dx.doi.org/10.2307/4153002.

Traphagan, John W. and John Knight. *Demographic Change and the Family in Japan's Aging Society*. Suny Series in Japan in Transition. Albany: State University of New York Press, 2003.

Traphagan, Tomoko. "Negotiating Internationalization in Kitasawa." In *Wearing Cultural Styles in Japan: Concepts of Tradition and Modernity in Practice*, edited by Christopher S. Thompson and John W. Traphagan, 96-123. Albany: State University of New York Press, 2006.

Tsukada, Noriko and Yasuhiko Saito. "Factors That Affect Older Japanese People's Reluctance to Use Home Help Care and Adult Day Care Services." *Journal of Cross-Cultural Gerontology* 21, no. 3/4 (2006): 121-37. http://dx.doi.org/10.1007/s10823-006-9028-9.

鵜飼秀徳. 寺院消滅 失われる「地方」と「宗教」[Vanishing Temples: The Loss of Regions and Religion] Tokyo: 日経BP社 [NikkeiBP], 2015.

Ushino, Tadashi. "Comprehensive District Plan by Inhabitants and "Kande" System." *Journal of Rural Planning Association* 1, no. 3 (1982): 19-29,62. http://dx.doi.org/10.2750/arp.1.3_19.

Uzama, Austin and Pierre Walter. "Incorporating Ecotourism into Social Education (Shakai Kyouiku 社会教育) and Lifelong Learning (Shougai Gakushuu 生涯学習) in Japan." *Journal of Adult and Continuing Education* 24, no. 1 (2018/05/01 2018): 18-36. Accessed 2019/02/11. http://dx.doi.org/10.1177/1477971417753975.

Vestel, Viggo. "Limits of Hybridity Versus Limits of Tradition? A Semiotics of Cultural Reproduction, Creativity, and Ambivalence among Multicultural Youth in Rudenga, East Side Oslo." *Ethos* 37, no. 4 (2009): 466-88. http://dx.doi.org/doi:10.1111/j.1548-1352.2009.01069.x.

Vogel, Ezra F. *Japan's New Middle Class: The Salary Man and His Family in a Tokyo Suburb.* Berkeley: University of California Press, 1971.

Walras, Léon, D.A. Walker, and J. van Daal. *Walras: Elements of Theoretical Economics: Or, the Theory of Social Wealth.* Translated by Donald A. Walker and Jan van Daal. Cambridge University Press, 2014.

Wang, Yiyuan. "Buddhist Cafe Gives Tokyo Caffeinated Enlightenment." *The Japan Times* 2016.

Wayama, Amanda. "Iwate and the ILC." Last modified 2017. Accessed 3 January, 2018. http://www.iwate-ilc.jp/eng/ktimes/the-ilc-is-not-a-gamble-33/.

Winkelmann, Karol, Filip Kłos, and Mateusz Rąpca. "Experimental Study and Numerical Optimization of Tensegrity Domes - a Case Study." *AIP Conference Proceedings* 1922, no. 1 (2017): 1-10. http://dx.doi.org/10.1063/1.5019127.

Wood, Donald C. *Ogata-Mura: Sowing Dissent and Reclaiming Identity in a Japanese Farming Village.* New York: Berghahn Books, 2012.

Woods, Michael. "The Local Politics of the Global Countryside: Boosterism, Aspirational Ruralism and the Contested Reconstitution of Queenstown, New Zealand." *GeoJournal* 76, no. 4 (2011/08/01 2011): 365-81. http://dx.doi.org/10.1007/s10708-009-9268-7.

Woss, Fleur. "*Pokkuri* Temples and Aging." In *Religion and Society in Modern Japan*, edited by Mark R. Mullins, Shimazono Susumu, and Paul L. Swanson, 191-202. Berkeley: Asian Humanities Press, 1993.

Yamada, Tatsuo, Hiroyuki Hattori, Ayako Miura, Mitunori Tanabe, and Yukio Yamori. "Prevalence of Alzheimer's Disease, Vascular Dementia and Dementia with Lewy Bodies in a Japanese Population." *Psychiatry and clinical neurosciences* 55, no. 1 (2001): 21-25.

Yamashita, Yusuke. "How Does the Restoration of Tōhoku Society Begin? Center and Periphery in the Great East Japan Earthquake." *International Journal of Japanese Sociology* 21, no. 1 (2012): 6-11.

Yano, Eiji, Kazue Yamaoka, and Nanako Tamiya. "Use of Home Health Services Covered by New Public Long-Term Care Insurance in Japan: Impact of the Presence and Kinship of Family Caregivers." *International Journal for Quality in Health Care* 14, no. 4 (2002): 295-303. Accessed 1/24/2019. http://dx.doi.org/10.1093/intqhc/14.4.295.

Yoshida, Akiko. *Unmarried Women in Japan: The Drift into Singlehood.* Taylor & Francis, 2016.

Yoshida, Mitsuhiro. "Contesting Powers: A Cultural Analysis of Water Distribution, Personhood, Gender and Ritual in a Japanese Hot Spring Town." University of Pittsburgh, 1997.

Yu, F., T. Takahashi, J. Moriya, K. Kawaura, J. Yamakawa, K. Kusaka, T. Itoh, S. Morimoto, N. Yamaguchi, and T. Kanda. "Traditional Chinese Medicine and Kampo: A Review from the Distant Past for the Future." *Journal of International Medical Research* 34, no. 3 (2006): 231-39. Accessed 2019/01/24. http://dx.doi.org/10.1177/147323000603400301.

Zlatev, Jordan. "Preconditions in Human Embodiment for the Evolution of Symbolic Communication." In *Embodiment in Evolution and Culture*, edited by Gregor Etzelmüller and Christian Tewes, 151-74: Mohr Siebeck GmbH and Co. KG, 2016.

Index

About the Author

John W. Traphagan is a professor of religious studies and in the program in Human Dimensions of Organizations at the University of Texas at Austin, where he is also Mitsubishi Fellow in Religious Studies. He holds a PhD from the University of Pittsburgh, an MAR from Yale University, and a BA from the University of Massachusetts Lowell. Dr. Traphagan's previous books on Japan include *Taming Oblivion: Aging Bodies and the Fear of Senility in Japan* and *The Practice of Concern: Ritual, Well-Being, and Aging in Rural Japan.*

Praise for the Book

"A very engaging and thoughtful work that will be of great interest to Japan scholars and to any social scientists with a concern for conditions of life in contemporary rural regions in many of the advanced industrial societies. This is a book about entrepreneurship, depopulation, and the nature of the contemporary rural. Each of these is of broad and comparative significance. The Japanese countryside doesn't look like the countryside of the sentimental imagination; it is a complex hybrid formation, much as we find in Europe and North America, giving the case a wide salience. Depopulation is a shorthand for several related trends of much consequence: population decline, yes, but rapid aging of the population and significant marriage delay, declining births, and solo living. This too is a feature of the rest of the 'developed' world, but Japan's trends are among the most advanced and there is much to learn from a judicious account such as this book. This is an impressive book, which should gain an enthusiastic and appreciative readership."

—Professor William Kelly, Yale University

"Traphagan's book should be required reading not just for Japan specialists but also for students, cultural anthropologists, gerontologists, demographers, and anybody in general interested in the topics indicated in its title. The richness of his ethnographic descriptions conveys many tasty morsels of insight into Japanese culture reflected within life in Kanegasaki, Iwate Prefecture—pertaining to pop culture, fashion, gender relations, food, religion, economics, and population loss—that are relevant to any locale. A very welcome practical and theoretical introduction to 'cosmopolitan rurality' in the context of Japan that is applicable globally today!"

—Professor Christopher Thompson, Ohio University

"Move over Tokyo and Osaka, the countryside is where real cosmopolitanism and entrepreneurship can be found in Japan. From Toyota factories making hybrid cars from the global marketplace to the new sharing economy of drone-controlled tractors plowing organic farms, John Traphagan makes a compelling case based on over thirty years of close ethnographic fieldwork in the rural northeast for the dynamisms that can be found in places formerly considered peripheral but should now be understood as deeply networked."

—Professor Karen Nakamura, University of California Berkeley

"John Traphagan, through his engaging account of six case studies of entrepreneurship in the remote northeastern Tohoku area of Japan, shows how the distinction between rustic and cosmopolitan, and rural and urban, is blurred by the hybridization of life and culture in contemporary Japan. The proliferation of the automobile gives people in the countryside access to the supermarkets, box stores and jobs in the suburbs or centers of the towns, sharing a life that differs little from the life of the town dwellers. The entrepreneurs in his case studies exhibit considerable creativity while also adhering to basic tenets of Japanese culture concerning family and community. All of this is taking place in an area of Japan that is experiencing worrisome depopulation with the ageing of society and the migration of young people to Tokyo and other large cities. This is an important and fascinating study showing basic changes in life and culture in Japan during the three decades of Traphagan's fieldwork."

—Professor L. Keith Brown, University of Pittsburgh

www.ingramcontent.com/pod-product-compliance
Lightning Source LLC
LaVergne TN
LVHW091526200926
848483LV00002B/315
* 9 7 8 1 6 2 1 9 6 5 0 2 2 *